EX LIBRIS

Name CHERYL PILEK

Study Guide to accompany

MACRO ECONOMICS

FOURTH CANADIAN EDITION

Study Guide to accompany

MACRO ECONOMICS

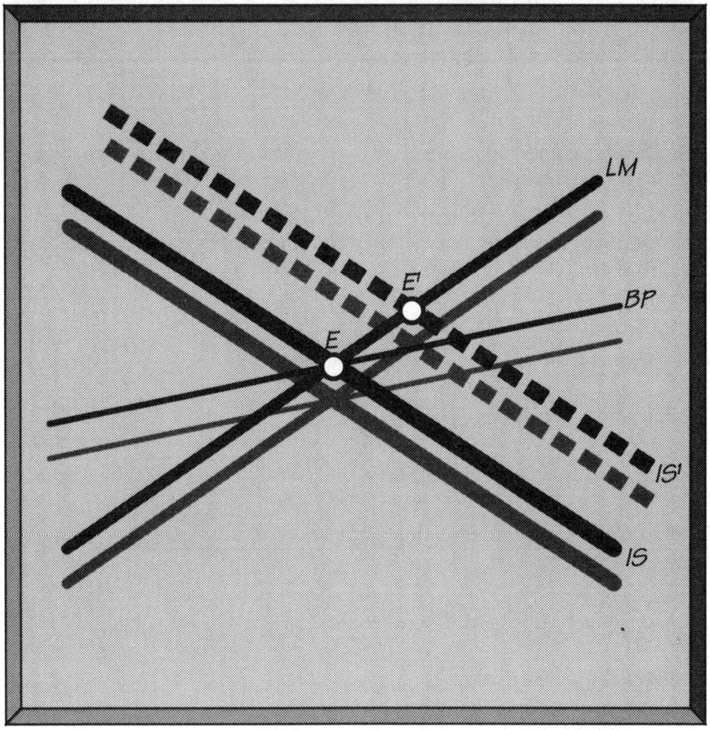

FOURTH CANADIAN EDITION

Richard Startz
University of Washington

Gordon R. Sparks
Queen's University

Frank Atkins
University of Calgary

McGraw-Hill Ryerson Limited
Toronto Montreal New York Auckland Bogotá Caracas Lisbon London Madrid Mexico Milan New Delhi Paris San Juan Singapore Sydney Tokyo

Study Guide to accompany
Macroeconomics
Fourth Canadian Edition

1 2 3 4 5 6 7 8 9 10 AP 2 1 0 9 8 7 6 5 4 3

Printed and bound in Canada

Sponsoring Editor: Jennifer Mix

Cover and Text Design: Mireault Images

Canadian Cataloguing in Publication Data
Startz, Richard
Study guide to accompany Macroeconomics, fourth Canadian edition

Supplement to: Dornbusch, Rudiger. Macroeconomics. 4th Canadian ed.
ISBN 0-07-551404-4

1. Macroeconomics. I. Sparks, Gordon R. II. Atkins, Frank J. (Frank Joseph), 1951– . III. Dornbusch, Rudiger. Macroeconomics. 4th Canadian ed. IV. Title.

HB172.5.D672 1993 339 C93-093148-3

CONTENTS

To the Student ix

Part 1: Determination of National Income

Chapter 1	Introduction	3
2	National Income Accounting	10
3	Income and Spending	17
4	Money, Interest, and Income	27
5	International Trade and Exchange Rates	39
6	International Capital Flows and Stabilization Policy	54

Part 2: Income and the Price Level

Chapter 7	Aggregate Supply and Demand: An Introduction	71
8	Aggregate Supply in the Short Run	81
9	Aggregate Supply and Demand in an Open Economy	91

Part 3: Aggregate Demand and Stabilization Policy

Chapter 10	Consumption and Saving	105
11	Investment Spending	113
12	The Demand for Money	124
13	The Money Supply Process	132
14	Problems of Stabilization Policy	141
15	Fiscal Policy and Public Finance	149

Part 4: Unemployment, Inflation, and Growth

Chapter 16	The Rate of Inflation in the Short and Long Run	157
17	Inflation and Unemployment	169

18 Money, Deficits, and Inflation 176
19 Monetarism and the Fight Against Inflation in Canada 187
20 Current Issues in Macroeconomic Policy 193
21 Long-Term Growth and Productivity 201

Answers to Study Guide Questions and Problems 208

Answers to Text Problems (even-numbered) 261

Notation in *Macroeconomics*, Fourth Canadian Edition 295

Economic Data Tables 299

To the Student

The *Study Guide* is designed for use with Dornbusch, Fischer, and Sparks, *Macroeconomics*, Fourth Canadian Edition. The only sensible reason for the existence of a study guide is to *make learning easier.*

Format

In the main section of this book, most of the twenty-one chapters have the following features:

- **Focus of the Chapter** gives a quick peek at the most important topics of the chapter.
- **Section Summaries** summarize each section of the text briefly.
- **Thinking Like an Economist** is a new feature of the *Study Guide* which is described in detail below.
- **Key Terms** lists the most important technical terms used in the chapter.
- **Graph It** asks you to plot data, complete a graph, or fill in a chart. Most of these are quite simple. Think of the Graph Its as being like warmup exercises before a run or limbering-up scales for piano practice. Taking a pencil in hand gets your mind loosened up and gets your mind focussed on the subject at hand.
- **Fill-In Questions** test the most important ideas and concepts of the chapter.
- **True-False Questions *and* Multiple-Choice Questions** test the detailed concepts of the chapter and sometimes require you to work out some simple problems.
- **Problems**, which finish up each chapter, require you to apply the concepts of the chapter.

There are also two **answer sections**, which provide (1) answers to every question in the *Study Guide* and (2) answers to the even-numbered problems that appear at the end of chapters of the main text.

There is a section on the mathematical **notation** used in the textbook. Finally, **tables** at the back of the book give various kinds of annual economic data for Canada; you may want to refer to them to get a feeling for what the real numbers in the economy are.

How to Study Macroeconomics

Do not! It wastes too much time. Instead:

Practise Macroeconomics

Practise, do not study. Many diligent students read and reread the text several times, underline all the important points, and spend hours and hours trying to memorize facts and theories, but they find that somehow they are not quite catching on. As the authors of the text say, *active learning* is the only way to learn. Do not waste valuable hours trying to remember masses of material; instead, spend a small amount of time trying to *focus* on its structure. This *Study Guide* has been created to provide you with very specific questions to practise on.

The questions in this book are not just lists of points to remember; most of them are intended to illustrate a basic principle. If you answer a question incorrectly, decide whether you have merely missed a minor point or whether you have overlooked some principle. The questions become progressively more difficult. Some of the problems are quite advanced. While you may be able to answer all the Fill-In Questions in two minutes, the problems take time to work through. When it becomes necessary to choose between rereading the text for the third time and spending 20 minutes doing a hard problem, do the problem.

Use this book to learn more in less time.

About the "Thinking Like an Economist" Sections

A special feature of the *Study Guide* is the "Thinking Like an Economist" sections found in each chapter. In these sections we place the material of each chapter into a wider framework to help you answer the question, "Why do macroeconomists appear to disagree so often?" You will see that macroeconomists don't disagree so much as place differing emphasis on certain questions. You will find this section especially helpful when it appears to you that the material you are currently studying bears no resemblance to anything you have previously studied in macroeconomics.

Toward the end of the course, you should go through all of the "Thinking Like an Economist" sections to get an overall grasp of the material.

Some Hints for Study

These hints are based on our experience teaching a large number of students with the previous editions of the text and *Study Guide*.

- Don't become overwhelmed by details. Concentrate instead on the overall structure. Though the text covers thousands of important details, there are only a dozen or so major themes. Think of these themes as the large branches of a tree, and of the details as its leaves. It is much easier to trace a specific detail by running out along the right branch than it is to build up an entire tree from a pile of leaves.

- Study with a pencil in your hand and scribble in the margins or on scrap paper as you go. Pictures show structures better than words do. When the *Study Guide* describes how two curves interact, scribble a graph right there in the *Guide*. The picture you draw will stay with you much better than any words we can use.

Study Guide to accompany

MACRO ECONOMICS

FOURTH CANADIAN EDITION

PART I *Determination of National Income*

CHAPTER 1 *Introduction*

Focus of the Chapter

- This introductory chapter is designed to acquaint you with the methodology used in the study of economics in general and macroeconomics in particular. Our study of macroeconomics begins with an introduction to the principal concepts of macroeconomics and an overview of the textbook. We look at the questions of gross domestic product, unemployment, inflation, economic growth, and the balance of international payments.
- We introduce the use of models for economic analysis. The fundamental model is that of Aggregate Demand and Aggregate Supply. A unifying theme in this *Study Guide* is that there are two schools of thought in macroeconomics, and that the two schools have different views concerning the shape of the demand and supply curves.

Section Summaries

Micro- and macroeconomics emphasize different aspects of the economy. For instance, microeconomics worries about the level of an individual product price *relative* to the level of another individual product price. In macroeconomics we are concerned with the *overall level of prices*. Similarly, microeconomics is concerned with supply and demand of, say, different types of labour, while macroeconomics assumes that all of the individual labour markets can be aggregated into one overall labour market in Canada.

The three central issues on the research agenda of macroeconomics are to explain persistent unemployment, to explain price inflation, and to understand the determinants of the rate of growth of output. A central question is whether the government *can* and *should* do something about altering the state of the economy, and if so *what* should be done.

1.1 *Gross domestic product* (GDP) is the value of all final goods and services produced in the economy during a given time period. *Nominal*, or *current dollar*, GDP is the value of output at current prices, while *real*, or *constant dollar*, GDP measures output at the prices of a base year (1986 is currently being used). In both the text and the *Study Guide*, GDP means real GDP unless we explicitly use the term "nominal GDP."

From 1970 to 1990, GDP grew at an average annual rate of 3.4 percent, though of course some years were good and some were bad. Trend growth in GDP is due to increased amounts of labour and capital and to increased efficiency in using these factors of production. Year-to-year movements around trend depend on how much of the available resources are used. When unemployment is high, less is produced.

Full-employment output, or *potential output*, is the level of GDP that the economy would produce if all resources were being used at just the right level. Actual output fluctuates around this level. The difference between potential output and actual output is called the *output gap*, or *GDP gap*.

Many economic variables exhibit seasonal patterns over time. *Seasonally adjusted* data is corrected for the typical seasonal pattern observed in the past and is a measure of the underlying cyclical movement.

The *balance of payments* is the record of transactions with other countries. It includes *merchandise trade* as well as borrowing and lending and exchange of assets.

The foreign exchange rate is the relative value of the currencies of two countries. Countries can operate under a *flexible* (or *floating*) *exchange rate* or under a *fixed rate*, which involves pegging the rate within narrow bounds around a preannounced value.

1.2 Output growth and unemployment are related by *Okun's Law*. The trend growth of GDP is roughly 3.4 percent per year. If output grows faster than trend, unemployment falls.

Inflation is the rate of increase in prices. When prices are going up, the level of inflation is positive. When (on those rare occasions) prices are going down, the level of inflation is negative.

The *Phillips curve* describes a relation between inflation and unemployment: the higher the rate of unemployment, the lower the rate of inflation. This relation is fairly reliable in the short run (say, two years). In the long run, there is no tradeoff worth speaking about between inflation and unemployment.

1.3 The overall concepts in studying unemployment, growth, and inflation are *aggregate demand* and *aggregate supply*. Basically, aggregate demand tells how much GDP consumers, business, and the government choose to buy given the overall level of prices. Aggregate supply tells how much output is produced at a given price level. If the aggregate demand curve were to shift to the right, and the aggregate supply curve were very steep, the economy would experience a rise in prices with very little change in output.

Chapters 3 through 6 concentrate on aggregate demand. Later chapters consider aggregate supply as well as aggregate demand. You should think of the lessons of these early chapters as applying best at high levels of unemployment, that is, when the aggregate supply curve is flat.

Remember: In Chapters 3 through 6, *GDP really means aggregate demand for a given price level.*

1.4 Policy makers can affect the economy through *monetary policy* and *fiscal policy*. The primary instruments of monetary policy, controlled by the Bank of Canada, are the stock of money and, through the stock of money, the interest rate. The primary instruments of fiscal policy are tax rates and government spending. *Stabilization policy* is used to smooth out fluctuations in the economy and is also called *countercyclical policy*. Political use of policy instruments to reduce unemployment right before an election leads to the idea of the *political business cycle*.

1.5 Macroeconomics has two main intellectual traditions: one school of thought believes markets clear if left to themselves, and the other believes that government intervention may be required to improve the operation of the economy. In the 1960s this debate was between the monetarists (nonintervention) and the Keynesians (government intervention). Since the 1970s this debate has been carried on by the *New Classical* economists versus the *New Keynesian* economists.

The three central tenants of New Classical macroeconomics are that all markets are always in equilibrium, agents are utility maximizing individuals, and all decisions, especially those with regard to expectations of future events, are made in a rational manner. This approach to macroeconomics, which is sometimes called the *rational expectations equilibrium approach*, leads to the view that government intervention is not only unnecessary, it may even worsen the performance of the economy.

New Keynesian economists are similar to the 1960s Keynesians in that they do not believe that markets always clear, and they seek to explain why this might be the case. Adherents to this approach believe that there is a need for government intervention.

Many people are confused by the fact that there are two schools of thought in macroeconomics. However, this should be thought of as a difference in emphasis rather than complete disagreement. New Keynesians may be placing more emphasis on the short run, while New Classicals emphasize the long run. For instance, there may be serious informational problems in the short run that impede wage and price setting, while in the long run these informational problems are overcome.

1.6 The easiest way to study macroeconomics is to try to think like an economist. In this *Study Guide* we will include a section, wherever applicable, titled "Thinking Like an Economist." The section will help you to work through the logic of the arguments presented. You should draw diagrams to explain the material and try to present counterarguments to the results presented in the text. This way you will understand the material as opposed to memorizing the material.

Thinking Like an Economist

Economics, like other disciplines, has theories of how the world works. We try to explain these theories using models. Models are simply a summary of how we think various economic variables fit together to produce some economic outcome. The main model that we will use involves aggregate demand (*AD*) and aggregate supply (*AS*).

Together these curves determine the equilibrium price level and level of output. In Figure 1-1 we have drawn the *AD/AS* diagram for two different assumptions concerning the shape of the *AS* curve.

In each of these cases consider what would happen if the government were to pursue, say, an expansionary monetary policy, which would shift the *AD* curve up and

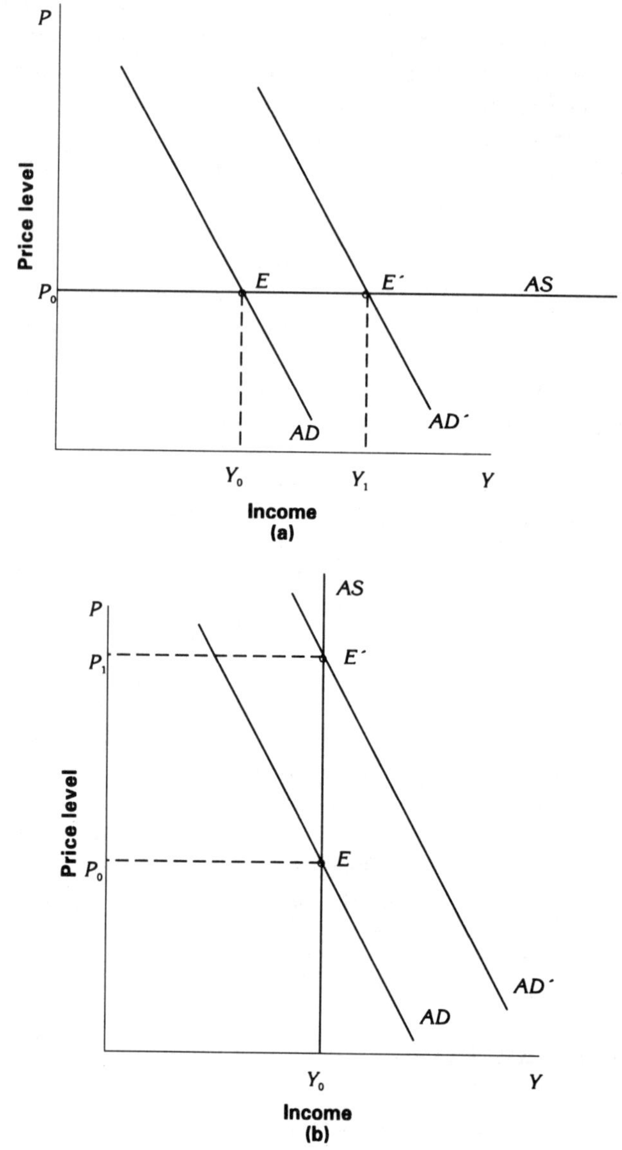

Figure 1-1

to the right. In Figure 1-1(a), the *AS* curve is completely horizontal. In this case, expansionary policy causes output to change while the price level remains constant. In Figure 1-1(b), the *AS* curve is completely vertical, and expansionary monetary policy causes the price level to rise, while output does not change.

So, which result is correct? The answer is that either of them could be correct in different situations. The result that only output will change in response to monetary policy could be thought of as a short-run result. This type of assumption will occupy us for the first six chapters of the text. The result that only price will change in response to monetary policy could be thought of as a long-run result, something that will happen once all of the rigidities have been worked out. We will see this result in later chapters of the text. This is our first example of the two schools of thought. Very strict Keynesians believe that Figure 1-1(a) is correct, while classical economists believe Figure 1-1(b) is correct.

Key Terms

Monetarists
Keynesians
New Classical macroeconomist
Rational expectations
GDP, nominal and real
Trend or potential output
Peak
Trough
Recovery or expansion
Recession
Output gap
Okun's Law
Seasonal variation
Supply shocks
Balance of payments
Exchange rate
Inflation
Supply-side economics
Growth
Unemployment
Business cycle
Phillips curve
Monetary policy
Fiscal policy
Stabilization policies
Activists
Aggregate demand and supply

Graph It 1

The easiest way to see whether the economy is doing well is to chart real GDP. If GDP is going up by more than its usual trend, the economy is doing well — and vice versa. In Chart 1-1 you are asked to graph the annual rate of change in GDP from 1971 through 1991. Over this period, GDP grew about 3.4 percent each year on average, though some years had faster growth and some lower.

In order to fill out the chart, you must first calculate the rates of change of GDP and then plot them. The relevant data that you need can be found in the Appendix of this *Study Guide*. For example, GDP was $303.5 billion in 1972 and $287.0 billion in

Table 1-1

Year	GDP	Percentage Change from Previous Year
1971	287.0	—
1972	303.5	5.7
1973	______	______
1974	______	______
1975	______	______
1976	______	______
1977	______	______
1978	______	______
1979	______	______
1980	______	______
1981	______	______
1982	______	______
1983	______	______
1984	______	______
1985	______	______
1986	______	______
1987	______	______
1988	______	______
1989	______	______
1990	______	______
1991	______	______

1971. Thus the annual growth rate was 100 × [(303.5 − 287.0)/287.0], or 5.7 percent. We've filled in several years on the table and chart. You do the rest.

Fill-In Questions

1. The value of production when all inputs are fully employed is ______ ______.
2. The difference between production with fully employed inputs and actual production is the ______.
3. The bottom of the business cycle is called the ______.
4. Economic policy makers may try to improve economic performance by changing government spending and taxes, which are types of ______ policy.

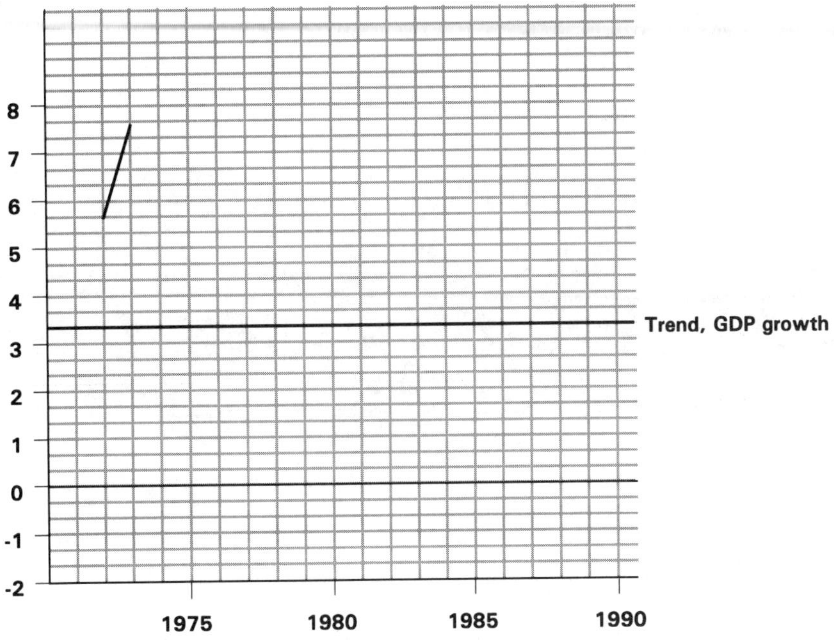

Chart 1-1

5. Or they may try to do so by changing the money supply or interest rates, which are examples of ________________ policy.
6. Both (4) and (5) are examples of ________________ .
7. GDP and unemployment are related through ________________ .
8. A time of high economic growth is called ________________ .
9. Times of economic weakness and contractions are termed ________________ .
10. New Classical economists believe that agents form expectations in a(n) ________________ manner.
11. New Keynesian economists believe that there is a need for ________________ ________________ in the economy.

True-False Questions

T F **1.** GDP growth and increases in the unemployment rate are positively related.

T F **2.** In the first six chapters of the text, prices are taken as being given.

CHAPTER 2 National Income Accounting

Focus of the Chapter

- Under the heading "National Income Accounting," we consider the several different ways in which the national economic pie can be sliced into its component parts.
- While we are taking apart GDP, we are also really learning how the different sources of aggregate demand can be added together to determine total national income.

Section Summaries

2.1 *Gross domestic product* (GDP) measures the value of all final output of the economy. We measure only the value of final goods because counting both the value of a car and the value of the steel in the car would be double-counting. Double-counting is avoided by working with the concept of *value added*. The Goods and Services Tax is an example of a value added tax. GDP includes the value of current production and excludes the sale of existing goods from inventory. Goods are valued at their market price.

GDP measures the value of goods produced within a country. *Gross national product* is also used as a measure of output; it is the value of goods and services produced by domestically owned factors of production. *Net national product* (NNP) is GNP minus depreciation — it is current production minus an allowance for the wearing-out of equipment.

2.2 For the nation as a whole, income must equal output. When one person buys an item, the money paid for it is part of another person's income. There are two qualifications to this. Replacement of worn machinery does not make a net addition to income because it is a cost of production. Sales and other indirect taxes also have to be deducted, since these payments are not directly part of anyone's income.

Net domestic income can be viewed as the sum of all payments to factors of production — wages, profits, and so on. National income can be further broken down into personal income and *personal disposable income* by subtracting those elements of income that do not accrue to individuals.

Personal disposable income must be either consumed or saved.

2.3 GDP can also be divided up into expenditure categories. The four sources of spending are consumption, investment, government expenditure on goods and services, and net exports.

2.4 Because prices change from year to year, we distinguish *real GDP* from *nominal GDP*. Nominal GDP is the value of output at current prices, while real GDP measures the physical quantity of output by valuing it at the prices of a base year.

Wherever we use the term "GDP" we mean real GDP, unless we specifically state "nominal GDP."

A *price index* is a measure of the average level of prices in the economy. It attempts to compare the price of goods on average in one year with the price of goods in a previous year. The most important price indexes are the *GDP implicit price index*, the *consumer price index*, and the *industrial product price index*.

2.5 GDP data are not perfect measures of economic output or welfare. This is because of the difficulties involved in measuring nonmarket activities such as volunteer work or housework.

2.6 Several important identities summarize the conventions of national income accounting. Be sure to understand the identities in terms of the economic concepts represented, not just as a set of abstract symbols.

$Y \equiv C + I + G + NX$	fundamental identity of aggregate demand
$YD \equiv Y + TR - TA$	sources of disposable income
$YD \equiv C + S$	uses of disposable income
$BD \equiv (G + TR) - TA$	budget deficit

Y = GDP	YD = disposable income
C = consumption	TR = transfers
I = investment	TA = taxes
G = government expenditure	S = savings
NX = net exports	BD = government budget deficit

All these are summarized by the basic macroeconomic identity:

$$C + G + I + NX \equiv Y \equiv YD + (TA - TR) \equiv C + S + (TA - TR)$$

Thinking Like an Economist

We introduced the concept of using models in Chapter 1 of this *Study Guide*. Each topic in the text involves analyzing some economic model. The overall model is the *AD/AS* model. At times we will have to break off small sectors of the economy to study in isolation. However, even these smaller models will involve some sort of demand and supply considerations. Recall that a model describes how we believe economic variables fit together to produce an economic outcome. We can think of variables in a model as being either *exogenous* or *endogenous*.

Some variables are taken as inputs to a model. These are called *exogenous*. There are three general types of exogenous variables. Some economic variables are given by nature (the weather, for example), or at least are taken to be outside the scope of study of the model (investor psychology, for instance). Some economic variables can be set by policy makers. These are called *policy variables*. The level of government spending and the level of the money stock are two important policy variables. Changes in these exogenous variables cause shifts in curves. For example, in Chapter 1 of this *Study Guide* we saw that an increase in the money supply, which is an increase in an exogenous policy variable, shifts out the aggregate demand curve.

Variables that may affect the reactions of the economy but that are not of any direct interest in and of themselves are called *parameters*. The marginal propensity to consume is an important economic parameter. (It will be introduced in Chapter 3.)

Endogenous variables are those that are determined internally by a given economic model. In the *AD/AS* model, price and real national income are the endogenous variables.

Exogenous variables determine the level of endogenous variables. The relation of exogenous to endogenous variables is one of cause to effect. Sensible questions are: "For a given change in an exogenous variable, what changes in the endogenous variables are expected?" and "In order to achieve a desired change in an endogenous variable, what change in a given exogenous variable would be required?" For example, how much will price and real national income change if the government were to increase the money supply? It is not sensible to ask about the effect of a change in an endogenous variable. A change in some endogenous variable is always the result of some more fundamental change in some exogenous variable.

Key Terms

Gross domestic product (GDP)
Final goods
Value added
Market prices
Factor cost
Gross national product (GNP)
Personal disposable income
Consumption
Government expenditure on goods and services
Investment
Net exports

Net national product (NNP)
Depreciation
Net domestic income
Factor shares
Personal income
Consumer durables
Real GDP
GDP Implicit Price Index
Consumer price index
Government budget deficit
Transfers

Graph It 2

Economists spend a lot of time drawing straight lines on graph paper. This chapter's Graph It asks you to draw a line just for practice. We've taken two possible relations between consumption and income from Chapter 10. We've graphed the first in Chart 2-1. You are asked to draw the second in Chart 2-2. The two possible relations are

$$C = 6 + 0.90Y \text{ (ours)}$$
$$C = 47 + 0.73Y \text{ (yours)}$$

One draws a straight line by finding two points on the line and then connecting them. One point is found easily by taking $Y = 0$, and so $C = 6$, and we put a dot at 6 on the

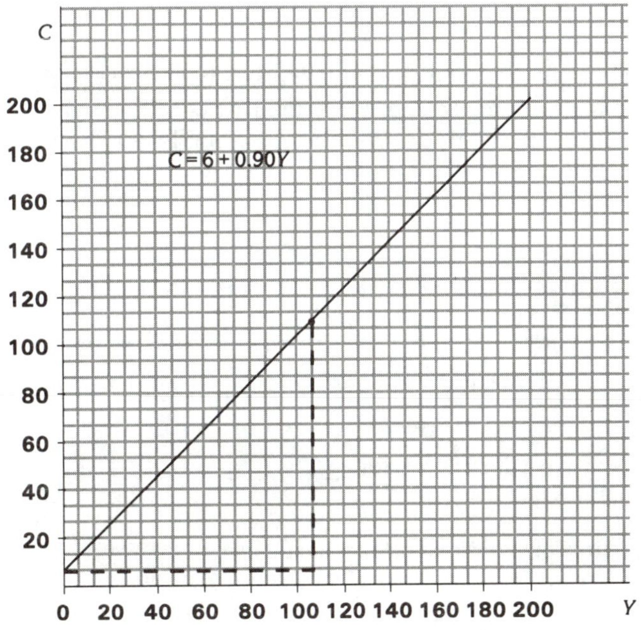

Chart 2-1

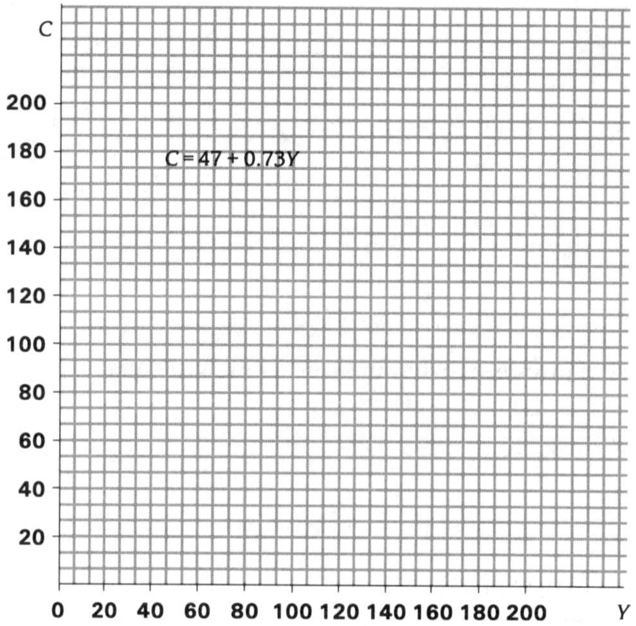

Chart 2-2

C axis. Since the slope of our relation is 0.90, consumption must go up 9 points for every 10 points that income goes up. From the first dot we counted off 10 positions to the right and then 9 positions up. We placed a second dot there and then drew the line connecting the two dots. Now you draw your relation on the blank graph.

Fill-In Questions

1. The value of all final goods and services produced in the economy is ____________ ____________.

2. It is necessary to adjust GNP for ____________ in order to calculate net national product.

3. GDP measures production within Canada using ____________ factors of production.

4. A person's disposable income is (basically) either ____________ or ____________.

5. The principal difference between net domestic income and disposable income is the addition of ____________________ and the subtraction of ____________________.

6. If all physical output and input were to stay constant while the money price of everything doubled, then ____________________ GDP would double, but more importantly, ____________________ GDP would be unchanged.

7. The ratio of nominal to real GDP is a useful price index called the ____________________.

8. The index we use to measure the cost of living is the ____________________.

9. The excess of private savings over investment must equal ____________________ plus ____________________.

10. Net exports is the excess of ____________________ over ____________________.

True-False Questions

T F 1. Investment equals private savings.

T F 2. Sale of a home adds to GDP.

T F 3. The real estate agent's commission on the sale of a home adds to GDP.

T F 4. Depreciation expenses are part of GDP.

T F 5. Depreciation expenses are part of disposable income.

T F 6. Purchase of common stock is part of investment.

T F 7. Purchase of a jeep by a camping enthusiast is part of consumption.

T F 8. Purchase of a jeep by a logging company is part of investment.

T F 9. The difference between gross investment and net investment is the same as the difference between GNP and NNP.

T F 10. Exports are part of GDP.

Multiple-Choice Questions

1. Which of the following is not part of aggregate demand?
   - (a) government expenditure
   - (b) taxes
   - (c) net exports
   - (d) investment

2. Which of the following is part of aggregate demand?
   (a) indirect taxes
   (b) transfers
   (c) consumption
   (d) imports

3. Social insurance payments are counted as part of
   (a) government expenditure
   (b) transfers
   (c) taxes
   (d) consumption

4. Benefits paid to government employees are counted as part of
   (a) government expenditure
   (b) transfers
   (c) taxes
   (d) consumption

5. Suppose investment and three of the following four items remain fixed. Which of the four might have risen?
   (a) government budget surplus
   (b) saving
   (c) net exports
   (d) tax rates

6. Suppose GNP and NNP both rise by the same amount while three of the following four remain fixed. Which of the four could have not risen?
   (a) gross investment
   (b) net investment
   (c) consumption
   (d) net exports

7. An increase in the price of bicycles will show up in
   (a) the GDP deflator
   (b) the consumer price index
   (c) the industry selling price index
   (d) both **(a)** and **(b)**

8. If the price of apples goes up and the price of oranges goes down, this change would most likely be reflected in an increase in
   (a) the GDP deflator
   (b) the consumer price index
   (c) the industry selling price index
   (d) none of these

9. Which of the following are part of net domestic income?
   (a) wages
   (b) profits
   (c) both wages and profits
   (d) neither wages nor profits

10. Which of the following is not part of net domestic income?
   (a) rental income
   (b) welfare payments
   (c) salaries
   (d) interest

Problems

1. This is a problem in national income accounting. You are given the following facts about the economy: consumption = \$1000; saving = \$100; government expenditure = \$300. The government budget is balanced. What is the value of GDP?

2. Suppose saving equals \$200, the budget deficit is \$50, and the trade deficit is \$10. What is the level of investment?

CHAPTER 3 *Income and Spending*

Focus of the Chapter

- The heart of Keynesian macroeconomic analysis is the idea that national income and the level of unemployment depend on aggregate demand. We have already seen that in the *AD/AS* model, both the price level and the level of real national income are endogenous. Recall, however, that in the first six chapters of the book, the *AS* curve is assumed to be horizontal. Therefore real national income is determined by aggregate demand and the price level is exogenous.

Section Summaries

3.1 The fundamental identity of aggregate demand, $Y \equiv C + I + G + NX$, shows that the *actual* level of output must always equal the sum of all the different sources of aggregate demand. However, we can imagine a situation in which the *planned* level of output is not equal to the *planned* levels of consumption, investment, and government spending. When the planned and actual levels are different, unintended inventory changes occur. When planned and actual levels are equal, the economy is in equilibrium. We use this fact to find the equilibrium of the economy by finding the level of GDP where planned output equals the sum of planned consumption, investment, and government expenditure.

3.2 Increased income causes increased consumption. When an individual receives an additional dollar of income, a fraction of that dollar is consumed and the remaining fraction is saved. The fraction of each additional dollar that is consumed is called the *marginal propensity to consume*, abbreviated to MPC.

Since saving is just the difference between income and consumption ($S \equiv Y - C$), a given consumption function implies a specific saving function. Saving and consumption cannot be looked at independently.

In order to determine the equilibrium level of output, we set income equal to planned consumption, which is itself a function of income, plus planned investment. The equilibrium of the economy is found by solving for income as a function of the autonomous components of consumption and investment. We can write aggregate demand as $AD = C + cY + I$, or letting $A = C + I$, as $AD = \overline{A} + cY$. For the economy to be in equilibrium, GDP must equal aggregate demand, or $AD = Y$.

The equilibrium level of GDP can be found by using the graphic technique illustrated in Figure 3-1 (text Figure 3-5). The 45° line represents the *equilibrium condition* $AD = Y$, and the second line is the graph of $AD = \overline{A} + cY$. The intersection of the two lines gives the equilibrium value of GDP.

Alternatively, and equivalently, equilibrium may be found by equating investment and savings ($I = S$). (Both methods of finding equilibrium will require some minor modification when the public and foreign sectors are put back into the model.)

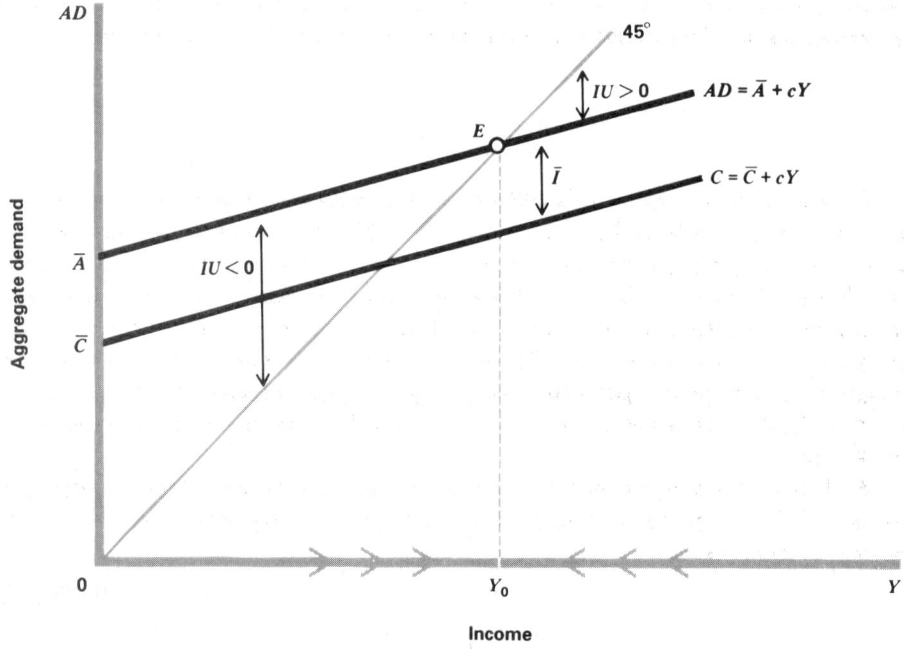

Figure 3-1

3.3 A dollar increase in autonomous spending does not in general increase GDP by a dollar. The original increase adds directly to aggregate demand and also induces further spending. If the marginal propensity to consume is c, then a dollar increase in autonomous spending brings a further increase of c — but this further increase itself induces yet a further increase, this increase causes yet another increase, and so forth. When all the increases are added up, the total addition to GDP is given by the multiplier. The value of the multiplier is $1/(1-c)$. The change in GDP as a result of the original change in autonomous spending is

$$\Delta Y = \frac{1}{1-c}\,\Delta\overline{A}$$

3.4 Reintroducing the government sector requires two major modifications to our model. First, government expenditure belongs in the adding-up identity for GDP. Second, consumption truly depends on disposable income. If the government uses an income tax, the multiplier is reduced to

$$\frac{1}{1-c(1-t)}$$

where the parameter t is the marginal income tax rate. As an example, if the MPC is 9/10 and the tax rate is 1/6, the multiplier will be 4. Because the multiplier is reduced, an income tax is called an *automatic stabilizer*. The multiplier for transfers is

$$\frac{c}{1-c(1-t)}$$

3.5 The budget surplus is the difference between government income and government outgo. Symbolically, $BS = TA - G - TR$. The surplus responds to both exogenous changes in government expenditure and endogenous changes in tax collections due to changes in GDP. The full-employment budget surplus measures what the surplus would be if the economy were at full employment, with current expenditure policy and current tax rates. The full-employment budget surplus responds to changes in government expenditure and in tax rates, but is immune to those changes in actual GDP that occur for other reasons, such as an increase in autonomous investment.

3.6 When the foreign sector is included, net exports are added to aggregate demand. Taking exports as autonomous and imports as dependent on income, the multiplier becomes

$$\frac{1}{1-c(1-t)+m}$$

where the parameter m is the marginal propensity to import.

Just as our model of the Canadian economy depends on our exports to other countries, so too the state of foreign economies depends on our imports from them. Thus all nations are interdependent. If our income rises, we import more and this leads to an expansion of foreign GDP, leading to more purchases of Canadian exports and a further increase in Canadian GDP. This is called the *repercussion effect*. It is one example of a *spillover effect*, in which an increase in one country's GDP increases imports, thus spilling over into increased GDP in other countries.

Thinking Like an Economist

It may seem odd to you that there appears to be no explicit treatment of aggregate demand equals aggregate supply in this chapter. However, the model in this chapter can be viewed in this framework. The national accounts identity

$$Y \equiv C + I + G + NX$$

can be viewed as current measured output, that is, the supply of goods and services at any point in time. The equilibrium condition that

$$AD = Y$$

can be viewed as the condition that aggregate demand equals aggregate supply. However, we cannot graph aggregate supply and demand on the same graph in this situation, as aggregate supply is simply measured output (Y) at any point in time. The 45° line therefore represents the equilibrium condition that aggregate demand equals aggregate supply.

A central result of this model is that a change in demand will bring about a change in supply. Because there is no explicit supply curve, only current measured output, there is no explicit story concerning where the increase in supply comes from. We simply assume that output goes up when demand goes up.

This model can be cast in the *AD/AS* framework that was introduced in Chapter 1, under the assumption that the aggregate supply curve is horizontal. This is illustrated in Figure 3-2.

Figure 3-2(a) is similar to Figure 3-8 in the text. The initial equilibrium is at *E*. If there is an increase in some autonomous portion of aggregate demand, the *AD* curve shifts up and real national income increases. The new equilibrium is at *E′*. Exactly the same result can be shown using Figure 3-2(b). The increase in autonomous aggregate demand shifts the *AD* curve outward. The *AS* curve is horizontal and therefore there is an increase in supply with no price level change. Accordingly, *E* and *E′* are the same points as in Figure 3-2(a).

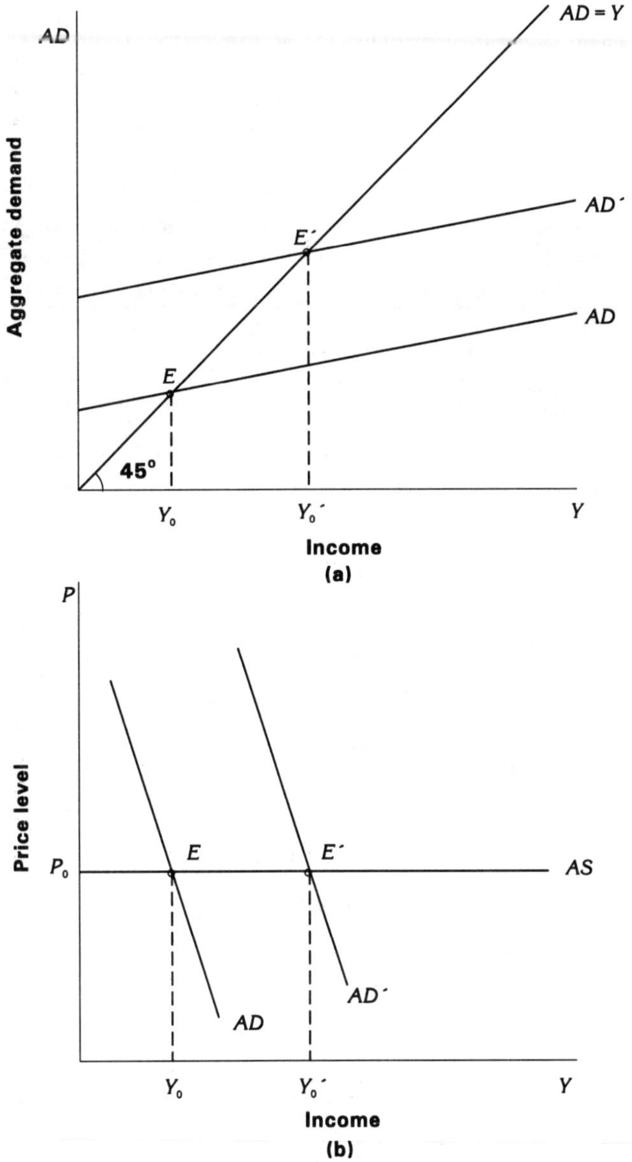
AD
AD = Y
Aggregate demand
AD´
E´
AD
E
45°
Y0
Y0´
Y
Income
(a)
P
Price level
E
E´
P0
AS
AD´
AD
Y0
Y0´
Y
Income
(b)

Figure 3-2

Key Terms

Aggregate demand
Equilibrium output
Unintended (undesired) inventory accumulation
Planned aggregate demand
Consumption function
Marginal propensity to consume
Marginal propensity to save
Multiplier
Automatic stabilizer
Budget surplus
Balanced budget multiplier
Full-employment (high-employment) surplus
Marginal propensity to import
Repercussion effect

Graph It 3

For this Graph It, you are asked to use a graph to prove the following proposition: *For a given change in* $\overline{A}$, *a large marginal propensity to consume means a large*

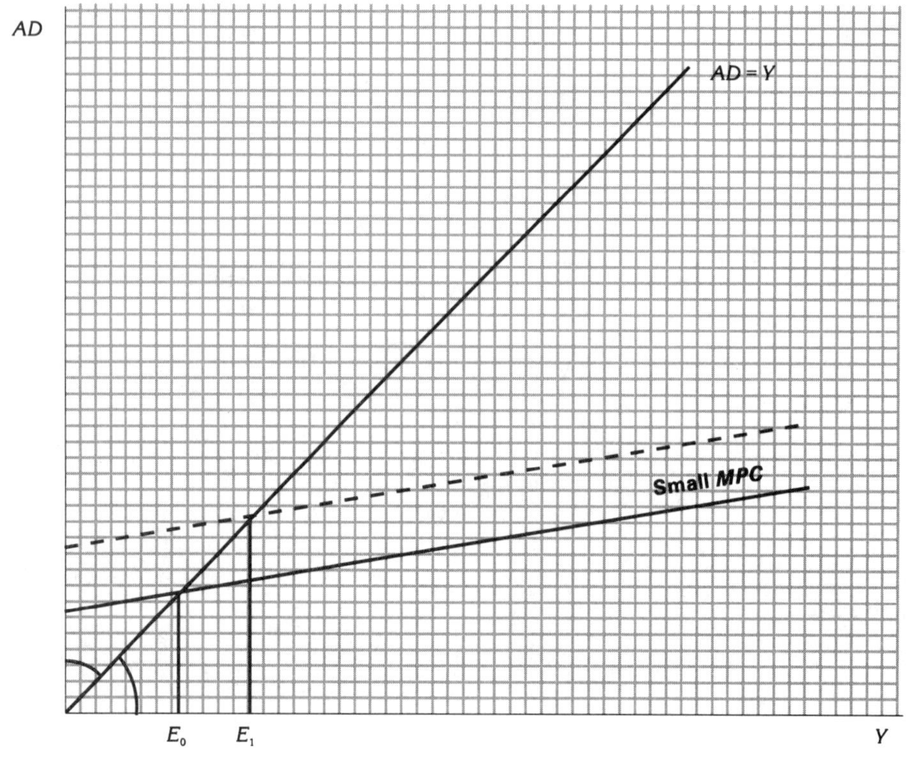

Chart 3-1

change in GDP. To prove this proposition requires a graph with five lines on it. We've provided the first three lines on Chart 3-1. You are asked to draw in the last two.

The first line we drew was the 45° line for $AD = Y$. Then we drew in the solid aggregate demand line for $AD = A_0 + cY$ and the dashed aggregate demand line for $AD = \overline{A}_1 + cY$, with $\overline{A}_1 > \overline{A}_0$. GDP is shown increasing from level E_0 to level E_1. Notice that both our aggregate demand lines were fairly shallow, indicating that the marginal propensity to consume is small.

Now you draw in a solid aggregate demand line that goes through point E_0 with a steep slope, indicating a large *MPC*. Then draw a dashed line parallel to your solid line, only moved higher by the same vertical distance as appears between the two lines we drew in. Mark the point where your dashed line hits the 45° line as E_2. You should be able to see that the distance from E_0 to E_2 is greater than the distance from E to E_1.

Fill-In Questions

1. When planned and actual spending are equal, the economy is in __________________.
2. The relation between consumption and income is called __________________.
3. A $10 increase in GDP induces an increase in consumption of $10 times the __________________ (in the absence of an income tax).
4. The complement of the marginal propensity to consume is the __________________.
5. An initial increase in autonomous spending has an effect on GDP that is magnified by the __________________.
6. The difference between government expenditure and taxes is the __________________.
7. A(n) __________________ is a program, such as the income tax, that reduces the impact of shocks to the economy without any direct government action.
8. The __________________ is the difference between tax receipts at full employment and government expenditure.
9. The balanced budget multiplier equals __________________.
10. In equilibrium, planned investment equals __________________ and __________________.

True-False Questions

Assume that the autonomous components of spending remain constant except as specified.

T F 1. Increasing transfers increases GDP.

T F 2. Increasing the income tax rate increases GDP.

T F 3. Increasing government expenditure increases savings.

T F 4. Increasing government expenditure, in the presence of a proportional income tax, increases the budget deficit.

T F 5. Increased autonomous consumption, in the presence of an income tax, increases the full-employment budget surplus.

T F 6. Increasing autonomous consumption increases savings.

T F 7. An increase in the marginal propensity to consume reduces income.

T F 8. In the absence of an income tax, an increase in government expenditure, together with an equal decrease in transfers, will increase GDP by the amount of the increase in government expenditure.

T F 9. In the presence of an income tax, an increase in government expenditure, together with an equal decrease in transfers, will increase GDP by the amount of the increase in government expenditure.

T F 10. The greater the marginal propensity to import, the greater the impact on GDP of a change in government expenditure.

Multiple-Choice Questions

1. If the marginal propensity to consume is 0.8, then, in the absence of an income tax, the multiplier is
   (a) 1 (c) 5
   (b) 2 (d) 10

2. If the *MPC* is 0.8, then, in the absence of an income tax, the multiplier relating changes in transfer payments to changes in national income is
   (a) 4 (c) 6
   (b) 5 (d) 8

3. In the presence of a *MPC* equal to 0.9 and a tax rate of 33 1/3 percent, the multiplier is
   (a) 1/2 (c) 5
   (b) 2 1/2 (d) 10

4. Using the same parameters as in question 3, a \$30 increase in government expenditure leads to a change in the budget surplus of

(a) –\$30 **(c)** \$5
(b) –\$5 **(d)** \$30

5. Using the information in question 4, the increase in the full-employment budget surplus is

(a) –\$30 **(c)** \$25
(b) –\$25 **(d)** \$30

6. If the *MPC* is 0.75, a \$10 tax increase leads to a change in savings of

(a) –\$30 **(c)** \$10
(b) –\$10 **(d)** \$30

7. In equilibrium, investment equals

(a) private savings **(c)** the sum of **(a)** and **(b)**
(b) the budget surplus **(d)** neither **(a)** nor **(b)**

8. An increase in the income tax rate causes the full-employment budget surplus to

(a) increase **(c)** the answer depends on t
(b) decrease **(d)** the answer depends on c

9. In the presence of an income tax, the effect on GDP of equal and opposite changes in government expenditure and transfers

(a) equals the change in government expenditure **(c)** depends on c
(b) depends on t **(d)** depends on both t and c

10. Comparing the effect of government expenditure on GDP in an economy with an income tax to the effect in an economy without an income tax, the effect in the former

(a) is greater **(c)** depends on *MPC*
(b) is less **(d)** cannot be determined

Problems

1. Government expenditure and taxes are \$500 and \$400, respectively. Investment equals \$200. The autonomous part of consumption is \$100. The marginal propensity to consume is 0.9. What is the level of GDP?

2. The marginal propensity to consume is 0.9. The income tax is 1/3 of income. The government decides to increase spending in order to increase GDP by \$750. How much should government spending increase? What happens to the budget deficit?

3. The *MPC* and the marginal income tax rate are 0.9 and 1/3, respectively. The budget deficit is observed to increase by $15.

(a) What amount of change in investment would account for this?

(b) What amount of change in government expenditure would account for this?

CHAPTER 4 *Money, Interest, and Income*

Focus of the Chapter

- *IS-LM* analysis is the core of the modern theory of aggregate demand. The *IS* curve is a locus of points in real national income, interest rate space for which the goods market is in equilibrium. It is derived by extending the simple model of Chapter 3 to include the interest rate as an endogenous variable.
- The *LM* curve is a locus of points in real national income, interest rate space for which the money market is in equilibrium.
- The effectiveness both of fiscal and of monetary policy depends on the slopes of the *IS* and *LM* curves.
- The fiscal policy/monetary policy mix determines the composition of output as well as the overall size of aggregate demand.
- In the final section, we algebraically combine the *IS* and *LM* schedules to determine the equation for aggregate demand in terms of autonomous spending and the real money supply.

Section Summaries

4.1 The *IS curve* represents equilibrium in the goods market. The *IS* curve shows all those combinations of income and interest at which the goods market is in balance, that is, where demand for goods and services equals supply of goods and services. The formula for the *IS* curve is found in the following manner. We start with the national accounts identity,

$$Y \equiv C + I + G$$

We saw in Chapter 3 of this *Study Guide* that this can be considered to be aggregate supply at any point in time. We then postulate a theory of aggregate demand:

$$AD = C^* + I^* + G^*$$

Variables with asterisks (*) denote descriptions of economic behaviour, and therefore we must have equations for each of them. We know from Chapter 3 that consumption depends on income. We assume that investment depends negatively on the interest rate. We also assume that government spending is exogenous.

$$\begin{aligned} C^* &= \overline{C} + cY \\ I^* &= \overline{I} - bi \\ G^* &= \overline{G} \end{aligned}$$

Substituting these three equations into the definition of aggregate demand gives us

$$AD = \overline{C} + cY + \overline{I} - bi + \overline{G}$$

which is the equation for our aggregate demand curve. The equilibrium condition is aggregate demand for goods and services equals aggregate supply of goods and services,

$$AD = Y$$

Substituting into the equilibrium condition gives

$$Y = \overline{C} + cY + \overline{I} - bi + \overline{G}$$

After collecting and rearranging terms we have the equation for the *IS* curve,

$$Y = \frac{1}{1-c}(\overline{C} + \overline{I} + \overline{G}) - \frac{b}{1-c}i$$

4.2 The *LM curve* represents equilibrium in the asset markets. The *LM* curve shows all those points of income and interest where money demand equals money supply. Given the wealth budget constraint we know that if the money market is in equilibrium, then the bond market is in equilibrium, and therefore all asset markets are in equilibrium. We can derive the *LM* curve in the following manner. Money demand is assumed to depend positively on income and negatively on the interest rate.

$$L = kY - hi$$

Money supply is taken to be exogenous. In this chapter we also assume that prices are fixed.

$$M^s/\overline{P} = \overline{M}/\overline{P}$$

The equilibrium condition is, as usual, demand equals supply.

$$L = \overline{M}/\overline{P}$$

Substituting into the equilibrium conditions gives the *LM* curve

$$\frac{\overline{M}}{\overline{P}} = kY - hi$$

or, rearranging terms,

$$i = -\frac{1}{h}\frac{\overline{M}}{\overline{P}} + \frac{k}{h}Y$$

The *LM* curve is often written this way, as we think of the money market as taking on the role of determining interest rates. This role is emphasized in the Thinking Like an Economist section below.

4.3 The *IS* and *LM* curves give us two independent relations between two endogenous variables, income and the interest rate. By solving the two equations simultaneously, we can find the equilibrium levels of income and interest. Figure 4-1 (text Figure 4-12) illustrates an *IS-LM* equilibrium.

Figure 4-2 (text Figure 4-13) uses the *IS-LM* apparatus to show the effects of an increase in autonomous spending. Note that an expansion in autonomous demand, such as an increase in government expenditure, increases both income and interest rates.

4.4 At any point other than the intersection of the *IS* and *LM* curves, the economy is out of equilibrium. The economy moves toward equilibrium according to whether there is an excess supply or demand for money and an excess supply or demand for goods. It is often reasonable to assume adjustment in the money market is very fast, so that the adjustment path to equilibrium moves along the *LM* curve.

4.5 When the Bank of Canada makes an *open market purchase*, it increases the money supply while reducing the outstanding supply of bonds. Notice that this operation reduces the interest rate but does not initially change private wealth. The

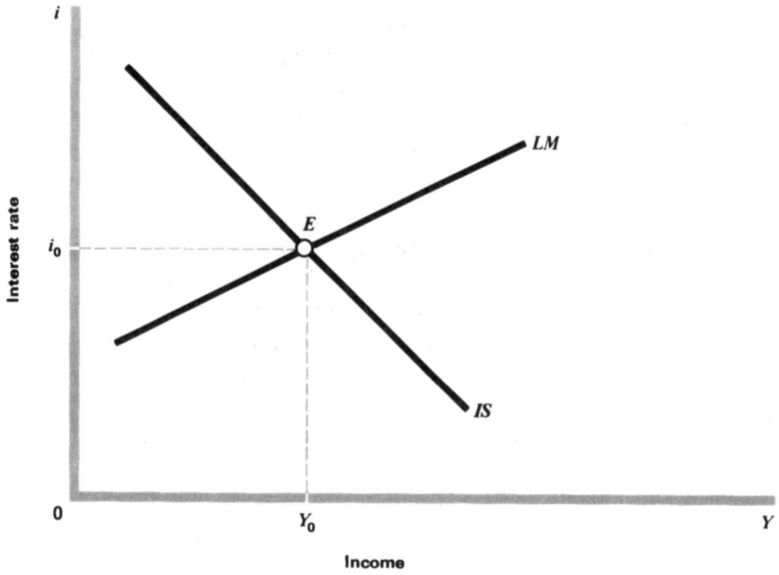

Figure 4-1

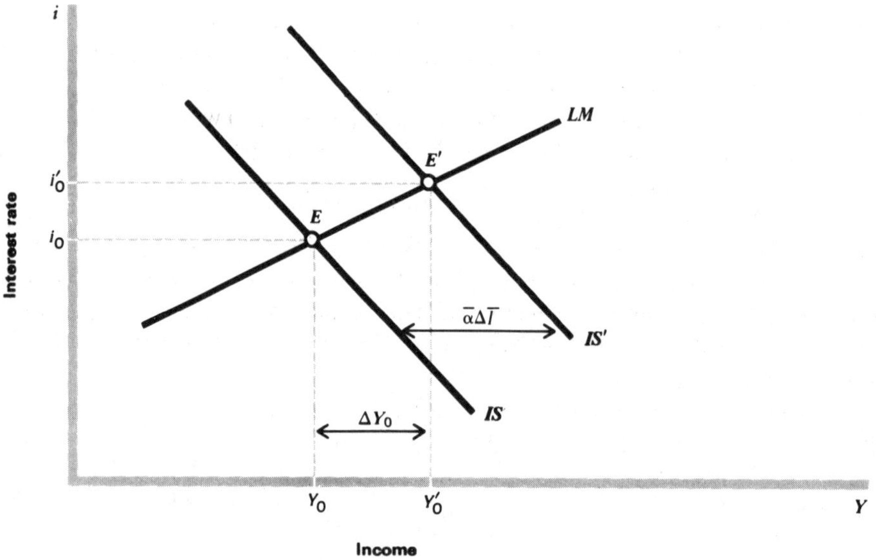

Figure 4-2

lower interest rate induces increased investment, which means that GDP rises. The flatter the slope of the *IS* curve, the greater the impact of an increase of the money supply on GDP.

With a horizontal *LM* curve, called the *liquidity trap*, an increase in the money supply does not move the *LM* curve, and so income is unaffected. A vertical *LM* curve, called the *classical case* or quantity theory case, gives the maximum effect of an increase in the money supply.

4.6 An increase in government spending increases GDP and the interest rate. The increased interest rate lowers investment. Thus, part of the increase in government spending is offset by a decrease in investment. This is called *crowding out*. In the quantity theory case, there is 100 percent crowding out; the increase in government spending is totally offset by a dropoff in investment, and so GDP does not increase at all. The flatter the *LM* schedule, the greater the increase in GDP. Thus fiscal policy has maximum power in the case of the liquidity trap and zero power in the quantity theory case.

Three rules summarize the effect of a fiscal expansion:

1. Income increases more, and interest rates increase less, the flatter the *LM* schedule.
2. Income increases more, and interest rates increase less, the flatter the *IS* schedule.
3. Income and interest rates increase more the larger the multiplier and thus the larger the horizontal shift of the *IS* schedule.

Will large government budget deficits crowd out investment? Not necessarily, since high budget deficits may be associated with higher income, and thus higher saving, rather than lower investment. In the real world the extent of crowding out depends on both the slope of the *LM* curve and the extent to which the central bank *accommodates* fiscal policy. The central bank accommodates fiscal policy when it increases the money supply (moves the *LM* curve right) to prevent interest rates from rising as the *IS* curve moves right.

4.7 Either fiscal or monetary policy can be used to expand aggregate demand. However, expansionary fiscal policy discourages investment, while expansionary monetary policy encourages investment. The choice of a policy mix, particularly between spending policy and tax policy, also depends on whether you favour a large government sector or a small one.

4.8 Since our *IS* and *LM* curves are both represented by linear equations, we can solve them together algebraically to find equilibrium income. The final equation for income in terms of all the exogenous variables is

$$Y = \frac{h\overline{\alpha}}{h + bk\overline{\alpha}}\overline{A} + \frac{b\overline{\alpha}}{h + bk\overline{\alpha}}\frac{\overline{M}}{\overline{P}}$$

In the text, this expression is simplified slightly further by defining

$$\psi = \frac{1}{h + bk\overline{\alpha}}$$

and writing the expression as

$$Y = \psi h\overline{\alpha}\,\overline{A} + \psi b\overline{\alpha}\,\frac{\overline{M}}{\overline{P}}$$

For obvious reasons, the first fraction is called the *fiscal policy multiplier* and the second is called the *monetary policy multiplier*; $\overline{\alpha}$ is the multiplier from Chapter 3, $\frac{1}{1-c}$ in the simplest model.

It is instructive to calculate the fiscal and monetary policy multipliers in the special cases of the liquidity trap and the classical case. The parameter h equals zero in the classical case, so the fiscal policy multiplier equals zero and the monetary policy multiplier reaches its maximum value, $1/k$. In a liquidity trap, the parameter h approaches infinity, and so the fiscal policy multiplier approaches the simple multiplier $\overline{\alpha}$ and the monetary policy multiplier goes to zero.

The final equation for the interest rate in terms of all the exogenous variables is

$$i = \psi k\overline{\alpha}\,\overline{A} - \psi\frac{\overline{M}}{\overline{P}}$$

Key Terms

_IS_ curve
_LM_ curve
Bond
Money
Portfolio decisions
Real balances (real money balances)
Wealth budget constraint
Open market operation
Transmission mechanism
Liquidity trap
Classical case
Crowding out
Monetary policy/fiscal policy mix
Investment subsidy

Thinking Like an Economist

The *IS-LM* model can be viewed as a form of general equilibrium model. That is, the model is a description of equilibrium in two markets at the same time. We have simultaneous equilibrium in the goods market ($Y = AD$) and the money market ($L = M^s/P$). In this section, we wish to investigate what happens to the general equilibrium nature of the model in adjustment towards equilibrium.

Consider how the model reacts to an increase in the money stock. This is described in Figure 4-3.

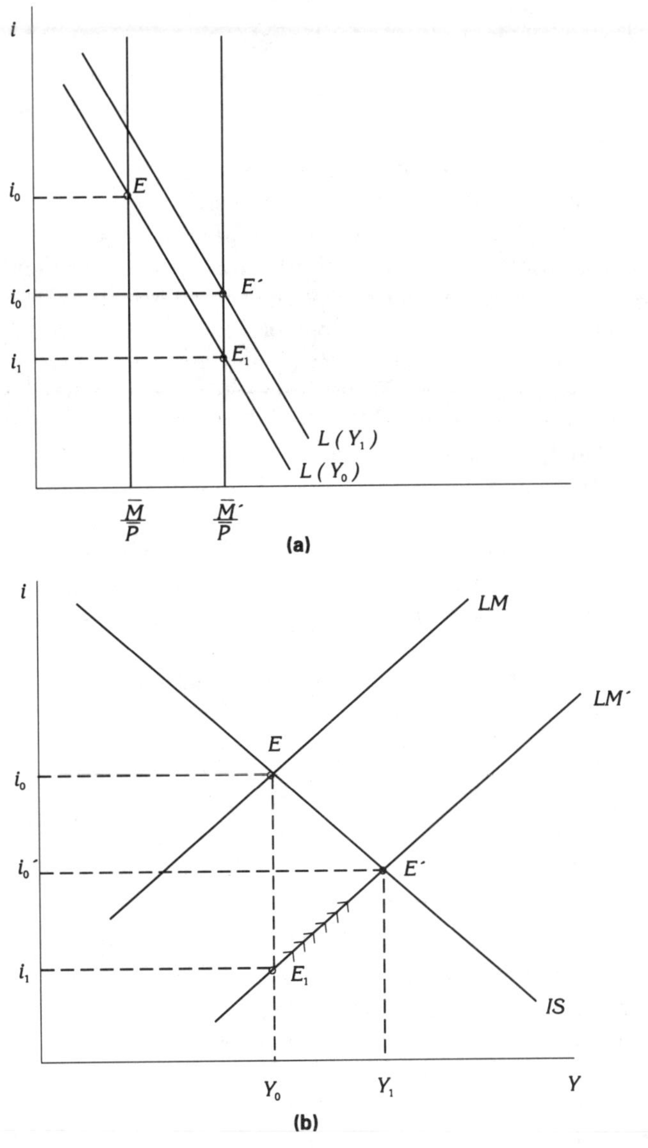

Figure 4-3

Figure 4-3(a) is a description of money market equilibrium, and Figure 4-3(b) is text Figure 4-16. The initial equilibrium is at point E where i_o and Y_o are consistent with equilibrium in both the goods and money markets. Now suppose that the monetary authorities increase the money stock to $\overline{M}'/\overline{P}$. Given the assumption of rapid money market adjustment, the interest rate immediately falls to i_1. Since income has not changed, the money demand function does not shift. The impact effect is a new equilibrium (i_1, Y_o) on the *new LM* curve. Notice here that the money market is in equilibrium while the goods market is not. That is, the combination (i_1, Y_o) which the model has produced as the new equilibrium interest rate and income is a point where money demand equals money supply; but, given that income has remained at Y_o, the interest rate i_1 is too low for goods market equilibrium. Therefore, there is excess demand in the goods market.

This points up an important feature of the *IS-LM* model: when there is an exogenous change which disturbs equilibrium, the money market clears before the goods market by producing a new (in this case lower) interest rate. Once the interest rate has fallen, the goods market reacts by increasing investment, and national income goes up. The increase in income causes money demand to increase (an upward shift in the money demand function), which increases the interest rate. Therefore, the adjustment path is upward *along* the *LM* curve.

The lesson to be learned here is that, in dynamic adjustment (that is, in describing the path that the economy takes toward equilibrium after an exogenous change), the role of the money market is to produce new interest rates, while taking changes in income as given, and the role of the goods market is to change income, while taking interest rate changes as given. This is one reason why we write the *LM* equation with the interest rate on the left-hand side, and we write the *IS* equation with income on the left-hand side.

Once all of the adjustments have occurred, the model is in general equilibrium again at E', where the same interest rate/income combination (i'_0, Y'_0) is consistent with equilibrium in both the goods and the money market.

Graph It 4

For this chapter's Graph It, we ask you to use graphs to demonstrate that an increase in the money stock generates a large increase in income if the *LM* curve is vertical (the *classical case*), a moderate increase in income if the *LM* curve has a moderate positive slope, and no change in income at all if the *LM* curve is horizontal (the *liquidity trap*). In Chart 4-1, we've provided three graphs, one under the other, with initial *IS* and *LM* curves filled in.

On the middle graph, we've also drawn in a dashed line showing the *LM* curve moved a distance Δ to the right. Note the equilibrium has moved from E_0 to E_2. Now you draw in new *LM* curves on the upper and lower graphs and show the new equilibria E_1 and E_3. You should find that the horizontal distance from E_0 to E_2 is less than the distance from E_0 to E_1 and greater than the distance from E_0 to E_3.

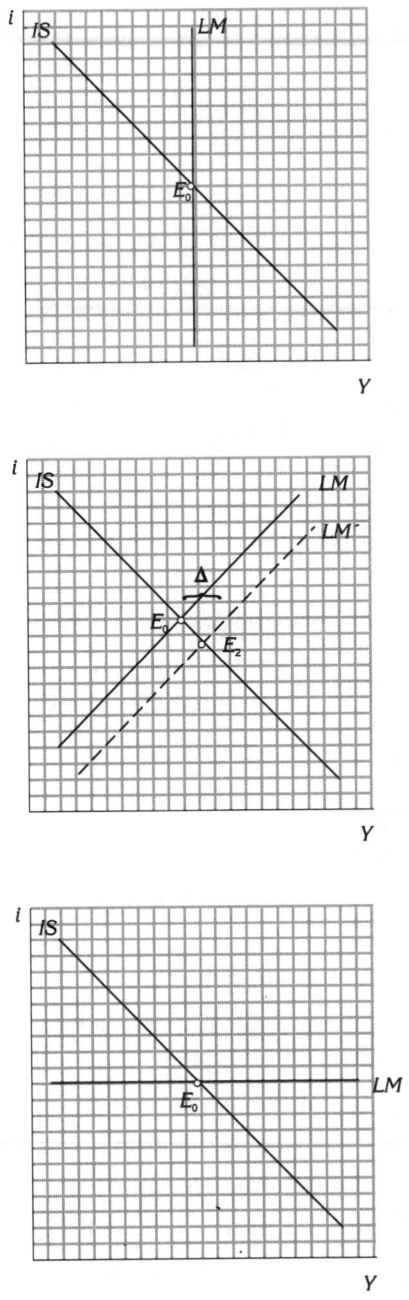

Chart 4-1

Fill-In Questions

1. Both the *IS* curve and the *LM* curve represent combinations of ________________ and the ________________.
2. The *IS* curve represents equilibrium in the ________________ market.
3. The *LM* curve represents equilibrium in the ________________ market.
4. A(n) ________________ produces an increase in the money supply and an equal decrease in outstanding bonds.
5. The interest rate rises when there exists an excess ________________ money.
6. A flat region of the *LM* curve is known as the ________________.
7. A vertical *LM* curve is called the ________________.
8. The key sector of aggregate demand linking the money market and the goods market is ________________.
9. The ratio of nominal money to the price level is called ________________.
10. Because of ________________, an increase in government spending increases GDP by less than one might think after reading Chapter 3.

True-False Questions

T F 1. Increased government spending moves the *IS* curve upward to the right.

T F 2. Increased money supply moves the *LM* curve downward to the right.

T F 3. For a given money supply, there is a positive relation between interest and income along the *LM* curve.

T F 4. For a given level of autonomous spending, there is a positive relation between interest and income along the *IS* curve.

T F 5. In the classical case, monetary policy has no effect on GDP.

T F 6. In the liquidity trap case, monetary policy has a large effect on GDP.

T F 7. Decreasing the money supply increases investment.

T F 8. Increasing government spending increases investment.

T F 9. Equal increases in government expenditure or transfers have the same effect on the *IS* curve.

T F 10. Tax rates do not matter in the *IS-LM* model.

Multiple-Choice Questions

1. Lower exogenous taxes lead to
   (a) higher income
   (b) higher interest
   (c) both
   (d) an increase in neither one

2. A lower money supply leads to
   (a) higher income
   (b) higher interest
   (c) both
   (d) an increase in neither one

3. An increase in the money supply increases
   (a) interest rates
   (b) investment
   (c) both
   (d) neither

4. An increase in government expenditure increases
   (a) interest rates
   (b) investment
   (c) both
   (d) neither

5. The steeper the *LM* curve, the more an increase in the money stock
   (a) increases GDP
   (b) lowers interest rates
   (c) both
   (d) neither

6. Rapid adjustment in the money market means the economy is always on
   (a) the *IS* curve
   (b) the *LM* curve
   (c) both
   (d) neither

7. Expansionary fiscal policy tends to
   (a) raise consumption
   (b) lower investment
   (c) both
   (d) neither

8. A high *MPC* means a relatively
   (a) steep *IS* curve
   (b) flat *IS* curve
   (c) steep *LM* curve
   (d) flat *LM* curve

9. A high interest sensitivity of investment means a relatively
   (a) steep *IS* curve
   (b) flat *IS* curve
   (c) steep *LM* curve
   (d) flat *LM* curve

10. A high income tax rate means a relatively
    (a) steep *IS* curve
    (b) flat *IS* curve
    (c) steep *LM* curve
    (d) flat *LM* curve

Problems

1. The following equations describe the economy.

$$C = 100 + 0.8Y \qquad \text{consumption}$$

$I = 200 - 1000i$	investment
$L = Y - 10\,000i$	money demand

Initially, government expenditure is \$550 and taxes are \$500. The real money supply equals \$900.

(a) Derive the formulas for the *IS* curve and the *LM* curve.

(b) What are the initial levels of GDP, the interest rate, consumption, and investment?

Owing to a drop in investor confidence, the autonomous component of investment drops by \$90.

(c) By how much do income, the interest rate, and investment drop?

(d) By how much should the money supply be changed in order to return GDP to its original level? What will the new interest rate be?

(e) Draw three graphs to illustrate the equilibria in **(b)**, **(c)**, and **(d)**.

2. The following equations describe the economy.

$C = 90 + 0.9Y$	consumption
$I = 200 - 1000i$	investment
$L = Y - 10\,000i$	money demand

There is a 33 percent proportional income tax. Government expenditure equals \$710. The real money supply is \$500.

(a) What are the initial values of investment and the budget deficit?

(b) How large a change in the money supply would give the government a balanced budget?

CHAPTER 5 *International Trade and Exchange Rates*

Focus of the Chapter

- All countries engage in foreign trade, exporting some goods to foreign countries and importing other goods from abroad. A country that engages in foreign trade is said to have an *open economy*.
- After introducing the concepts of the *exchange rate* and the *balance of payments*, we extend our *IS-LM* model to include the effects of foreign trade on the state of economy.

Section Summaries

5.1 The *balance of payments* measures the difference between total payments to foreigners and total receipts from foreigners. The two principal parts of the balance are the *current account* and the *capital account*. The current account is made up of the *merchandise trade balance*, the difference between exports and imports of goods, plus net exports of services, plus net transfers abroad. The *capital account* is the difference between investment abroad and foreign investment in Canada, including both real and financial investment. During the last twenty years, Canada has typically had a surplus on merchandise trade more than offset by a deficit on services and transfers, leaving a current account deficit. When there is an overall deficit in the balance of payments, the foreign currency required to fill the gap is supplied out of the *official reserves* held by the Bank of Canada on behalf of the government.

A bilateral nominal exchange rate is a price for exchanging the currency of one country for the currency of another country. Since this exchange involves two different currencies, the value of the exchange rate can be expressed in two ways. For instance, the Canada/U.S. exchange rate can be defined either as the Canadian dollar price of one U.S. dollar (e.g., \$1.25 Canadian) or as the U.S. dollar price of a Canadian dollar (\$0.80 U.S.). A *depreciation* of the domestic currency means that it becomes worth less in terms of foreign currency. This means that it would take more Canadian dollars to buy a U.S. dollar, or the Canadian dollar price *increases*. An *equivalent* statement of a depreciation is that it would take less U.S. dollars to buy one Canadian dollar, so the U.S. dollar price *decreases*. Conversely, an *appreciation* means that the domestic currency becomes worth more in terms of the foreign currency. An appreciation means that the Canadian dollar price of a U.S. dollar *decreases*, or equivalently the U.S. dollar price of a Canadian dollar *increases*.

Under a *fixed exchange rate* regime, central banks peg the prices of their currencies. For example, from 1962 to 1970 the Canadian dollar was fixed at 92.5 U.S. cents, so that the Bank of Canada was committed to buy or sell foreign currency to maintain that rate. If a country is in persistent deficit, it may run out of reserves, and it must either borrow reserves from other central banks or lower the value of its currency.

Under *flexible exchange rates*, the prices of different currencies are determined by the laws of supply and demand. Since 1970 the value of the Canadian dollar has changed continually in the same manner as the prices of stocks on the stock exchange. In a *clean floating* system, the central banks allow supply and demand to operate without interference. In practice the world operates on a system of *managed* or *dirty floating*, in which central banks intervene in a limited way.

Occasionally, we wish to characterize the value of the Canadian dollar relative to several other currencies in a single index. This is known as a *multilateral exchange rate*.

The above sections discussed the nominal exchange rate. It is termed *nominal* because it only involves currencies. If we wished to know whether goods produced in, for example, the U.S. were cheaper than goods produced in Canada, we would have to use the real exchange rate. We could not simply compare prices in each country, because the prices are measured in two different currencies. However, we can convert a U.S. dollar price of a good to Canadian dollars by multiplying the U.S. price by the nominal exchange rate (measured as the Canadian dollar price of a U.S. dollar). Accordingly, the real exchange rate is defined as

$$\text{Real exchange rate} = \frac{eP^*}{P}$$

5.2 We return now to our *IS-LM* model and *add back in* net exports *NX*. For this section, we assume a fixed exchange rate. We differentiate between spending by domestic residents and total spending on domestic goods. Aggregate demand for domestically produced goods is

$$AD = C + I + G + NX$$

where NX is the trade balance (net exports). Our behavioural equation for net exports assumes that exports are fixed and that imports depend on income.

$$NX = \overline{X} - \overline{Q} - mY$$

With these modifications, the equation for the *IS* curve becomes

$$Y = \overline{\overline{\alpha}}(\overline{A} - bi)$$

where autonomous spending now includes exports minus the autonomous component of imports and is thus given by

$$\overline{A} = \overline{C} - c\overline{TR} + \overline{I} + \overline{G} + \overline{X} - \overline{Q}$$

This *IS* curve can be combined with the *LM* curve of Chapter 4 to find overall equilibrium. Once we know equilibrium income, we can compare exports and imports to find the overall trade surplus. Figure 5-1 (text Figure 5-4) shows the equilibrium of the economy at point *E* and also the level of income at which $NX = 0$. Since point *E* is shown to the left of the $NX = 0$ line, the economy has a trade surplus.

We can use this extended *IS-LM* diagram to explore the impact of several economic changes on income and the trade balance. Consider an increase in autonomous spending on domestic goods, for example, by the use of expansionary fiscal policy. This moves the *IS* curve as shown in Figure 5-2 (text Figure 5-5), increasing income and reducing the trade surplus.

Consider now an increase in exports. As shown in Figure 5-3 (text Figure 5-6), this moves the *IS* curve to *IS′* and also moves the $NX = 0$ line right, since it now requires more imports (and therefore higher income) to have balanced trade. Income increases, and the trade surplus also improves as shown.

A change in the composition of demand will have the same effect as a change in exports.

5.3 In this section we modify the above analysis to consider changes in the exchange rate. Maintaining the assumption that the domestic price level is fixed, and assuming that the foreign price level is exogenous, any change in the nominal exchange rate will change the real exchange rate. Of course, any change in the real exchange rate is a change in the relative price of domestic and foreign goods. For instance, a devaluation (or depreciation under flexible exchange rates) will cause the real exchange rate to increase. This increases the relative price of imported goods domestically, and decreases the relative price of exports in the foreign market. For this reason, the real exchange rate is often also called the *terms of trade*.

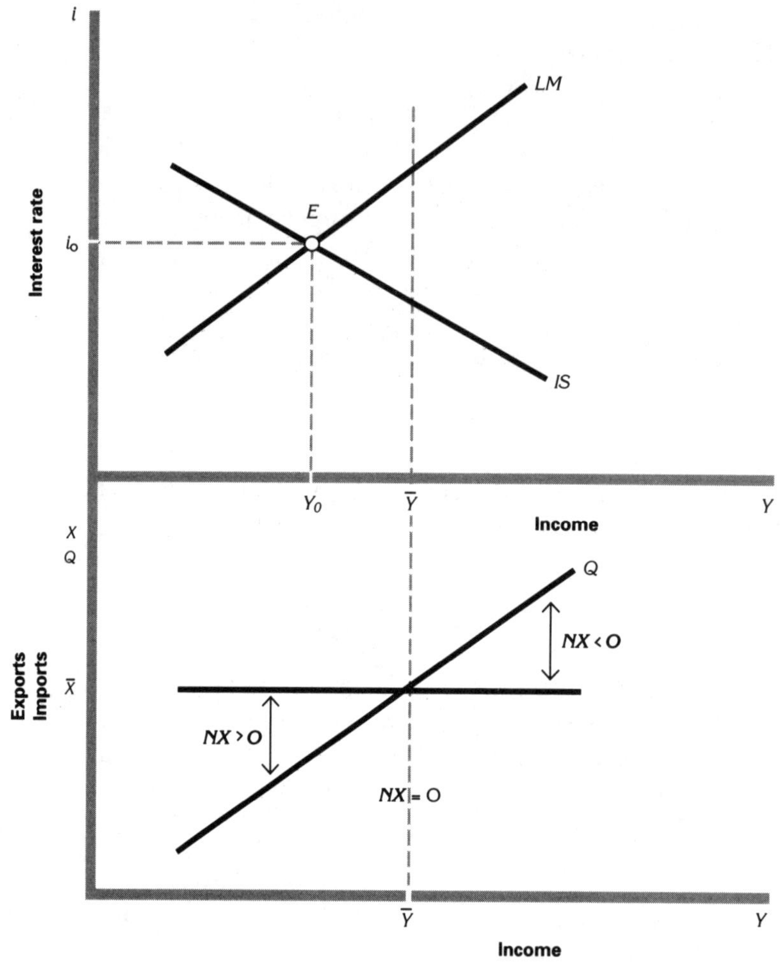

Figure 5-1

This change can be incorporated into our equation for net exports by adding a term for changes in the real exchange rate.

$$NX = \bar{X} - \bar{Q} - mY + q\frac{eP*}{P}$$

Using this information, the equation for the *IS* curve becomes

$$y = \bar{\bar{\alpha}}(\bar{A} - bi + q\frac{eP*}{P})$$

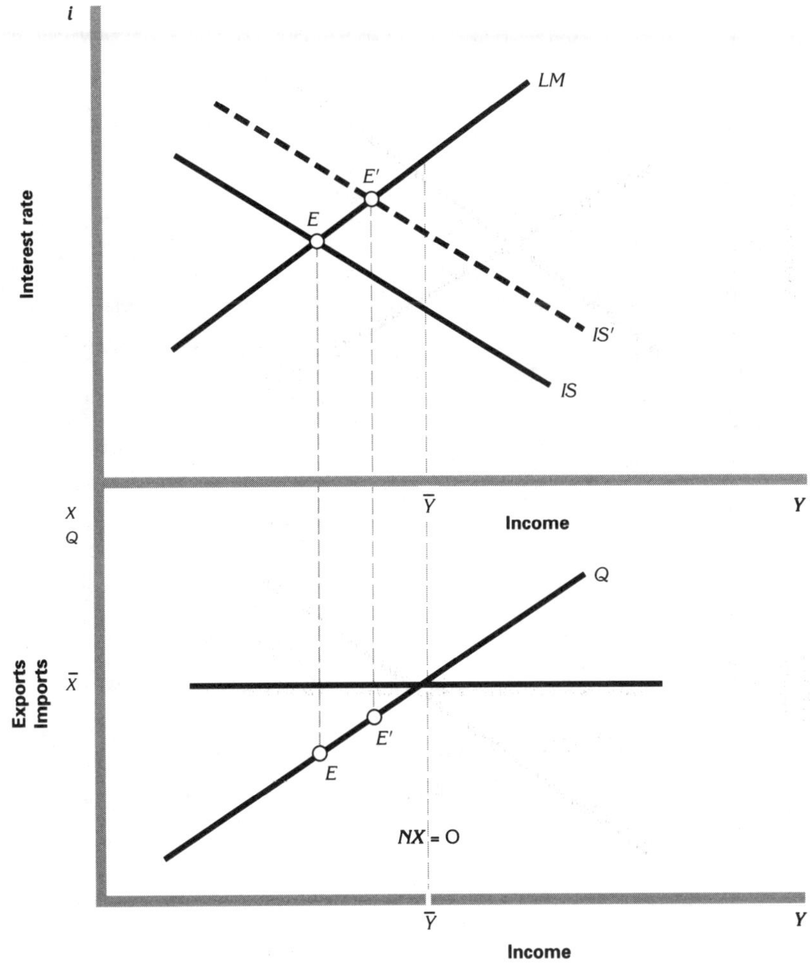

Figure 5-2

This new *IS* curve is shown in Figure 5-4 (text Figure 5-7). A devaluation or depreciation will shift the new *IS* curve up and to the right and a revaluation or appreciation will shift the *IS* curve down and to the left.

As shown in Figure 5-2, expansionary aggregate demand policies increase income but lower the trade surplus. If the economy is running a trade deficit and is below full employment, there is a *policy dilemma*, since aggregate demand policy can improve one problem only at the expense of making the other worse. Aggregate demand policy can provide *internal balance* or *external balance* — but not both. The solution

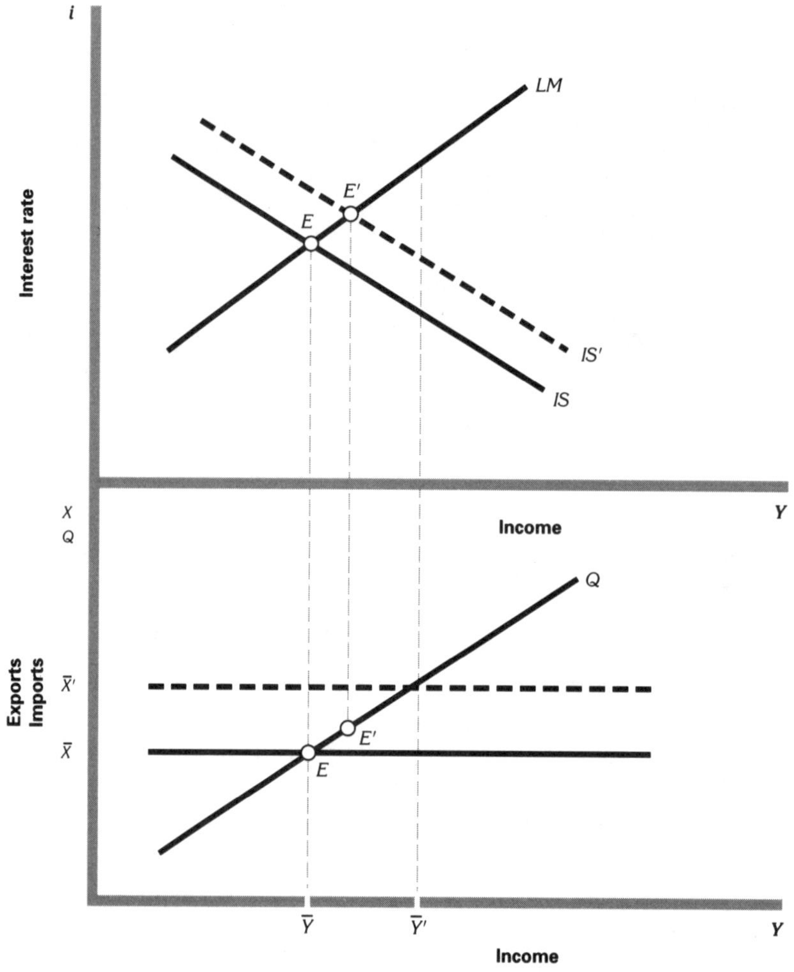

Figure 5-3

is to find an additional policy instrument. An important instrument for dealing with a trade deficit under fixed exchange rates is *devaluation*. By lowering the value of the Canadian dollar in terms of foreign currency, imports are made more expensive in Canada and our exports become more attractive abroad. Thus net exports increase, and the trade deficit is reduced. Since this result also stimulates domestic income, devaluation is generally accompanied by more restrictive fiscal and monetary policy than would otherwise be used. This is an example of combining *expenditure switching policies* with *expenditure reducing policies*.

Current account adjustment through devaluation is not costless. Since foreign goods become more expensive in Canada, our standard of living is reduced.

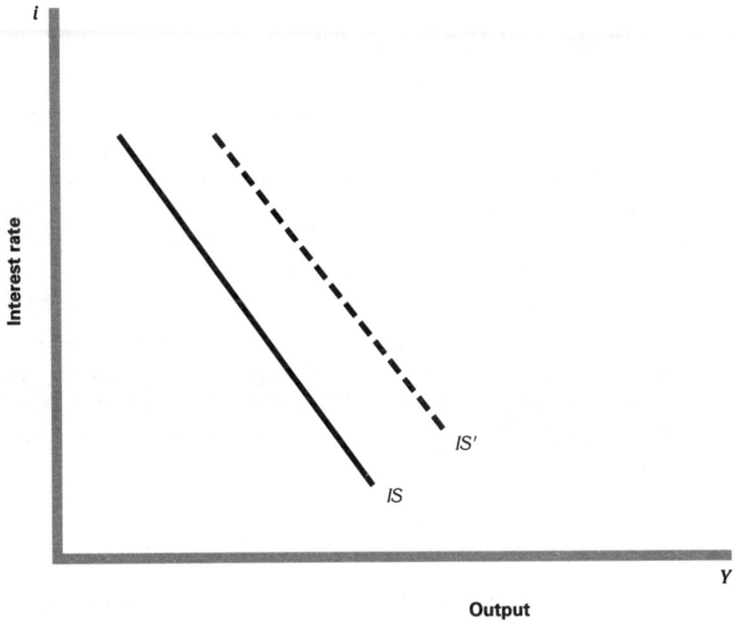

Figure 5-4

Key Terms

Fixed exchange rates
Flexible exchange rates
Balance of payments
Current account
Capital account
Trade balance
Intervention
Devaluation
Revaluation
Currency depreciation
Currency appreciation
Internal and external balance
Multilateral exchange rate
Real exchange rate
Clean floating
Dirty (managed) floating

Thinking Like an Economist

In this section we are going to look at foreign exchange rate determination more closely. As is almost always the case in economics, the tools of analysis will be supply and demand. Recall that a bilateral nominal exchange rate is the relative price of two currencies. Assume that we are interested in the Canada/U.S. exchange rate. If you wish to buy U.S. dollars in this market, then you wish to pay for them with Canadian dollars. Therefore, demanders of Canadian dollars are simultaneously suppliers of

U.S. dollars. In a similar manner, demanders of U.S. dollars are simultaneously suppliers of Canadian dollars. Therefore, when modelling the exchange rate we could model the supply and demand of Canadian dollars in the foreign exchange market, or the supply and demand of U.S. dollars. To complicate matters further, the exchange rate could be measured in either Canadian or U.S. dollars! In actual fact, it does not matter which quantity (Canadian or U.S. dollars) or which exchange rate (Canadian or U.S. dollars) is used, as long as the analysis consistently uses one exchange rate and one quantity. We will follow the methodology used in text Figure 5-2: the exchange rate is measured as the Canadian dollar price of foreign exchange and the quantity is the quantity of foreign exchange.

Consider first the demanders of foreign exchange. Foreign exchange is needed to pay for imports into Canada and to take financial capital out of Canada. To simplify the analysis we assume no capital flows. The Canadian dollar price of imports into Canada can be thought of as having two components: the price that the foreign manufacturer of the good charges in foreign currency and the nominal exchange rate.

$$P^m = \tilde{P}^x * e$$

where P^m is the Canadian dollar price of imports, $\tilde{P}^x$ is the foreign currency price of exports from the foreign country, and e is the nominal exchange rate. To see why the demand curve for foreign exchange is downward-sloping, consider Figure 5-5.

In Figure 5-5(a) we have assumed that there is a downward-sloping demand curve for imports in Canada. Assume that the initial price is P_0^m and quantity is Q_0^m. (We implicitly assume that the foreign country will supply whatever is demanded at each price.) The Canadian dollar price is composed of foreign currency price $\tilde{P}_0^x$ and exchange rate e_0. We assume that Q_0^m amount of imports gives rise to Q_0 amount of foreign exchange demand to pay for these imports. Therefore, in Figure 5-5(b) point E^0 is one point on the demand curve for foreign exchange. Suppose that the nominal exchange rate were to depreciate to e_1, while the foreign price P_0^x were to remain the same. The result would be an increase in the domestic price of imports to P_1^m, and a decrease in the quantity of imports demanded to Q_1^m. This decrease in demand for imports would lead to a decrease in the demand for Canadian dollars to Q_1. E^1 is another point on the demand curve for foreign exchange. Therefore, the demand curve for foreign exchange is downward-sloping.

Recall that individuals who are demanding foreign exchange are willing to buy it with Canadian dollars, and therefore they are suppliers of Canadian dollars. The above discussion would be the same if we were deriving the supply of Canadian dollars. Be sure that you understand that *the demand curve for foreign exchange is equivalent to the supply curve for Canadian dollars*.

The supply of foreign exchange comes from the need for foreign countries to pay for exports from Canada (which are imports into the foreign country). The foreign currency price of Canadian exports is made up of the Canadian dollar price and the nominal exchange rate.

$$\tilde{P}^m = \frac{P^x}{e}$$

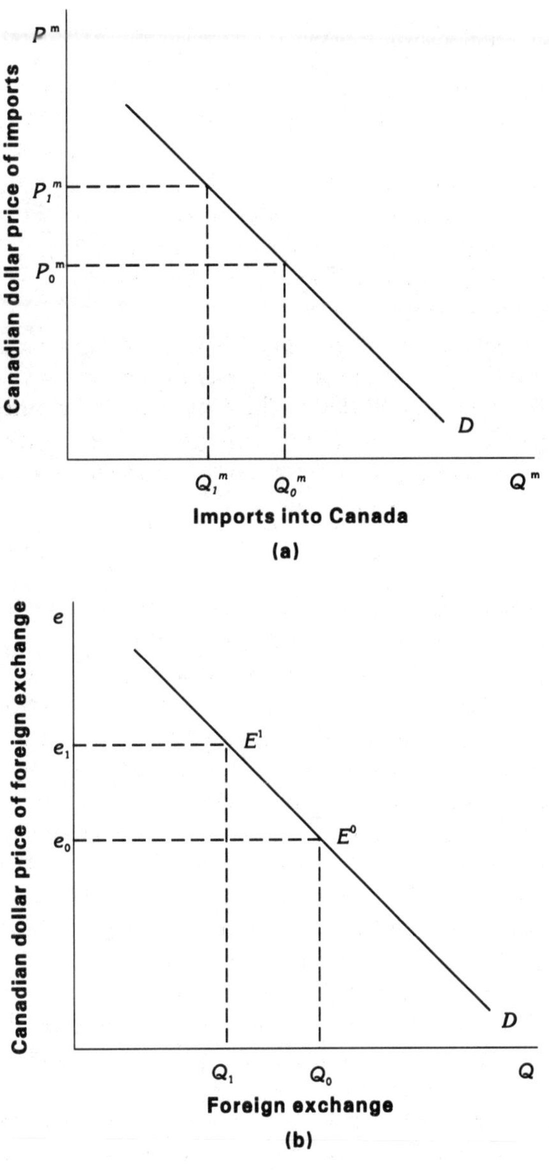

Figure 5-5

where $\bar{P}^m$ is the foreign currency price of Canadian exports, P^x is the Canadian dollar price of our exports, and e is the nominal exchange rate. To see why the supply curve for foreign exchange is upward-sloping, consider Figure 5.6.

In Figure 5-6 we assume that the demand curve for exports from Canada is downward-sloping in foreign countries. Assume that the initial foreign currency price

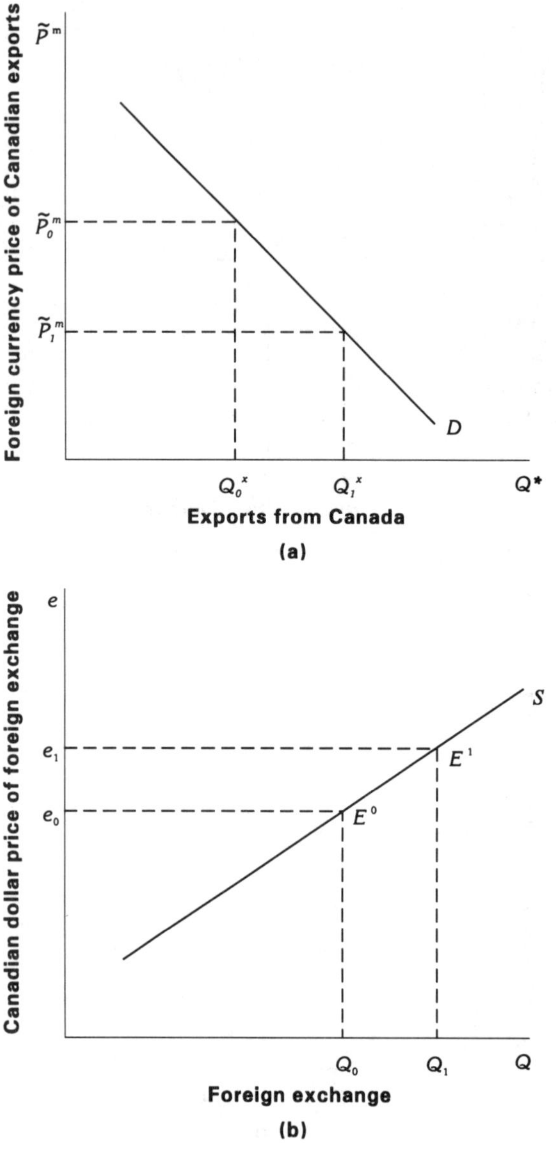

Figure 5-6

is $\tilde{P}_0^m$ which gives rise to Q_0^x quantity of exports demanded. (We assume that Canada exogenously supplies whatever exports are demanded.) The foreign currency price is composed of P_0^x Canadian dollar price and e_0 nominal exchange rate. We assume that Q_0^x amount of exports gives rise to Q_0 amount of foreign currency supplied to pay for these exports. Therefore, in Figure 5-6(b) E_0 is one point on the supply curve for foreign exchange. Assume that the Canadian dollar depreciates, which lowers the foreign currency price of Canadian exports to $\tilde{P}_1^m$. This increases the demand for Canadian exports to Q_1^x, which increases the supply of foreign exchange to Q_1. E^1 is another point on the supply curve for foreign exchange. Therefore, the supply curve for foreign exchange is upward-sloping. Again, be sure that you understand that *the supply curve for foreign exchange is equivalent to the demand curve for Canadian dollars*.

In Figure 5-7, we have drawn the demand and supply curves together, and assumed an initial equilibrium at an exchange rate of e_0. Assume that there is an exogenous increase in the demand for imports in Canada, which would shift out the demand curve for foreign exchange in Figure 5-7. In equilibrium this would lead to a *depreciation* in the exchange rate. Why does the exchange rate depreciate? The increase in demand for foreign exchange is equivalent to an increase in *supply* of Canadian dollars. The excess supply of Canadian dollars leads to a decrease in the relative value of the Canadian dollar, which is exactly what a depreciation is.

Now suppose that the Bank of Canada, for whatever reason, did not wish to let the nominal exchange rate depreciate. At e_0 there is an excess demand for foreign exchange. If the central bank wishes to maintain e_0, it must supply this foreign exchange to the market. It does this by buying up Canadian dollars with foreign exchange. Clearly, this can only be a short-run solution; otherwise the Bank of Canada would run out of foreign exchange. So, under what situation would the central bank be justified in fixing the exchange rate at e_0? The answer is: Only in a situation where the shift in demand is temporary — that is, if e_0 is the equilibrium

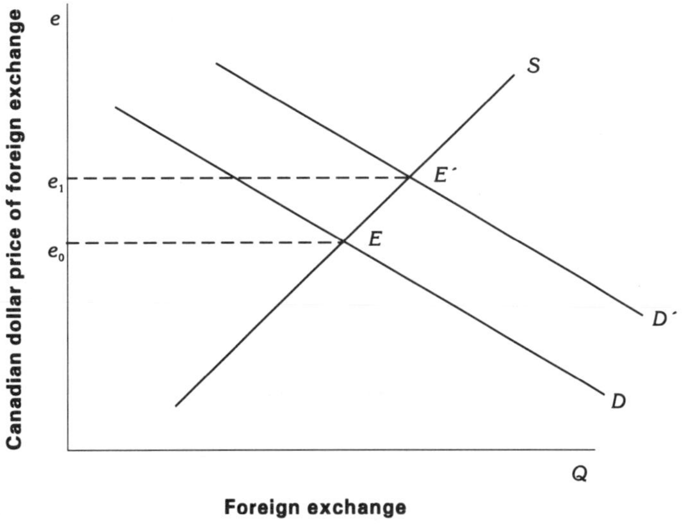

Figure 5-7

value of the exchange rate, and it is known that the demand shift will be shortly reversed. If the demand shift is permanent, then the new equilibrium value of the exchange rate is e_1 and the Bank of Canada cannot hold the exchange rate at e_0 forever.

Graph It 5

You are now asked to use the following numerical example to show that an increase in exports results in an increase in the trade surplus but by an amount that is less than the increase in exports. We assume that aggregate demand is given by $AD = 0.6Y + 200 + X - Q$, and that imports are determined by $Q = 25 + 0.1Y$. On Chart 5-1, we show the 45° line and an initial level of exports, $X = 75$.

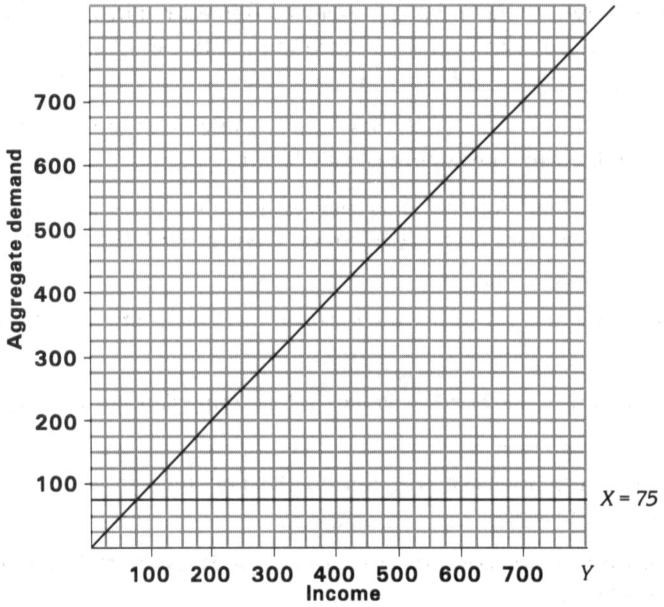

Chart 5-1

Draw in the aggregate demand line and the import function. At the equilibrium level of income, you should find that the trade balance is zero.

Now suppose that exports increase by 100 to 175. Show this by drawing a new horizontal line at $X = 175$ and draw a new aggregate demand line by shifting the initial one upward by 100. Use your diagram to compare the increase in exports with the increase in the trade surplus.

Fill-In Questions

1. The value of foreign currency in terms of domestic currency is the ________________ ________________.

2. The net flow of goods and services and transfers from here abroad forms the ________________ ________________ of the balance of payments.

3. The net flow of investments from here to foreign countries forms the ________________ ________________.

4. The total flow of transactions between countries makes up the ________________ ________________.

5. A system in which the relative values of domestic and foreign currency are determined by the various governments involved is called a(n) ________________.

6. When the relative values of domestic and foreign currency are determined by supply and demand, the system is called a(n) ________________.

7. A system in which relative currency values are determined mostly through supply and demand but with some government intervention is called ________________.

8. A decrease in the value of domestic currency vis-à-vis other currencies is called ________________.

9. When initiated under fixed exchange rates, depreciation by the government is called ________________.

10. A policy that aims to encourage consumption of domestic goods and discourage imports is called a(n) ________________.

11. The relative price of domestic to foreign goods, expressed in a common currency, is called the ________________.

True-False Questions

T F **1.** Expansionary fiscal policy increases the trade surplus.

T F **2.** A decrease in the Canadian dollar price of a U.S. dollar is a depreciation of the Canadian currency.

T F **3.** Devaluation improves the trade balance.

T F **4.** Devaluation increases GDP.

T F **5.** The central bank can meet a temporary balance of payments deficit by using up reserves of foreign exchange.

T F **6.** An increase in autonomous spending on domestic goods increases income and the trade balance.

T F **7.** A policy which causes a shift in demand from foreign to domestic goods is called an expenditure-increasing policy.

T F **8.** A decrease in the real exchange rate increases the relative price of imports in the domestic economy.

T F **9.** A permanent balance of payments surplus means a country is forgoing some consumption.

Multiple-Choice Questions

1. High domestic GDP leads to
(a) high exports
(b) high imports
(c) both high exports and imports
(d) neither one

2. High U.S. GDP leads to
(a) high Canadian exports
(b) high Canadian imports
(c) both
(d) neither one

3. Contractionary fiscal policy increases
(a) the current account surplus
(b) the capital account surplus
(c) both types of surplus
(d) neither type of surplus

4. An economy is facing a policy dilemma if it has
(a) a trade deficit and is above full employment
(b) a trade surplus and is below full employment
(c) a trade deficit and is below full employment
(d) a trade balance and is at full employment

5. If the deutschmark is initially worth 25 cents and Germany revalues its currency by 50 percent, the exchange rate
(a) rises
(b) falls
(c) remains unchanged
(d) cannot be determined from the information given

6. In an open economy, the simple multiplier is ____________________ in a closed economy.
(a) larger than
(b) smaller than
(c) no different from that
(d) any of **(a)**, **(b)**, or **(c)**

7. If the central bank wishes to fix the exchange rate above its equilibrium value (measured in Canadian dollars) it must
   - **(a)** buy foreign exchange and sell Canadian dollars
   - **(b)** sell foreign exchange and buy Canadian dollars
   - **(c)** sell foreign exchange and sell Canadian dollars
   - **(d)** buy foreign exchange and buy Canadian dollars

8. A depreciation of the currency shifts the
   - **(a)** *IS* curve to the left
   - **(b)** *IS* curve to the right
   - **(c)** *LM* curve to the right
   - **(d)** *LM* curve to the left

9. An increase in foreign demand for our exports
   - **(a)** causes an appreciation of the currency
   - **(b)** causes a depreciation of the currency
   - **(c)** has no effect on the currency
   - **(d)** causes an equal increase in imports

Problems

1. Initially, the deutschmark is worth 25 cents. Suppose the Canadian dollar is devalued by 50 percent and then by an additional 20 percent. What is the new exchange rate?

2. The marginal propensity to consume is 0.9, investment and exports are autonomous, and imports are as described below. What is the multiplier on government spending?

$$Q = \overline{Q} + 0.1Y \text{ (Canadian imports)}$$

3. Suppose that the Canadian economy is as described in problem 2, and that the German economy has an *MPC* of 0.8, investment is purely autonomous, and German imports are as given below. Further assume that all trade between Germany and Canada is bilateral. What is the multiplier of Canadian government spending on Canadian GDP? What is the multiplier of Canadian government spending on German GDP?

$$Q_G = \overline{Q}_G + 0.2Y_G \text{ (German imports)}$$

CHAPTER 6 *International Capital Flows and Stabilization Policy*

Focus of the Chapter

- In this chapter we consider the role of capital account in determining the balance of payments and equilibrium income.
- We study the relationship between capital flows and interest rates, and show how monetary and fiscal policy operate under the assumptions of imperfect capital mobility and perfect capital mobility.
- The last section extends the model to take account of exchange rate expectations.

Section Summaries

6.1 In this section we assume that capital flows respond to the difference between the domestic and foreign interest rate. For a given foreign interest rate, the higher the domestic interest rate, the greater will be the capital inflow. Of course, if the domestic interest rate is below the foreign, there will be capital outflow. This is described by the equation

$$CF = a(i - i^*)$$

Combining this equation with the balance of payments equilibrium equation from Chapter 5, we obtain the following equation for the overall balance of payments surplus *BP*:

$$BP = \overline{X} - \overline{Q} - mY + q\frac{eP*}{P} + a(i - i^*)$$

Along the *BP* curve the balance of payments surplus is zero. Therefore, setting the above equation equal to zero, and rearranging terms, we obtain the equation

$$i = i^* + \frac{m}{a}Y - \frac{1}{a}(\overline{X} - \overline{Q} + q\frac{eP*}{P})$$

It can easily be seen that the slope of the *BP* curve depends on *m*, the marginal propensity to import, and *a*, the degree of capital mobility. Since *m* and *a* are positive, the *BP* curve has a positive slope. For points above the *BP* curve we have a balance of payments surplus, and for points below the curve we have a deficit.

As shown in Figure 6-1 (text Figure 6-4), an expansionary fiscal policy increases income and the interest rate. The trade account worsens, since higher income increases imports, while the capital account improves, since a higher domestic interest rate increases capital inflow. The net effect is an improvement in the overall balance of payments under the assumption that capital is highly mobile. Figure 6-2 (text Figure 6-5) shows that an increase in the money supply worsens the balance of payments. The rise in income increases imports and the fall in the domestic interest rate reduces capital inflow.

The internal-external balance dilemma that we saw in Chapter 5 can now be solved by using an appropriate mix of monetary and fiscal policy. We can use fiscal policy to eliminate unemployment, and we can vary interest rates through monetary policy to achieve balance of payments equilibrium. However, a country is unlikely to be indifferent to the level of domestic interest rates or to the composition of its balance of payments. In particular, a capital account surplus means an increase in net foreign debt.

6.2 The preceding analysis involves the implicit assumption that the link between the balance of payments and the domestic money supply is eliminated through *sterilization*. In the absence of sterilization, monetary policy has no effect, since the money supply is automatically determined by the balance of payments and cannot be controlled by the central bank. In general, the equilibrium point is determined by the intersection of the *IS* and *BP* curves, since the *LM* curve shifts automatically in response to the balance of payments surplus or deficit. Thus an expansionary fiscal

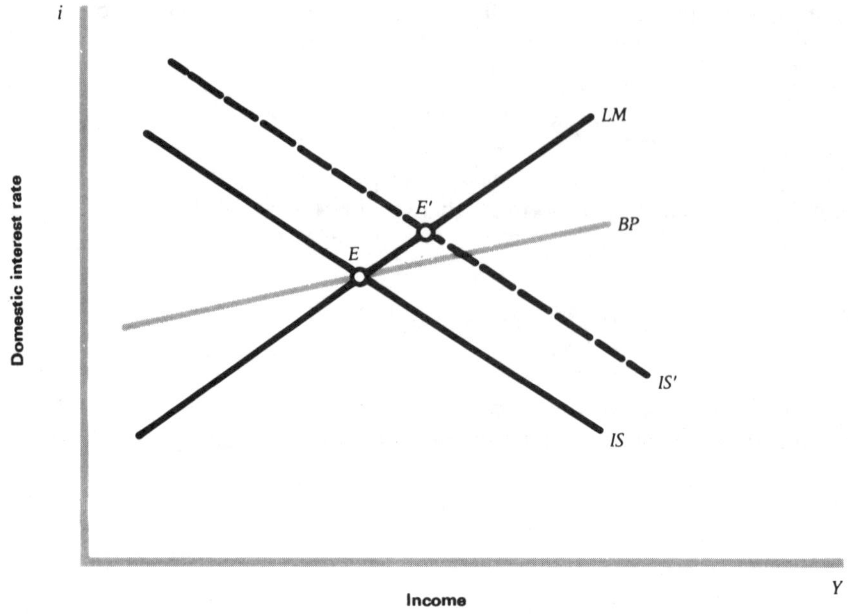

Figure 6-1

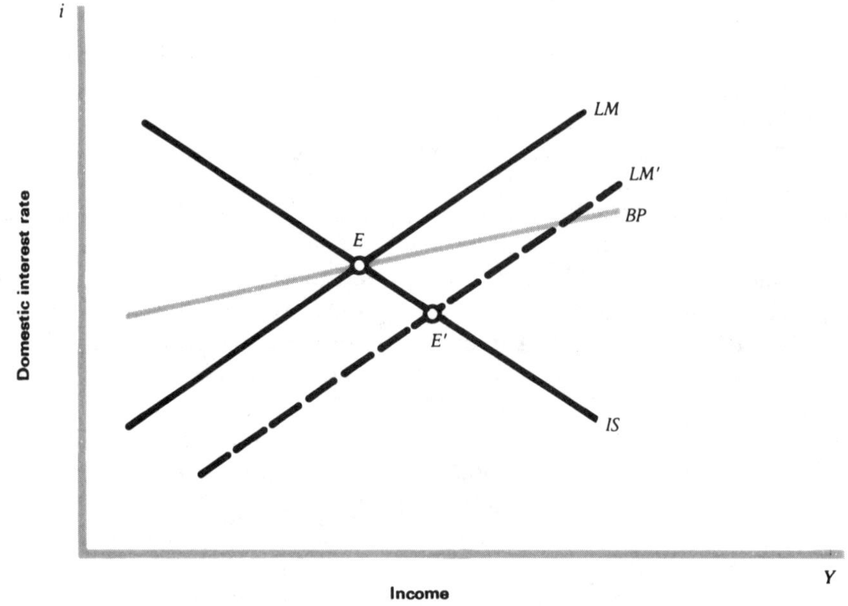

Figure 6-2

policy that shifts out the *IS* curve will cause the *LM* curve to shift until all three curves intersect at the same point.

6.3 In this section we apply the above model to an economy with a flexible exchange rate. Figure 6-3 (text Figure 6-9) shows the effects of an increase in the money supply. When the *LM* curve shifts outward, there is a balance of payments deficit; therefore, the currency depreciates and the *IS* and *BP* curves shift to the right. The net effect is an increase in income and a fall in the interest rate. Figure 6-4 (text Figure 6-10) illustrates the effects of a fiscal expansion. The *IS* curve shifts to the right, causing a balance of payments surplus. The domestic currency appreciates, causing the *IS* and *BP* curves to shift to the left. The net effect is a higher income and interest rate.

Notice that in each of these cases income is higher. However, the composition of income is different for the monetary and the fiscal expansion. In the monetary expansion, the exchange rate depreciates and net exports are higher. In the fiscal expansion, government spending is higher but the resultant appreciation has lowered net exports. Therefore, the monetary expansion has caused *crowding in* of net exports while the fiscal expansion has caused *crowding out* of net exports.

6.4 For the remainder of this chapter we adopt the assumption of perfect capital mobility. Under this assumption the capital flows curve in text Figure 6-2 is com-

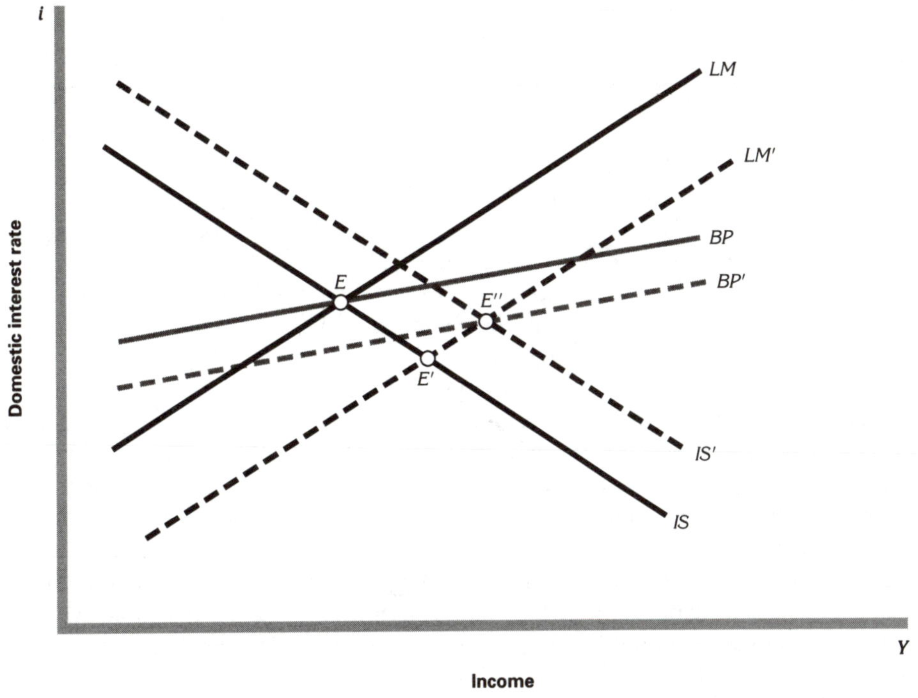

Figure 6-3

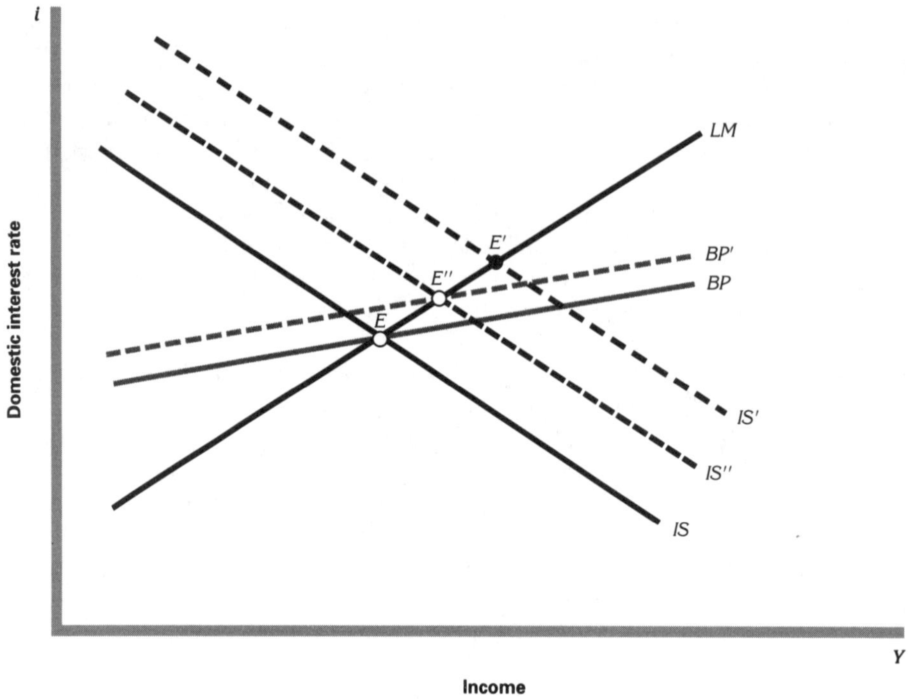

Figure 6-4

pletely horizontal, which causes the *BP* curve to be horizontal at the given level of the foreign interest rate. Therefore, the only situation in which the balance of payments is in equilibrium is when the domestic interest rate equals the foreign interest rate. If, for instance, the domestic interest rate were below the foreign, there would be massive capital flows out of the domestic economy, which would only cease once the domestic interest rate equalled the foreign.

The effects of expansionary monetary policy under capital mobility are illustrated in Figure 6-5 (text Figure 6-11). Consider first the fixed exchange rate case. We know that expansionary monetary policy will lower domestic interest rates. However, with perfect capital mobility, as soon as the domestic interest rate is below the foreign interest rate there will be massive capital flows out of the domestic economy. These capital flows will cause depreciation pressure on the exchange rate. Given that the monetary authorities are running a fixed exchange rate, this would be a contradictory policy, as the expansionary monetary policy would cause a depreciation, which is exactly what monetary policy is trying to avoid by running a fixed exchange rate. With perfect capital mobility the only way to keep the exchange rate fixed is for monetary policy to keep the domestic interest rate equal to the foreign interest rate. Therefore, monetary policy is not free to do anything else, such as changing domestic income.

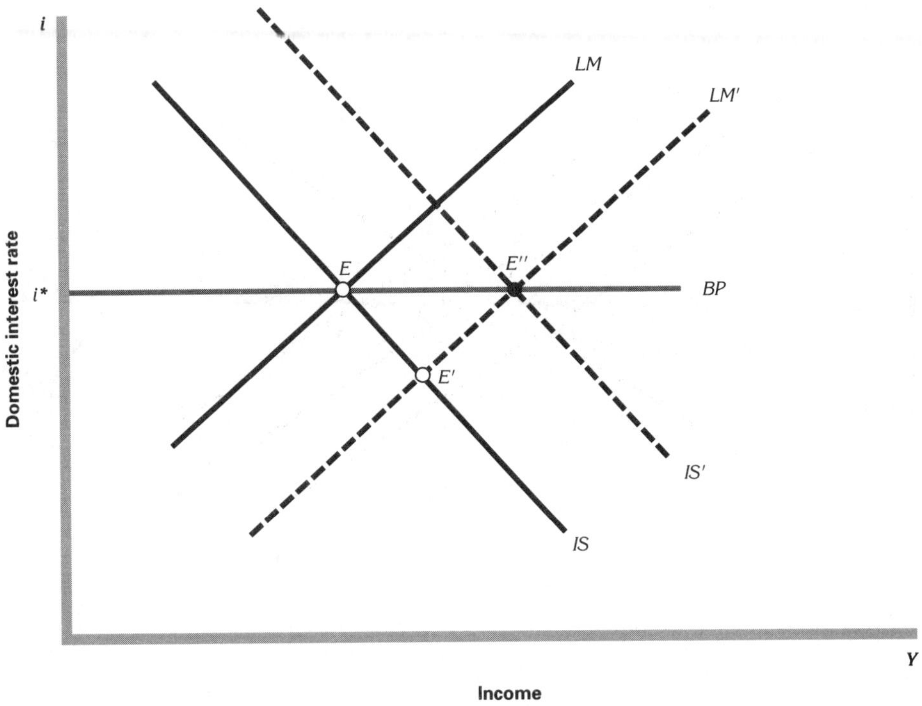

Figure 6-5

Now consider monetary policy under a flexible exchange rate. This shifts out the *LM* curve to *E′* on Figure 6-5. This lower domestic interest rate causes capital outflow, which causes the nominal exchange rate to depreciate. Since prices are fixed domestically, and the foreign price level is exogenous, a nominal exchange rate depreciation is equivalent to an increase in the real exchange rate. Therefore, the *IS* curve shifts outward, and the new equilibrium is at point *E″*. In this case, because monetary policy is not used to keep the exchange rate fixed, it is able to change domestic income.

Notice that, since our net exports increase, foreigners' net exports decrease, tending to reduce GDP abroad. If all countries try to stimulate their economies by depreciating at the same time, the result is a *beggar-thy-neighbour* policy. These *competitive depreciations* only serve to reallocate world aggregate demand without expanding it in total.

Figure 6-6 (text Figure 6-12) illustrates the effects of fiscal policy with perfect capital mobility. Expansionary fiscal policy causes the domestic interest rate to increase, which causes massive capital inflows and appreciation pressure on the exchange rate. Recall that running a fixed exchange rate with perfect capital mobility requires that the monetary authorities keep the domestic interest rate equal to the

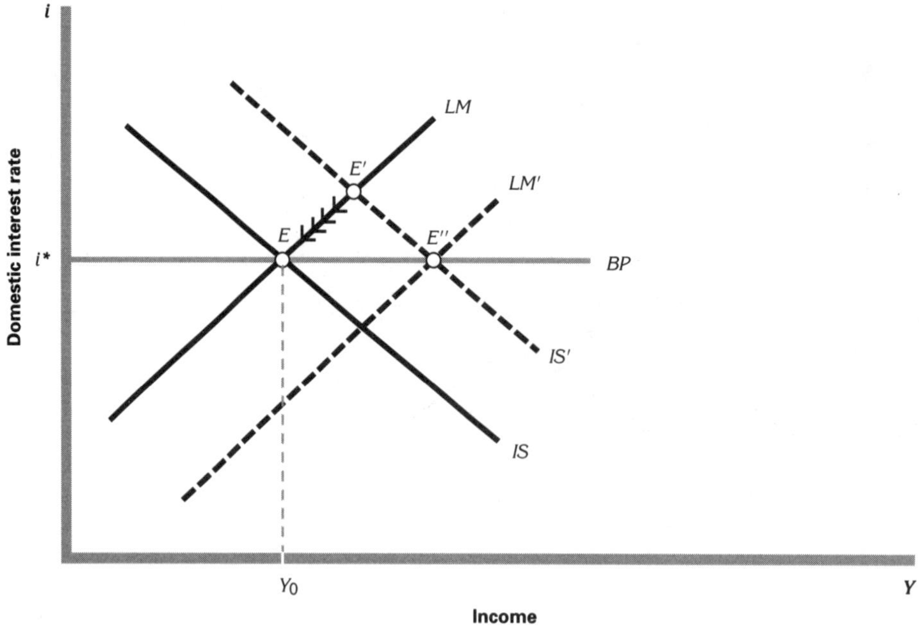

Figure 6-6

foreign interest rate. Therefore, expansionary fiscal policy, which raises interest rates, must be accompanied by expansionary monetary policy, which lowers interest rates, if the exchange rate is to be fixed. Therefore, the new equilibrium is at E'' with a higher level of income.

Now consider expansionary fiscal policy with a flexible exchange rate. In Figure 6-6 interest rates increase to E', which causes capital inflow and exchange rate appreciation. Given the fixed price assumptions, this leads to a decrease in the real exchange rate, which causes net exports to decrease and the *IS* curve shifts back to its original position, and the level of income does not change. However, the composition of income changes, as the increase in government spending has crowded out net export spending.

6.5 When exchange rate expectations are taken into account, balance of payments equilibrium is described by the interest parity condition, which equates the domestic interest rate with the foreign rate plus the expected rate of depreciation.

$$i = i^* + x$$

This condition implies that a change in the money supply leads to overshooting of the exchange rate. As shown in Figure 6-7 (text Figure 6-15), when the money supply is increased the economy initially moves to E, where $i < i^*$, and investors anticipate an

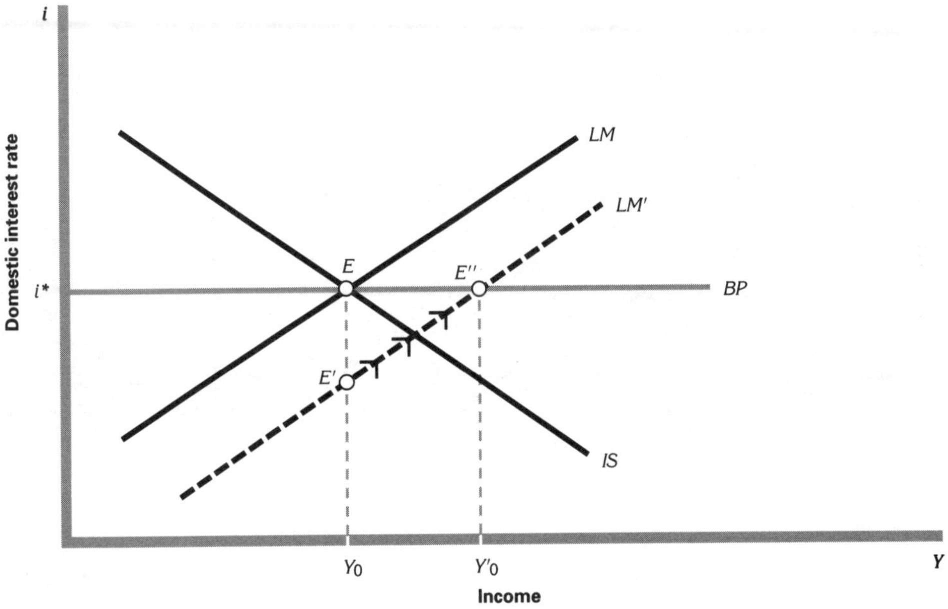

Figure 6-7

appreciation of the currency. As we move to *E*, income increases, the currency appreciates, and *i* rises back to the level of i^*.

Key Terms

***BP* curve**
Sterilization
Perfect capital mobility
Beggar-thy-neighbour policy
Competitive depreciation
Interest parity condition
Exchange rate overshooting

Thinking Like an Economist

In this section we are going to take a closer look at stabilization policy with perfect capital mobility. We have seen that with perfect capital mobility the *BP* curve is horizontal at the given level of the foreign interest rate. The *BP* curve imposes a type of constraint on policy formulation. That is, perfect capital mobility forces the domestic interest rate to equal the foreign interest rate. If you wish to pursue a policy which

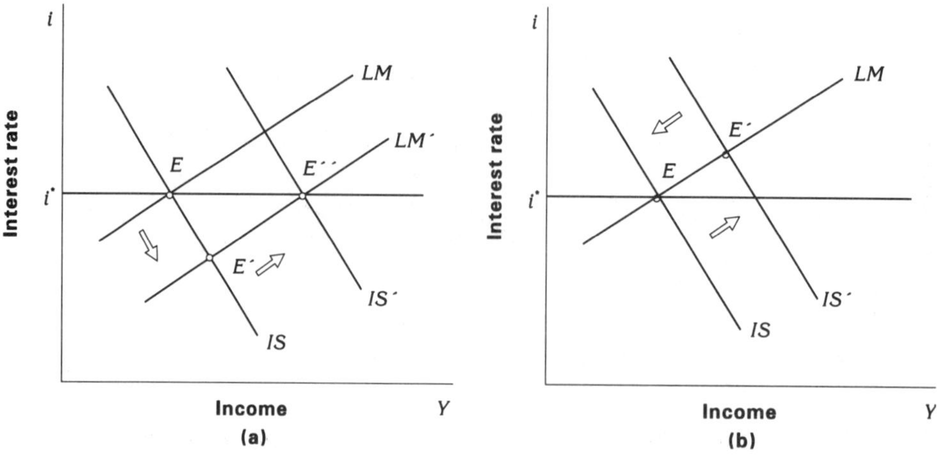

Figure 6-8

drives the Canadian interest rate away from the foreign, you must be willing to accept the exchange rate consequences.

There are two possible policy targets in the *IS/LM/BP* model. Policy could be aimed at controlling the domestic economy or at fixing the exchange rate.

Figure 6-8 describes the effects of expansionary monetary and fiscal policy. Notice that each of these expansionary policies causes a change in interest rates. However, the exchange rate ramifications of each policy are different. Monetary policy lowers interest rates, and causes capital outflow and exchange rate *depreciation* pressure, while fiscal policy raises interest rates, and causes capital inflows and exchange rate *appreciation* pressure. Therefore, expansionary monetary policy *crowds in* net exports, shifting the *IS* curve to the right, while expansionary fiscal policy *crowds out* net exports, shifting the *IS* curve to the left. In each of these cases policy has affected the domestic economy: monetary policy has changed the level of income, while fiscal policy has changed the composition of income. Notice that external balance has been taken care of by the flexible exchange rate. That is, if you are willing to have a flexible exchange rate, external balance is automatically taken care of by movements in the exchange rate.

Now consider a fixed exchange rate. With perfect capital mobility the exchange rate can only be fixed by keeping the domestic interest rate equal to the foreign. This is accomplished through monetary policy. Figure 6-9 describes how this is done.

Figure 6-9(a) shows that, if the money supply were held constant, every time there was a change in money demand interest rates would change. These changes in the interest rate could be avoided by changing the money supply every time money demand changed. In Figure 6-9(b) this is shown as a horizontal money supply curve. Thus fixing the exchange rate is equivalent to holding the interest rate constant at the level of the foreign interest rate. Therefore, monetary policy is not free to do anything

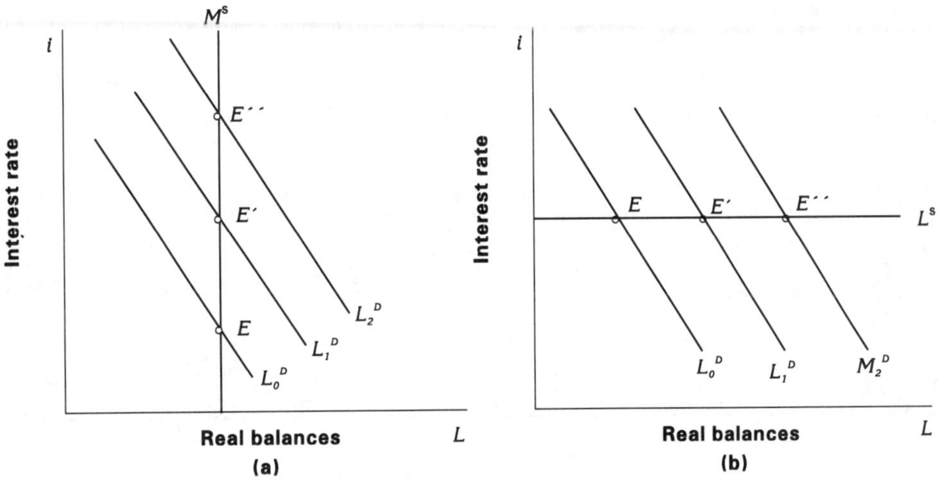

Figure 6-9

else other than keep interest rates constant, to keep the exchange rate constant. Monetary policy is aimed at the exchange rate, and only fiscal policy can be used to control the domestic economy, as shown in Figure 6-10. Expansionary fiscal policy raises income which increases money demand. Monetary policy accommodates this increase in money demand by increasing the money supply, and income increases.

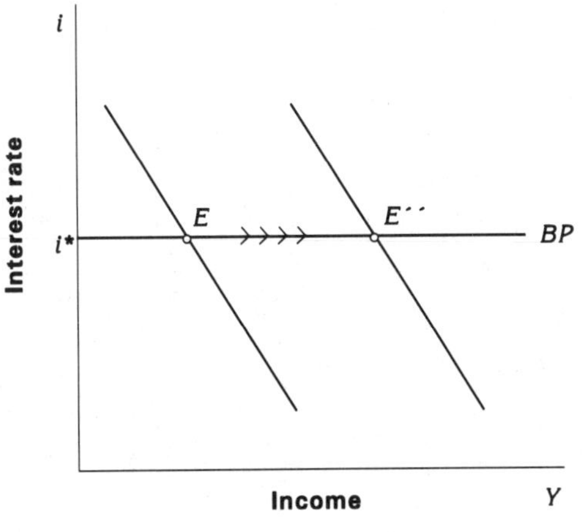

Figure 6-10

Graph It 6

As can be seen in text Figure 6-8, the 12-month period beginning in the fourth quarter of 1979 was one of unusual swings in U.S. interest rates and the spread between Canadian and U.S. rates. To see the effects on the exchange rate, plot on Chart 6-1 a graph of the interest differential against the exchange rate.

The interest parity condition states a relationship between the interest differential and the expected future change in the exchange rate. Indicate which quadrant in your graph corresponds to an expected appreciation and which corresponds to an expected depreciation.

Table 6-1

		Interest Rates		
Year and Quarter	**Exchange Rate**	**U.S.**	**Canada**	**Differential**
1979 4	116.7	14.20	13.97	0.23
1980 1	119.6	15.25	17.93	−2.68
2	115.1	11.50	8.30	3.20
3	117.0	10.90	11.51	−0.61

Source: Bank of Canada Review.

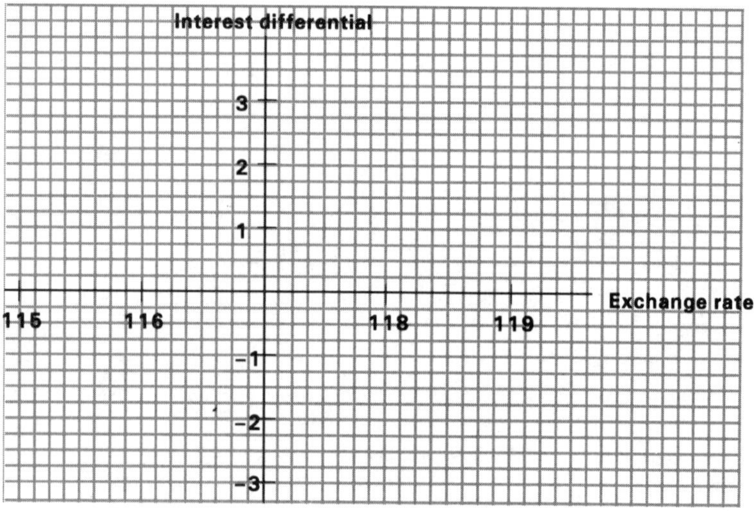

Chart 6-1

Fill-In Questions

1. A depreciation of the currency leads to a gain in ________________ .

2. ________________ ________________ implies that there will be very large capital flows when the domestic interest rate deviates from foreign rates.

3. On the other hand, ________________ implies limited capital flows in response to interest differentials.

4. A(n) ________________ policy is an attempt to increase domestic income at the expense of income in other countries.

5. Canada operated under a(n) ________________ exchange rate in the 1950s.

6. The relationship between interest rates and exchange rate expectations is called the ________________ .

7. If domestic interest rates are higher than foreign rates, investors must be expecting a currency ________________ .

8. An increase in the domestic money supply leads to exchange rate ________________ in the short run.

True-False Questions

T F 1. Fiscal policy is ineffective under fixed exchange rates and perfect capital mobility.

T F 2. An increase in the U.S. interest rate leads to an improvement in Canada's balance of payments.

T F 3. An increase in the exchange rate increases domestic aggregate demand.

T F 4. Under perfect capital mobility the *LM* curve is horizontal.

T F 5. An increase in Canadian government spending causes the Canadian dollar to appreciate.

T F 6. With perfect capital mobility, an increase in Canadian government spending increases Canadian GDP.

T F 7. With perfect capital mobility, an increase in government spending increases net exports.

T F 8. Under flexible exchange rates, the central bank has no control over the money supply.

T F 9. With perfect capital mobility, an increase in the money supply increases aggregate demand.

T F 10. With perfect capital mobility, an increase in the money supply causes the currency to depreciate.

Multiple-Choice Questions

1. In the absence of sterilization operations
   - **(a)** only fiscal policy is effective
   - **(b)** only monetary policy is effective
   - **(c)** both are effective
   - **(d)** neither is effective

2. With fixed exchange rates and perfect capital mobility
   - **(a)** only fiscal policy is effective
   - **(b)** only monetary policy is effective
   - **(c)** both are effective
   - **(d)** neither is effective

3. An increase in foreign demand for our exports
   - **(a)** causes an appreciation of the currency
   - **(b)** causes a depreciation of the currency
   - **(c)** has no effect on the currency
   - **(d)** causes an equal increase in imports

4. Under perfect capital mobility, an increase in government spending crowds out private spending as a result of
   - **(a)** an increase in the domestic interest rate
   - **(b)** an increase in the foreign interest rate
   - **(c)** an appreciation of the currency
   - **(d)** a depreciation of the currency

5. Under perfect capital mobility, an increase in the money supply increases aggregate demand through
   - **(a)** a fall in the domestic interest rate
   - **(b)** a fall in the foreign interest rate
   - **(c)** an appreciation of the currency
   - **(d)** a depreciation of the currency

6. An increase in the money supply increases
   - **(a)** exports
   - **(b)** capital inflow
   - **(c)** government spending
   - **(d)** none of the above

7. The central bank has no control over the money supply under
   - **(a)** perfect capital mobility and a fixed exchange rate
   - **(b)** imperfect capital mobility and a flexible rate
   - **(c)** perfect capital mobility and a flexible rate
   - **(d)** imperfect capital mobility and a fixed rate

8. Capital flows into Canada when the Canadian interest rate (adjusted for expected changes in the exchange rate) is ________________ foreign interest rates.
   (a) greater than
   (b) equal to
   (c) less than
   (d) either greater than or less than

9. Contractionary monetary policy increases
   (a) the current account surplus
   (b) the capital account surplus
   (c) both types of surplus
   (d) neither type of surplus

10. Imperfect capital mobility suggests that the Canadian interest rate ________________ foreign interest rates.
    (a) is greater than
    (b) equals
    (c) is less than
    (d) may be greater than, equal to, or less than

Problems

1. The interest rate in Germany is 10 percent and the interest rate in Canada is 12 percent. If the current value of the deutschmark is 50 cents, what is the exchange rate expected to be in a year?
2. When capital is perfectly mobile and exchange rates are perfectly flexible, by what mechanism does an increase in the money stock raise GDP?
3. With perfect capital mobility and fixed exchange rates, how will the domestic economy be affected by an increase in government spending and an increase in the money stock so as to keep interest rates constant?

PART 2 *Income and the Price Level*

CHAPTER 7 *Aggregate Supply and Demand: An Introduction*

Focus of the Chapter

- *Aggregate supply and aggregate demand* each give a relationship between the overall price level and output. Together, the aggregate supply and demand schedules determine GDP and the price level.
- The aggregate supply schedule describes how much output firms are willing to supply at a given price level.
- The aggregate demand schedule summarizes the *IS-LM* equilibrium of Chapter 4, with the *LM* curve repositioned for changing price levels.

Section Summaries

7.1 The slope of the aggregate supply schedule splits movements of the aggregate demand schedule into changes in prices and changes in output. If the aggregate supply schedule is relatively flat, as in Figure 7-1(a) (text Figure 7-3), an increase in aggregate demand mostly increases GDP and leaves prices relatively unchanged. If

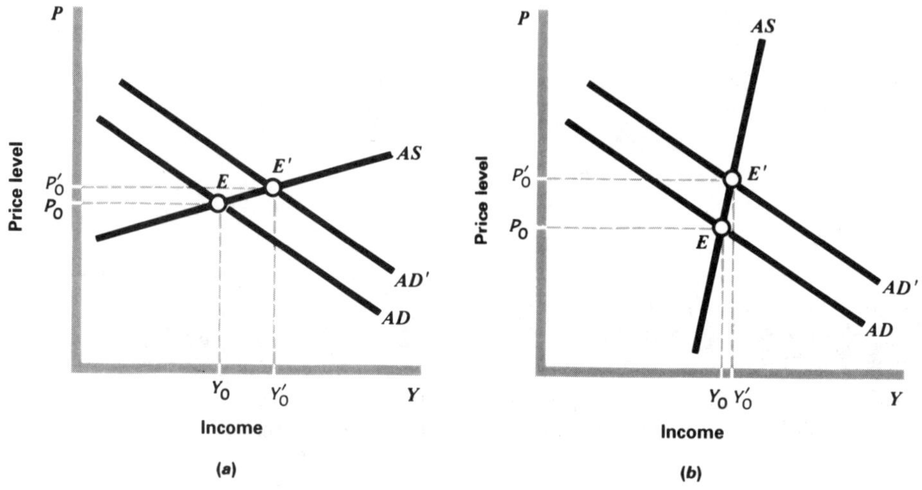

Figure 7-1

the aggregate supply schedule is steep, as in Figure 7-1(b), an increase in aggregate demand mostly increases prices and leaves GDP relatively unchanged. The two special cases of aggregate supply are the *Keynesian case*, a perfectly horizontal aggregate supply curve, and the *classical case*, a perfectly vertical aggregate supply curve.

7.2 In the *frictionless neoclassical model of the labour market*, all firms are competitive and produce with a fixed amount of capital. Each firm's demand curve for labour slopes downward, a result of the fact that the marginal product of labour falls as additional workers are used in production. Firms hire labour up to the point where the marginal cost of labour — the real wage — is equal to the marginal product of labour.

The supply curve of labour to the economy is an upward-sloping function of the real wage rate. As the real wage rises, more workers enter the labour force.

The economy-wide real wage rate is determined by the intersection of the aggregate demand curve for labour and the supply curve of labour to the economy.

Employment is always at its *full-employment level* in the frictionless neoclassical model. Any disturbance that causes the price level to rise or fall produces immediate pressure in the labour market for the money wage rate to rise by the same proportion. Output and employment immediately return to their full-employment levels. The aggregate supply curve is vertical.

Even at full employment there will be frictional unemployment. Frictional unemployment is associated with normal turnover in the labour market. The unemployment rate at full employment is called the *natural rate of unemployment*.

7.3 The aggregate demand curve summarizes the *IS-LM* model for given fiscal and monetary policy, but changing price levels. At a high price level, the real money supply is low, so aggregate demand is low. Thus the aggregate demand curve slopes downward. The slope of the aggregate demand curve is determined by the *monetary policy multiplier* of Chapter 4. If the monetary policy multiplier is large, then the aggregate demand curve is relatively flat, and vice versa. Expansionary fiscal or monetary policy shifts the *IS-LM* equilibrium out at a given price level and thus shifts the aggregate demand curve to the right.

7.4 With a Keynesian-case aggregate supply curve, prices are constant, and the conclusions in Chapter 4 of the text hold without modification. With a classical aggregate supply curve, prices rise when aggregate demand increases. In the case of expansionary fiscal policy, there is full crowding out and interest rates rise so much that investment falls by an amount equal to the increase in government spending. With expansionary monetary policy, the price level rises in proportion to the increase in the money supply, and so the real money supply and GDP are unchanged.

7.5 The *quantity theory* emphasizes the idea that changes in the money supply are responsible for most changes in the price level. Money is said to be *neutral* if an increase in money increases prices but leaves all real variables — GDP, unemployment, and the interest rate — unchanged. The pure quantity theory is equivalent to the notion that the velocity of money is constant and that real GDP is unaffected by changes in money — neither of which is true. Modern quantity theorists believe that the aggregate supply curve is vertical in the long run, but sloped in the short run. Thus the money supply will affect GDP in the short run but not in the long run.

Appendix The production function is a technological relation telling us how much output can be produced for a given combination of factor inputs. In the short run, when cooperating factors of production are in fixed supply, the marginal product of labour will be falling as more labour is added to the production process. The marginal product of labour measures the contribution to total output of an additional unit of labour (another worker). Firms will hire a worker as long as the contribution to total output is greater than the cost of hiring, which is the real wage.

Key Terms

Aggregate supply curve
Aggregate demand curve
Keynesian aggregate supply curve
Classical aggregate supply curve
Frictionless neoclassical model
Frictional unemployment
Full crowding out
Quantity theory of money
Neutrality of money
Monetarism
Natural rate of unemployment

Thinking Like an Economist

For the first six chapters of the text all of our models have been constructed using the Keynesian assumption that the price level is fixed. Chapter 7 is the first chapter that we have allowed the price level to be determined endogenously within the model. The opposite extreme of the Keynesian fixed price assumption, which gives rise to a horizontal aggregate supply curve, is the classical assumption that the price level is completely flexible, which gives rise to a vertical aggregate supply curve.

In this section we are going to look more closely at the workings of a very simple classical macroeconomic model. The essence of any classical macroeconomic model is that agents are rational utility maximizers, and prices are completely flexible. These assumptions ensure that all markets will be in continuous equilibrium.

In a classical macroeconomic model, the quantity theory of money holds. The quantity theory of money states that any change in the nominal money stock will lead to a change in the price level, with no change in any real variables, given the assumption that velocity is constant. This is known as *money neutrality*.

It is worth thinking more closely about the quantity theory. Suppose that the government were to pursue expansionary monetary policy, creating an excess supply of money. In a classical model, this results in an increase in the price level. That is, the price level is completely flexible, and plays the crucial role of ensuring that money demand equals money supply.

Notice how this result is different from the Keynesian *IS-LM* model. In the *IS-LM* model, the price level is fixed, and therefore it cannot respond to disequilibrium in the money market, such as excess supply of money. Therefore, in the *IS-LM* model it is the interest rate that moves to ensure money demand equals money supply.

We now wish to investigate how it is that changes in the nominal money stock will not change real output in a classical model. In Figure 7-2(a) we have drawn the demand and supply curves for labour.

Notice that the nominal wage is on the vertical axis. We know that in classical macroeconomics labour supply and demand depend on the real wage. Therefore, the price level acts as a shift parameter on the labour demand and supply curves. In Figure 7-1(a) E is the initial equilibrium. The equilibrium nominal wage is W_0, the price level is P_0, and therefore, the real wage is W_0/P_0. The price level P_0 comes from the money market, where P_0 ensures that money demand equals money supply. Equilibrium labour use is N_0. Recall that in a classical model, output depends on the production function

$$Y_0 = F(N_0, \overline{K})$$

where we assume that the capital stock, $\overline{K}$, is fixed. Therefore, output is Y_0, and in Figure 7-2(b) P_0, Y_0 is one point on the classical aggregate supply curve.

Now consider expansionary monetary policy, which creates an excess supply of money. The price level increases to P_1 to ensure that the money market is in equilibrium. The important question is, what happens to the labour market? Both the labour demand and the labour supply curve shift upwards, by the change in the price level. The nominal wage goes up to W_1, but the real wage remains the same because $W_1/P_1 = W_0/P_0$. Therefore, equilibrium labour use remains the same and output remains the same. Therefore P_1, Y_0 is another point on the aggregate supply curve and the classical aggregate supply curve is vertical.

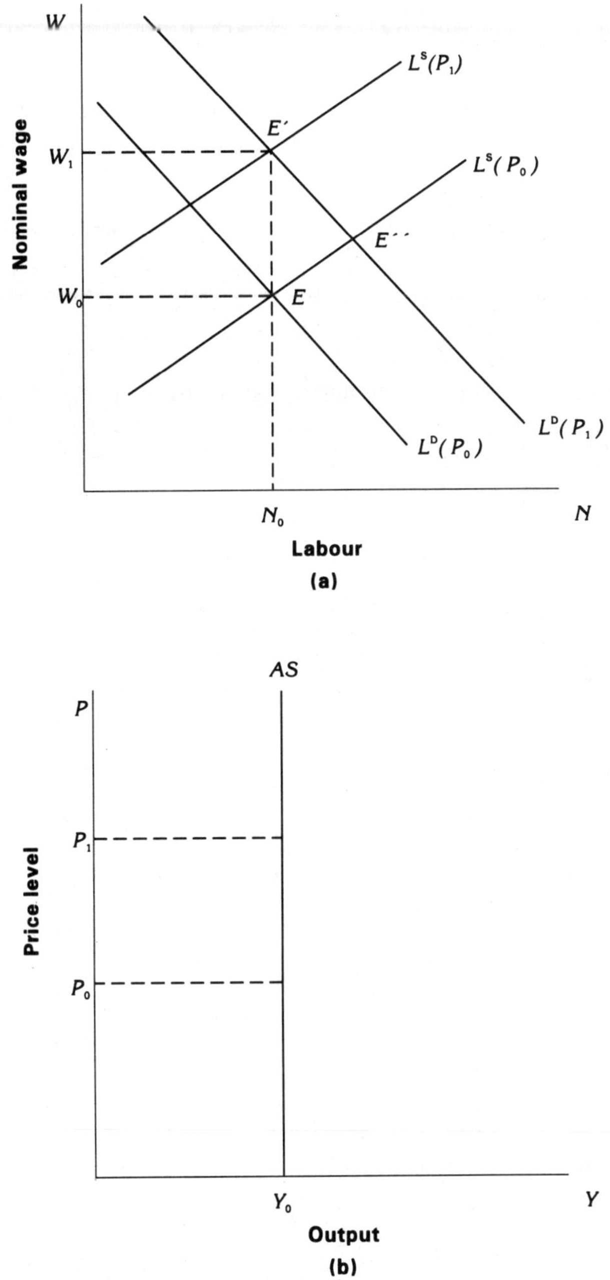
W
Nominal wage
W1
W0
E′
E′′
E
$L^S(P_1)$
$L^S(P_0)$
$L^D(P_0)$
$L^D(P_1)$
N0
N
Labour
(a)
AS
P
Price level
P1
P0
Y0
Y
Output
(b)

Figure 7-2

It is important that you understand why point E'' cannot be a classical equilibrium point. At E'' the nominal wage is higher, but the price level has increased by more than the nominal wage has increased, and therefore the real wage is lower. If point E'' were an equilibrium, it would mean that workers would be supplying more labour for a lower real wage. In this model firms and workers have full information, so it would

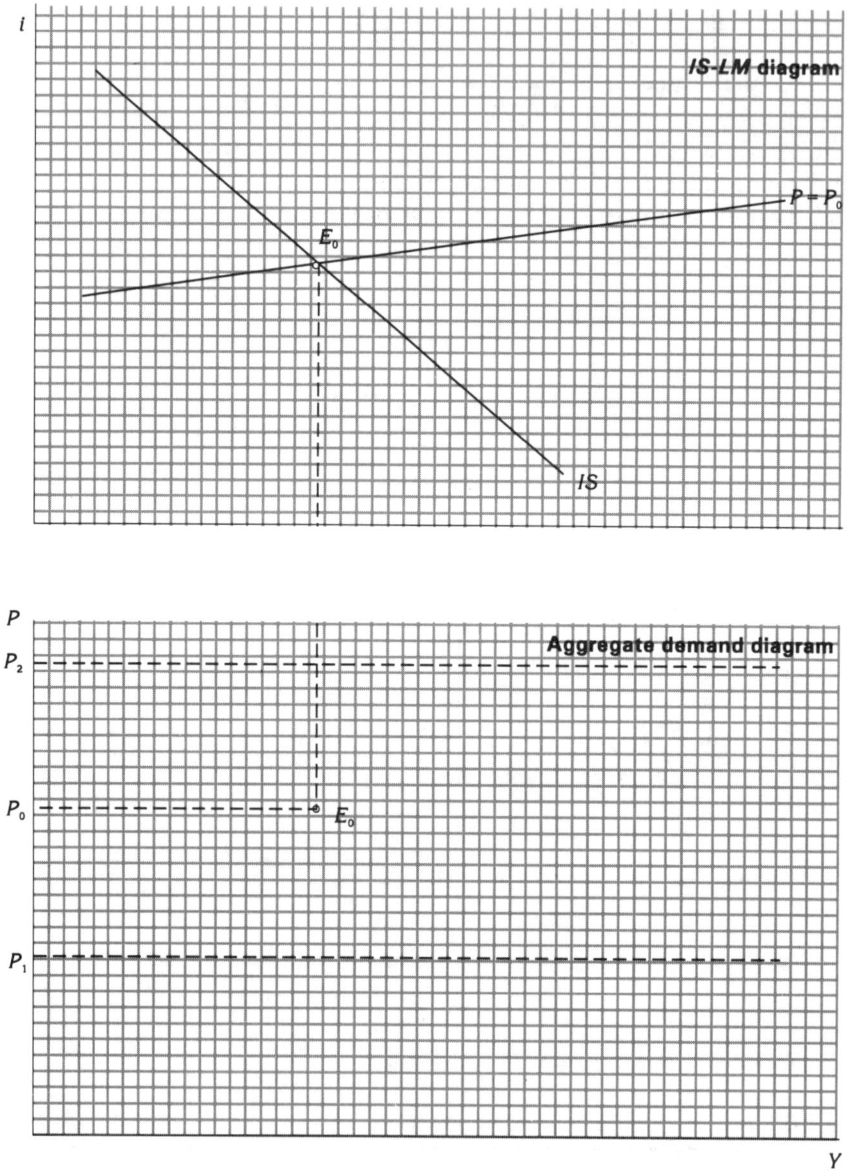

Chart 7-1

be irrational for labour to move to point E''. In the next chapter, we will see that *New-Classical* macroeconomics attempts to explain how point E'' could be a temporary equilibrium, if workers had less information about the price level than firms.

Graph It 7

The aggregate schedule represents the solutions of the *IS-LM* system at different price levels. Chart 7-1 shows an *IS-LM* diagram drawn above an aggregate demand diagram. We've drawn on an *IS* curve and an *LM* curve based on a price level P_0. The equilibrium income is E_0. We've marked off this same income level on the aggregate demand diagram at price P_0. This gives us one point on the aggregate demand schedule. Now you draw in two new *LM* curves, one based on $P_1 < P_0$ and another based on $P_2 > P_0$. Mark the points E_1 and E_2 and drop vertical lines to mark the points on the aggregate demand diagram. Connect the three points on the aggregate demand diagram and mark the line *AD*.

Fill-In Questions

1. The aggregate demand function depends on ________________ .

2. It also depends on ________________ .

3. The aggregate demand function represents those combinations of income and price level found through ________________ analysis.

4. The displacement of investment by government spending is called ________________ .

5. The proposition that proportional changes in the nominal money supply and the price level have no real effect is referred to as ________________ .

6. The relation between output and prices that summarizes the economy's ability to produce goods and services is the ________________ schedule.

7. The relation between output and prices that summarizes the various possible *IS-LM* equilibria is the ________________ schedule.

8. In the Keynesian model, the aggregate supply curve is ________________ .

9. In the classical model, the aggregate supply curve is ________________ .

10. According to the ________________ , prices are flexible and prices and output are determined by perfect competition.

True-False Questions

T F 1. Movements up and left along the aggregate demand schedule correspond to decreasing interest rates in the *IS-LM* equilibrium.

T F 2. A flat aggregate demand schedule results from a low *MPC*.

T F 3. A flat aggregate demand schedule results from a low interest sensitivity of money demand.

T F 4. A flat aggregate demand schedule results from a low interest sensitivity of investment.

T F 5. Aggregate demand (*AD*) is increased by increased government spending.

T F 6. Combinations of *IS* and *LM* curves can be used to trace out the aggregate supply curve.

T F 7. Increased government spending increases interest rates if the aggregate supply curve is Keynesian.

T F 8. Increased government spending increases interest rates if the aggregate supply curve is classical.

T F 9. Increased nominal money supply decreases interest rates if the aggregate supply curve is Keynesian.

T F 10. Increased nominal money supply decreases interest rates if the aggregate supply curve is classical.

T F 11. The frictionless classical model is a reasonably good short-run description of the economy.

Multiple-Choice Questions

The price level is held constant in questions 1, 2, and 3.

1. Increasing the money supply
   (a) increases aggregate supply
   (b) decreases aggregate supply
   (c) increases aggregate demand
   (d) decreases aggregate demand

2. Increasing government spending
   (a) increases aggregate supply
   (b) decreases aggregate supply
   (c) increases aggregate demand
   (d) decreases aggregate demand

3. There is a positive relation between GDP and the price level along
   (a) the aggregate demand curve
   (b) the aggregate supply curve
   (c) both these curves
   (d) neither of these curves

4. There is a negative relation between GDP and the price level along
- **(a)** the aggregate demand curve
- **(b)** the aggregate supply curve
- **(c)** both these curves
- **(d)** neither of these curves

5. There is a negative relation between GDP and the interest rate along
- **(a)** the aggregate demand curve
- **(b)** the aggregate supply curve
- **(c)** both these curves
- **(d)** neither of these curves

6. A high marginal propensity to save implies
- **(a)** that the aggregate supply curve is relatively flat
- **(b)** that it is relatively steep
- **(c)** that it is relatively flat only if *MPS* is greater than 1/2
- **(d)** nothing about aggregate supply

7. If the nominal money supply doubles, eventually the price level will
- **(a)** remain unchanged
- **(b)** double
- **(c)** increase by a factor of less than 2
- **(d)** increase by a factor of more than 2

8. If autonomous spending doubles, eventually the price level
- **(a)** will remain unchanged
- **(b)** will double
- **(c)** will more than double
- **(d)** cannot be determined without more information

9. An increase in the nominal money supply will cause investment to increase in
- **(a)** the long run
- **(b)** the short run
- **(c)** both the short and the long run
- **(d)** neither one

10. An increase in government spending will cause investment to decrease in
- **(a)** the long run
- **(b)** the short run
- **(c)** both the short and the long run
- **(d)** neither one

11. In the frictionless neoclassical model, the real wage
- **(a)** is unchanging over time
- **(b)** equals the marginal product of labour
- **(c)** equals the nominal wage
- **(d)** is higher than in the Keynesian model

Problems

Use the following equations for each of the questions below:

$Y = 2A + 4(M_{-1}/P_{-1})$	aggregate demand
$P = P_{-1}[1 - 0.8(1 - (Y/Y_p)]$	aggregate supply
$I = 1000 - 2000i$	investment

In the long run, assume the supply curve is classical and $P = P_{-1}$. Also, note that we assume there is a one-period lag before monetary policy works.

Potential GDP is 4000. Initial levels are $A = 1000$, $M = 50\ 000$, and $P = 100$. Consumption is a function only of current income.

1. Suppose government spending increases by 500. What are the levels of GDP and the price index in the year of the increase? In the two following years?
2. What is the price level in the long run? By how much does investment change? The interest rate?
3. Suppose, instead of increasing government spending, the money supply had been doubled. In the long run, what would be the level of the price index, the change in investment, and the change in the interest rate?

CHAPTER 8 *Aggregate Supply in the Short Run*

Focus of the Chapter

- In this chapter we first consider the New Classical approach, which combines the Lucas supply curve with the assumption of rational expectations.
- We then consider a model that assumes that money wages adjust slowly. When the wage differs from its long-run value, GDP differs from potential GDP.
- The Phillips curve describes the relation between wage change and unemployment. The aggregate supply curve is derived from the Phillips curve by looking at the relation of prices to wages and output to employment.
- The aggregate supply curve is inherently dynamic. In the long run it will move to bring the economy to full employment.

Section Summaries

8.1 The market-clearing approach has two essential components: the Lucas supply curve and the assumption of rational expectations.

Derivation of the Lucas supply curve starts with the assertion that at any point in time workers do not know the aggregate price level. Therefore, when they are faced with a nominal wage offer, they must make an expectation of the unknown price level.

In other words, workers offer their labour services on the basis of the *expected* real wage. This can be explained using Figure 8-1.

The following discussion starts where Chapter 7's Thinking Like an Economist section finished. You may find it helpful to review the discussion concerning Figure 7-2 in this *Study Guide*. In Figure 8-1, the nominal wage is measured on the vertical axis. Since workers offer labour on the basis of the expected real wage, we use the *expected* price level as a shift parameter on the labour supply function. In the initial equilibrium at point E_0, the expected real wage is W_0/P_0, and equilibrium labour use is N_0. Assume that the government pursues expansionary monetary policy which causes the price level to increase to P_1. Firms are assumed to know that price level has increased, and therefore the labour demand curve shifts out, and workers are faced with a higher nominal wage offer, W'. If workers correctly anticipate that the price level has increased, the labour supply function will shift outwards, the nominal wage will be bid up to W_1, and the expected real wage and equilibrium labour use will be the same at E_1, as at the original equilibrium E_0. If workers anticipate that the price level has not changed, they will work more as their *expected* real wage has increased. Therefore, whether or not output goes up, *in response to the nominal price change*, depends on whether or not labour correctly anticipates the price level change.

The Lucas supply function can be written as

$$Y = Y^* + \gamma(P - P^e)$$

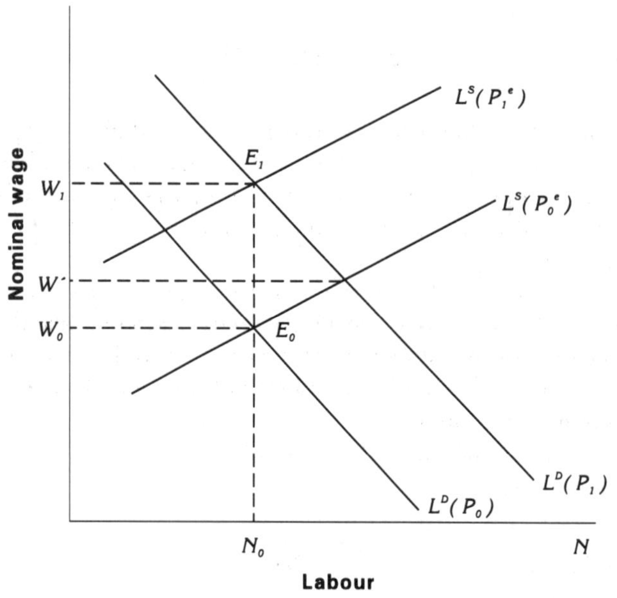

Figure 8-1

The second ingredient of the market-clearing approach is the assumption the expectations are formed rationally. Rational expectations assumes that agents use all relevant information in forming expectations of economic variables. The essence of this assumption is that workers can make errors, but they will not make systematic errors.

Combining the market-clearing approach with the assumption of rational expectations leads to the result that anticipated changes in the money supply have no real effects, while unanticipated changes in the money supply can have real effects. Notice that unanticipated changes in the money supply have real effects which are short-lived, as rational expectations states that agents will learn quickly from their errors and correct their mistakes.

8.2 Unemployment fluctuates much more than neoclassical theory implies should be the case. Furthermore, money wage rates respond slowly to shifts in aggregate demand, which again is inconsistent with the neoclassical model. Shifts in aggregate demand appear to affect output and employment well before they affect prices and money wages.

Letting W be the wage this period and W_{-1} be the wage last period, the rate of wage inflation, g_W, is

$$g_W = \frac{W - W_{-1}}{W_{-1}}$$

The Phillips curve

$$g_W = -\varepsilon(u - u^*)$$

makes precise the notion that wages respond slowly to shifts in aggregate demand (unemployment). As u rises above u^* (the natural rate of unemployment), money wages fall. As u falls below u^*, money wage rates rise. The rate at which money wages change from last period's level depends upon ε as well as $u - u^*$. The larger ε is, the more rapidly wages change.

At one time it was argued that policy makers could choose any combination of inflation and unemployment along the Phillips curve. Friedman and Phelps argued that the Phillips curve was not stable over time and that in the long run the economy would return to the natural rate of unemployment. Econometric evidence supports Friedman and Phelps's argument.

Using the definition of the unemployment rate

$$u = \frac{N^* - N}{N^*}$$

where N^* is the full-employment level of employment and N is the actual level of employment, we can rewrite the Phillips curve in terms of the level of employment:

$$g_W = \frac{W - W_{-1}}{W_{-1}} = -\varepsilon(\frac{N* - N}{N*})$$

Wages rise ($W > W_{-1}$) whenever employment is above full employment ($N > N^*$).

Wage employment contracts are renegotiated only periodically, since negotiation is costly. Renegotiation dates are usually staggered, so that at any point in time, only a fraction of all workers' wages are rising or falling in response to current changes in the cost of living or productivity. Wages in economies with low inflation rates are usually set in nominal terms, so that real wages do not adjust to changes in goods' prices immediately. Therefore, nominal wage contracts cause real wages to fluctuate over time, even though nominal wages may remain fixed for long periods. Fluctuations in the real wage cause the terms on which employers can hire workers to change over time, and thus produce fluctuations in employment.

8.3 The aggregate supply curve relates prices and output. Prices depend on costs, which we can think of as unit labour costs $1/a$ times the money wage w plus a percentage markup z, to cover the costs of materials, capital, and profits.

$$P = w/a(1 + z)$$

Now we substitute, in the wage adjustment equation, prices for wages and GDP for labour to get aggregate supply.

$$P = P_{-1}\,(1 + \lambda(Y - Y^*))$$

Note three properties of aggregate supply:

1. If wage adjustment is slow, the aggregate supply curve is relatively flat.
2. The position of the aggregate supply curve depends on the past history of prices.
3. The aggregate supply curve shifts over time because today's price becomes yesterday's price tomorrow. (Reread the last sentence if necessary. It actually does make sense.) A different P_{-1} tomorrow means that the aggregate supply curve has a new position tomorrow.

8.4 Figure 8-2 (text Figure 8-12) shows the response of the economy to an increase in the money stock. The aggregate demand curve shifts to the right. At first, prices rise very little and output goes up almost as much as the horizontal shift in aggregate demand. Since we are now above full employment, prices rise and the aggregate supply curve gradually shifts up. The aggregate supply curve keeps shifting up until output returns to potential GDP, at a higher price than when we started. At the new equilibrium point E''', all real variables are the same as they were at the initial equilibrium, E. That is, money is neutral *in the long run*. A classical model would say that you go directly from E to E''', while this *sticky price* model says that, although you do get to E''', there is a significant adjustment process.

8.5 An aggregate supply shock, such as an increase in the real price of oil, shifts the supply curve up. This increases prices and reduces output. If potential GDP has

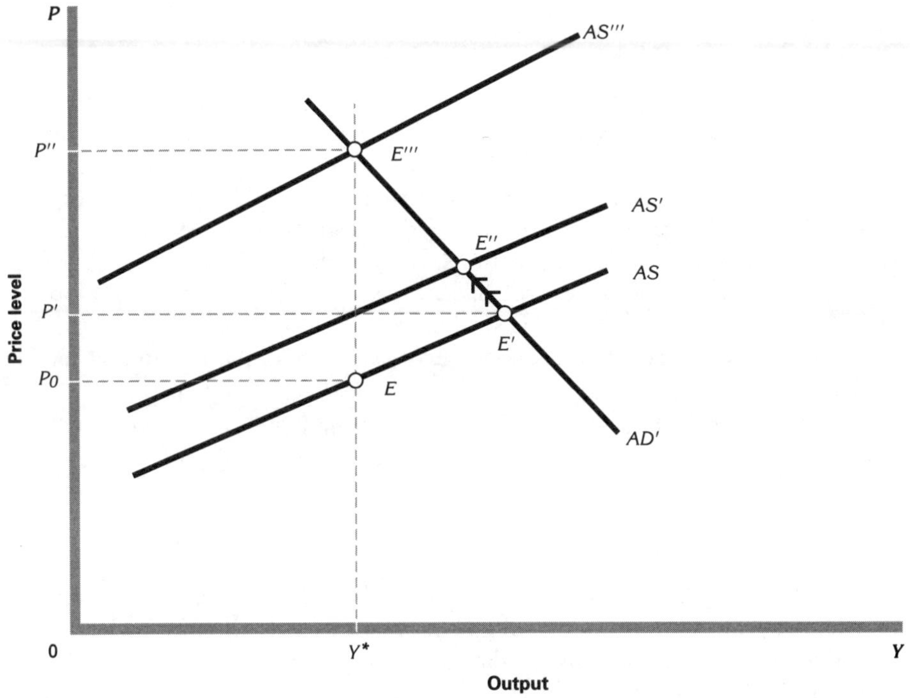

Figure 8-2

not fallen (and it may have), the aggregate supply curve will eventually return to its initial position. Aggregate demand policy can be used to accommodate supply shocks, stabilizing output but raising prices. The introduction of the federal Goods and Services Tax can be viewed as another example of an adverse supply shock.

8.6 The theory of aggregate supply is still unsettled in economics. Most theories aim to show that the aggregate supply curve slopes upward in the short run and is vertical in the long run. The Lucas supply curve depends on the real wage being countercyclical, which does not appear to be consistent with the empirical evidence.

Key Terms

Market clearing approach
Lucas supply curve
Rational expectations equilibrium
Phillips curve
Labour productivity
Unit labour costs
Markup
Sticky prices
Adverse supply shock
Accommodation of supply shocks

Thinking Like an Economist

Recall the discussion in Chapter 1, where we saw that there are two schools of thought in macroeconomics. One school believes that markets are in equilibrium all of the time, while the other school believes that markets may be out of equilibrium for a substantial amount of time. Clearly, the assumption used in the first six chapters of the book that the price level is fixed and that the aggregate supply curve is horizontal is a non-market-clearing assumption. The classical assumption that wages and prices are completely flexible, which leads to a vertical aggregate supply curve, is a market-clearing assumption. In this section we wish to investigate where the New Classical model and the sticky price model belong in terms of market- or non-market-clearing.

Consider first the sticky price model, which has an aggregate supply curve given by the following equation.

$$P = P_{-1}\,(1 + \lambda(Y - Y^*))$$

In Figure 8-2 above we saw that monetary policy has real effects in the short run, but not in the long run. Therefore, this model has features of both market-clearing and non-market-clearing assumptions. In the short run prices and wages are sticky, and therefore there are markets which are not clearing. However, in the long run all the stickiness works out of the economy and the model is a full market-clearing model.

Now consider the New Classical model. The Lucas supply function is given by the equation

$$Y = Y^* + \gamma(P - P^e)$$

We have seen that, if we combine the Lucas supply function with the assumption of rational expectations, monetary policy cannot *systematically* affect real income. The word "systematically" is very important in this context. To see this, consider once again monetary policy as described in Figure 8-2. In the sticky price model, points like E' can always be attained in the short run through expansionary monetary policy. In the New Classical model, a point like E' could be attained by an *unanticipated* increase in the nominal money stock. However, rational expectations would say that an error in expectations becomes part of your information set and accordingly the monetary authorities could not engineer the same unanticipated increase next period because rational agents would know about it. Therefore, the monetary authorities cannot systematically drive the economy to points like E'.

The above discussion shows that the New Classical model is very definitely a market-clearing model. This is because the Lucas supply function is a market-clearing aggregate supply function, and the assumption of rational expectations is also a market-clearing assumption. The result that monetary policy has no systematic effect on real income depends on both of these assumptions. To see this, consider again the Lucas supply function

$$Y = Y^* + \gamma(P - P_{-1})$$

Now, instead of rational expectations, consider the following way of thinking about expectations.

$$P^e = P_{-1}$$

This is known as *static expectations*. Notice that static expectations has the property that, as long as the price level is moving, agents are always wrong in their expectations about the price level. Therefore, this "market" is not clearing. Substitute this expression into the Lucas supply function.

$$Y = Y^* + \gamma(P - P_{-1})$$

Now rearrange terms to get the following expression.

$$P = P_{-1} + \gamma(Y - Y^*)$$

This is an equation which has properties identical to those of the sticky price aggregate supply function. Therefore, to have a full market-clearing model, all markets must clear. If at least one market does not clear, then the model will generate a Keynesian-type result.

Graph It 8

Graph It 8 asks you to implement fiscal policy (or at least to figure out how far to move the *IS* curve). Chart 8-1 shows *IS* and *LM* curves on the top diagram and aggregate supply and demand curves on the bottom diagram. Initially, equilibrium is at point E_0. Then a supply shock moves the aggregate supply curve up. The new equilibrium, with lower output and higher prices, is at point E_1. Draw in a new IS' curve that will move the economy to point E_2 and mark off the horizontal distance by which you moved the *IS* curve.

Hold it! Not so fast! Prices are higher at E_1 than at E_0. This means that real balances are lower and that the *LM* curve has already shifted left. Draw in the curve LM' corresponding to this movement along the aggregate demand curve. Then draw in IS' and measure the distance.

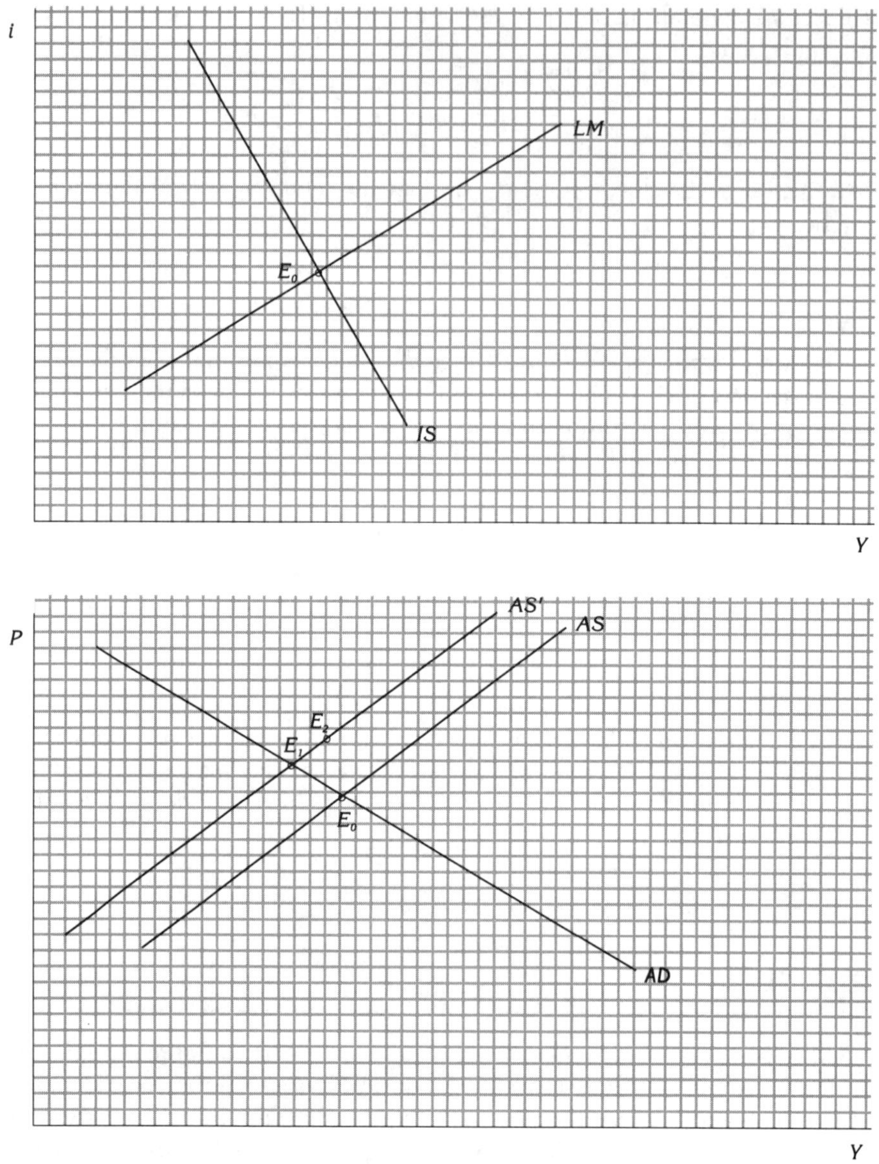

Chart 8-1

Fill-In Questions

1. The fact that wages change slowly is due to ________________ .
2. The rate of ________________ is the percentage change in the general price level per annum.
3. The ________________ is the relation between inflation and unemployment derived from the aggregate supply curve.
4. According to the New Classical model, monetary policy cannot ________________ affect the level of real income.
5. The ratio of output to labour input is called ________________ .
6. The theory that prices are set by a constant percentage over variable costs is the ________________ theory.
7. Events that change costs or shift the supply or demand for labour are called ________________ .

True-False Questions

T F 1. Average output per worker generally rises during a boom.

T F 2. The concept of diminishing returns indicates that additional labour leads to lower output.

T F 3. Aggregate supply (*AS*) is increased by increased potential GDP.

T F 4. *AS* is increased by an increased labour force.

T F 5. An increase in materials prices pushes the aggregate supply curve up.

T F 6. Unit labour cost is the inverse of labour productivity.

T F 7. The government should always accommodate an adverse supply shock.

T F 8. If expectations are rational, agents use all available information.

T F 9. The Lucas supply function states that a fully anticipated increase in the nominal money stock will raise real income.

Multiple-Choice Questions

1. In the New Classical model, if $P > P^e$
   (a) $W > W^e$
   (b) $W < W^e$
   (c) $W = W^e$
   (d) $Y < Y^*$

2. Adverse supply shocks
(a) increase prices and increase output
(b) decrease prices and increase output
(c) increase prices and decrease output
(d) decrease prices and decrease output

3. Movement of the aggregate supply curve moves the economy to potential GDP
(a) instantly
(b) quite quickly
(c) slowly
(d) never

4. An increase in the money stock increases GDP in
(a) the short run
(b) the long run
(c) both
(d) neither

5. A drop in autonomous spending decreases GDP in
(a) the short run
(b) the long run
(c) both
(d) neither

6. The position of the aggregate supply curve depends on
(a) potential GDP
(b) past prices
(c) both
(d) neither

Problems

1. Suppose that the fraction of the labour force that becomes unemployed for each percent deviation of GDP from potential GDP is 0.4. Further assume that nominal wages drop 2 percent for each 1 percent increase in unemployment. Initially, the economy is at full employment and the consumer price index (CPI) is 100. If the government increases GDP by 10 percent and maintains it at its new level, what will the CPI be after one year? After two years?

2. According to the sticky wage and price aggregate supply curve theory developed in this chapter, what is the inflation rate when the economy is at full employment?

3. We know that the classical vertical aggregate supply model, the New Classical model, and the sticky wage and price model, will all give the same long-run result with respect to expansionary monetary policy. Carefully describe the differences in the dynamics of adjustment inherent in each model.

CHAPTER 9 *Aggregate Supply and Demand in an Open Economy*

Focus of the Chapter

- The model of Chapters 5 and 6 is extended by incorporating aggregate demand and supply so as to determine the domestic price level in an open economy.
- We show that, with perfect capital mobility and flexible prices, monetary and fiscal policy cannot alter the long-run level of real income.
- The relationships between the trade balance, the exchange rate, and the domestic price level can cause problems in adjusting to disturbances.

Section Summaries

9.1 The equilibrium income and price level in an open economy with a fixed exchange rate are illustrated in Figure 9-1 (text Figure 9-1). In this case, aggregate demand is reduced by an increase in the price level through a reduction in domestic competitiveness as well as through a reduction in real balances. The external balance

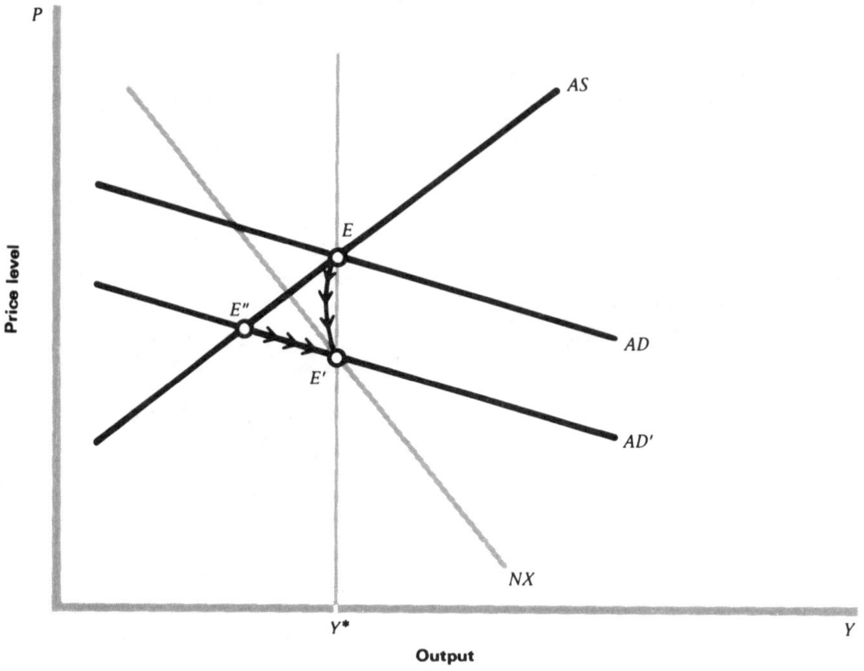

Figure 9-1

schedule *NX* shows the set of combinations of income and the price level along which we have a zero balance of trade.

The figure shows the adjustment starting at the point *E* where aggregate demand and supply are equal at full employment, but the price level is too high so that we have a trade deficit. External balance can be achieved by contractionary policy that leads to a short-run equilibrium at E'' and an adjustment path along AD' to E'. Alternatively the trade deficit can be eliminated through the *classical adjustment process*. In the absence of sterilization, the money supply will decline automatically and the economy will move from *E* to E' along the path shown. The protracted recession required to bring about a decline in the domestic price level can be avoided by restoring competitiveness immediately through a devaluation.

If there is an increase in the foreign price level, a proportionate increase in the domestic price level must occur to restore internal and external balance. This proposition has the important implication that a country on a fixed exchange rate ties its price level to that of its trading partners and is forced to import foreign inflation. Divergent policies and inflation rates among countries led to the collapse of the *Bretton Woods* system of fixed exchange rates in the early 1970s.

9.2 This section considers fiscal policy with fixed exchange rates and perfect capital mobility. Recall the result of Chapter 6, where we saw that with perfect capital

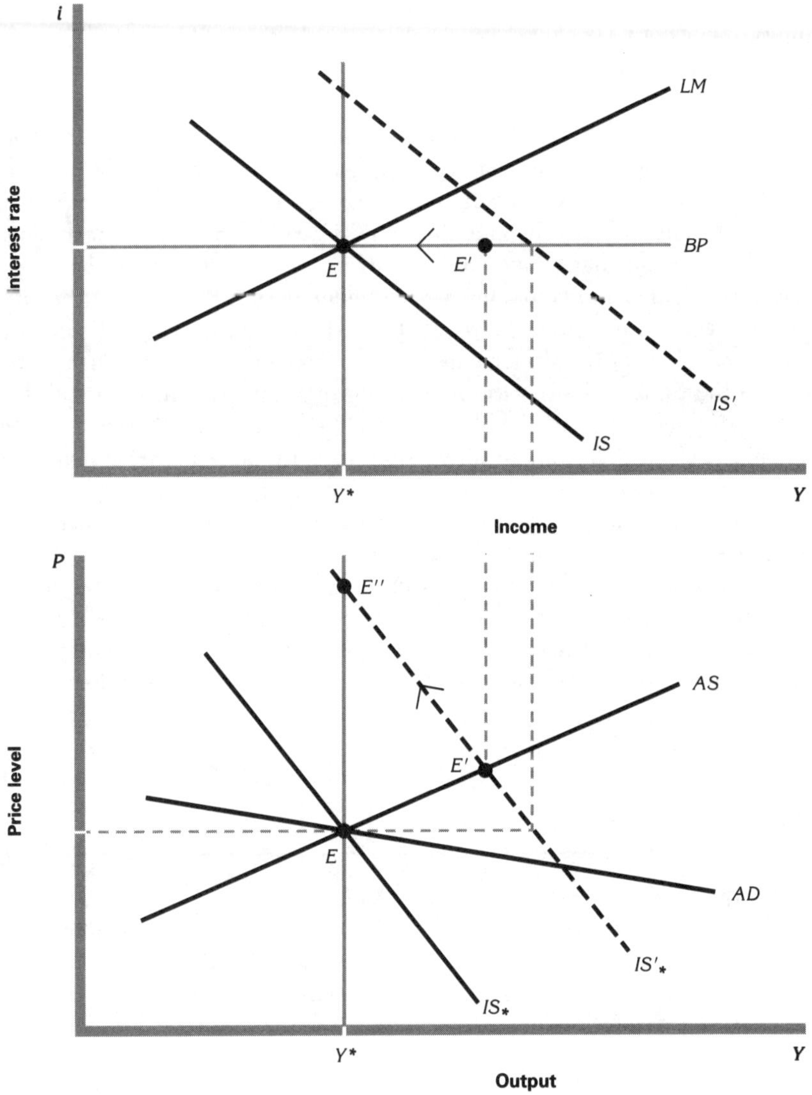

Figure 9-2

mobility and a fixed exchange rate, the money supply is endogenous, and therefore there is no role for monetary policy in domestic stabilization. Therefore, we only consider fiscal policy in this section. The effects of expansionary fiscal policy with perfect capital mobility are shown in Figure 9-2 (text Figure 9-4). Expansionary fiscal policy pushes the domestic economy beyond full employment, which raises the domestic price level. With a fixed exchange rate and a given foreign price level, the real exchange rate, eP^*/P, decreases, which crowds out net exports. Therefore, in the new equilibrium, at E'' in the lower panel, the level of income is the same, but the composition has changed. As well, the price level is higher and the real exchange rate is lower.

9.3 Figure 9-3 (text Figure 9-5) describes the effects of expansionary monetary policy with perfect capital mobility and a flexible exchange rate. The short-run effect of a monetary expansion is to depreciate the currency, which causes an improvement in the terms of trade, and results in an increase in net exports and domestic income. This is the same result that we derived in Chapter 6. However, now that the price level is flexible, expansionary monetary policy, which pushes the economy beyond full employment, causes the price level to rise. In the long run the economy moves to E'' in the lower panel (E in the upper panel), where money is neutral. That is, all real variables are the same as before the monetary expansion (real income and the real exchange rate), while nominal variables have changed (the nominal exchange rate and the nominal price level). This neutrality result leads to the *purchasing power parity* theory of exchange rates, which states that, *in the long run*, exchange rates move primarily as a result of differences in price level behaviour between countries in such a way as to keep the real exchange rate constant.

9.4 It used to be argued that floating exchange rates allowed nations to pursue totally independent macroeconomic policies. We now know that *spillover* effects are caused by the changes in a nation's competitive position. Thus *interdependence* suggests that countries can benefit from coordination of macroeconomic policies.

Key Terms

Real exchange rate
Classical adjustment process
Bretton Woods system
Purchasing power parity
J curve
Monetary theory of exchange rates
Imported inflation
Interdependence

Thinking Like an Economist

In Chapters 7 to 9 a recurrent theme has been that the nominal wage and price levels may exhibit sluggish adjustment in the short run. Recall that one method of distinguishing between long-run (classical) analysis and short run (Keynesian) analysis is that in the long-run all markets clear, while in the short run at least one market does not clear. The assumption that the price level may not adjust quickly in the short run distinguishes these two schools of thought, as sluggish adjustment by definition is non-market-clearing. Of course, the two schools agree about the long-run effects of, say, expansionary monetary policy, but disagree on the adjustment path of the econ-

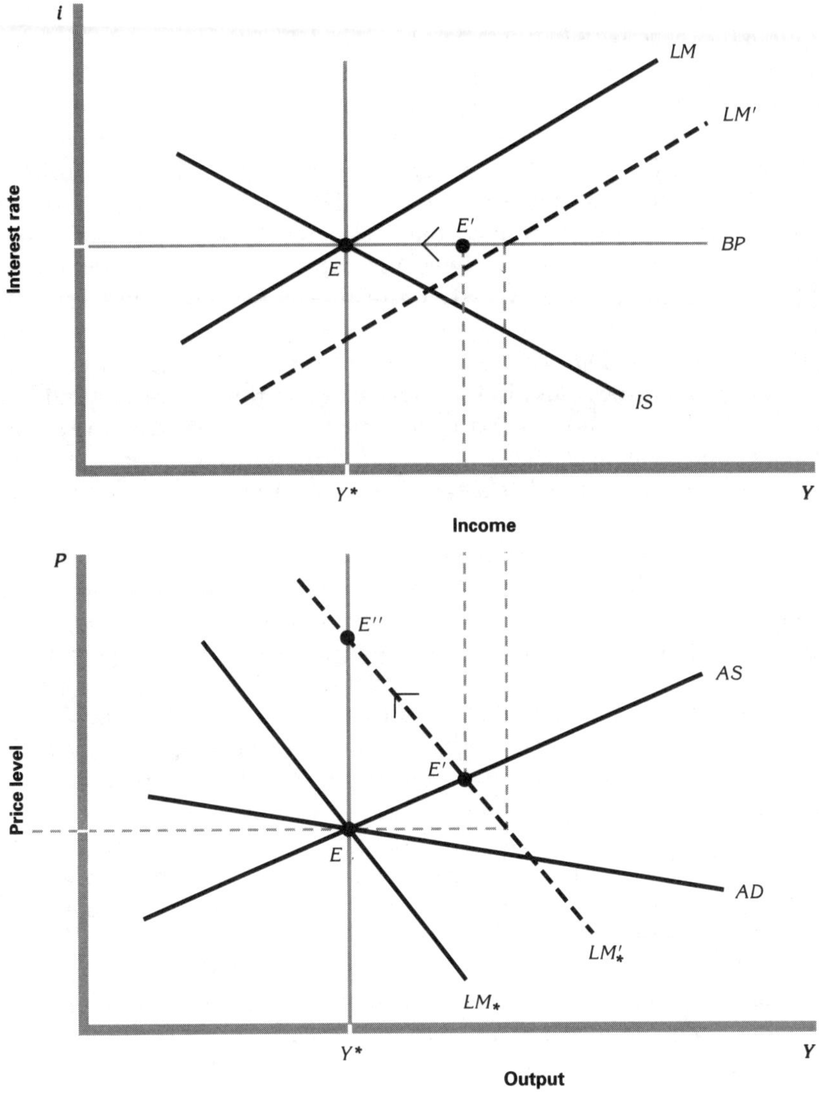

Figure 9-3

omy toward a new long-run equilibrium. A classical economist would say that the price level increases *instantly*, while a Keynesian economist would say that the price level increases *eventually*. This distinction has important ramifications for monetary policy.

Consider first how a classical economist would analyze expansionary monetary policy in an open economy. With flexible prices the classical quantity theory of money holds, and therefore an increase in the quantity of money increases the level of prices, so that the money market remains in equilibrium. (If you do not understand this, it will be helpful to review the Thinking Like an Economist section from Chapter 7 of this *Study Guide*.) Assuming that the foreign economy does not pursue a similar expansionary policy, this will result in $M > M^*$ and $P > P^*$. Purchasing power parity then predicts that, because domestic prices are greater than foreign prices, the nominal exchange rate must depreciate (that is, the Canadian dollar price of foreign exchange must increase) in order to equate international price levels. Therefore, the real exchange rate, eP^*/P, does not change, as e increases in proportion to the increase in P. Accordingly, net exports and real income remain constant, and only nominal variables, M, P, and e, change.

In the above analysis, no market exhibits sluggish adjustment. Therefore, a change in the *nominal* money stock only brings about changes in other *nominal* variables, and real variables do not respond to this nominal change. Therefore, we can think of purchasing power parity as being *open economy* quantity theory of money: a change in the nominal money stock only changes the nominal price level and the *nominal* exchange rate.

Now consider how a Keneysian economist would analyze the same expansionary monetary policy. The Keynesian economist assumes that in the short run price level adjustment is sluggish, and therefore an increase in the nominal money stock cannot bring about an immediate price level increase as it does in the classical model, but rather brings forth a decrease in the nominal interest rate. Therefore, expansionary monetary policy causes the domestic interest rate to be below the foreign interest rate, which causes capital outflow, and the nominal exchange rate depreciates. Because prices are sluggish in the short run, the terms of trade improve (the real exchange rate increases), which causes net exports and real income to increase. This increase in real income, which pushes the economy beyond the classical full-employment level, eventually causes the price level to increase, and the terms of trade worsen (eP^*/P decreases). When all of the adjustment is over, the economy ends up at exactly the same long-run equilibrium.

It is worth emphasizing that, although the long-run equilibrium is the same under each analysis, the path toward that long-run equilibrium is different. In the Keynesian analysis, the change in the nominal money stock brings about changes in real variables *because the price level is sluggish in the short run*. In the classical analysis, the change in the nominal money stock does not cause any real variables to change, *because all markets are assumed to clear*.

Graph It 9

Graphic Solution of a Two-Equation Model

Many economic models can be reduced to a problem of two unknown variables described by two equations. *IS-LM* analysis and supply-and-demand analysis are the best-known examples of such systems. In this Graph It we use graphs to solve a two-equation model and then to show how the equilibrium of the system shifts when exogenous parameters shift.

Equations 9-1 and 9-2 are a pair of simultaneous equations. The unknown variables are X and Y. Q and Z are exogenous variables. The coefficients are all positive.

$$Y = a_1X + a_2Z \tag{9-1}$$
$$X = -b_1Y - b_2Z + b_3Q \tag{9-2}$$

Notice that these are totally made-up equations. (We want you to work on technical tools for the moment and not use your economic intuition.) If you find algebraic coefficients such as "a" distracting, you can scratch them out and replace "a" with "7," "a_2" with "3," or whatever you like.

The two equations are graphed in Figure 9-4. The intersection of the two lines, the point (Y^*, X^*), is the one combination of X and Y that satisfies both equations.

We are frequently concerned with discovering how the solution to a system of equations is changed by a shift in one of the exogenous variables. Discovering the changes in income and the interest rate induced by an increase in government spending, which are predicted by the *IS-LM* model, is a typical example. We illustrate effects of increasing the exogenous variable Q in Figure 9-5. Equation 9-2 shifts upward to the right to the dashed line. At the new equilibrium (Y', X'), both X and Y are higher than at the original equilibrium. Notice that we are able to make very strong qualitative statements about the direction of change of the unknown variables even though we have very limited information about the two equations. In principle, we could find exact numerical solutions by drawing the graph with sufficient care. Practically speaking, we rarely do this. Graphs are used mainly for qualitative analysis.

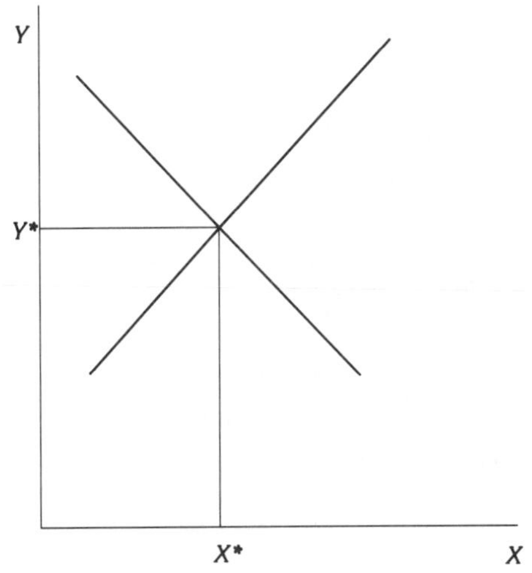

Figure 9-4

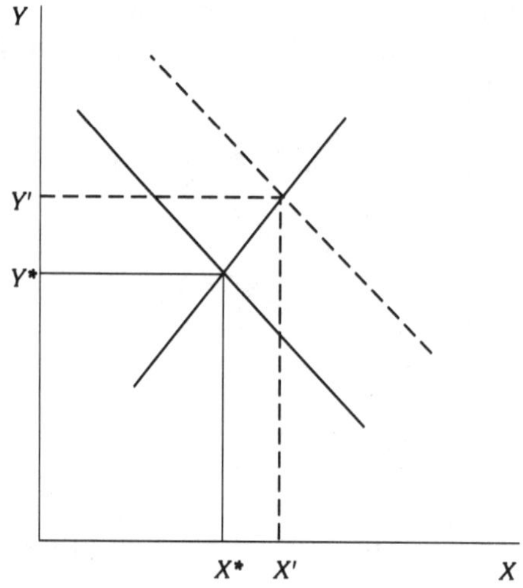

Figure 9-5

If Z increases, both equations shift. As illustrated in Figure 9-6, Equation 9-1 shifts upward to the left and Equation 9-2 shifts downward to the left. Since both equations shift to the left, the equilibrium surely shifts to the left; in other words, X will be lower. On the other hand, since one equation shifts up and the other shifts down, the new intersection might be either above or below the original point. The change in Y

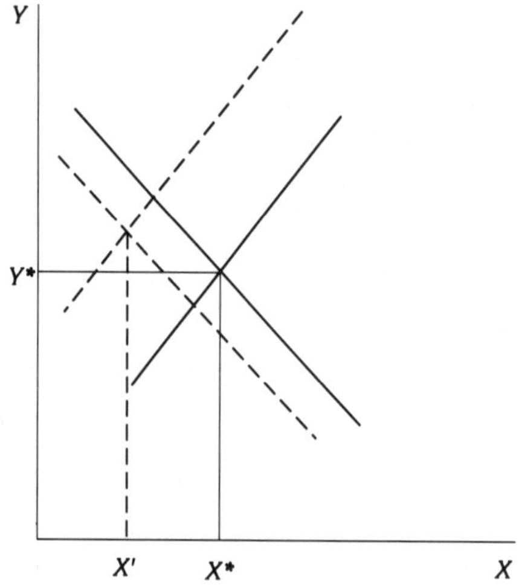

Figure 9-6

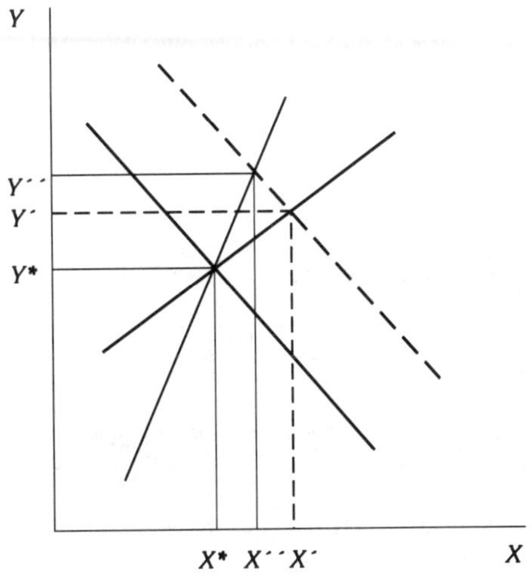

Figure 9-7

might be either positive or negative. In order to know the change unambiguously, we would need to know the relative values of a_2 and b_2.

The slope of Equation 9-1 determines how a shift in Equation 9-2 changes X and Y. A practical example of this is the question of how the slope of the *IS* curve determines the effectiveness of monetary policy. Figure 9-7 illustrates two different hypothetical versions of Equation 9-1.

The dashed line represents a line with a higher value for a_1, and therefore a greater slope, than the original Equation 9-1. (Y^*, X^*) to (Y', X') is the change that would occur with the original value of a_1. The point (Y'', X'') illustrates the change caused by the hypothetically higher value of a_1. The higher slope of Equation 9-1 results in a larger shift in Y and a smaller shift in X.

Fill-In Questions

1. The ____________________ show the relative prices of imports as compared with domestically produced goods.

2. With fixed exchange rates and no sterilization the economy reaches internal and external balance via the ____________________ adjustment process.

3. The fixed exchange rate system that was established after World War II was called the ____________________ .

4. If the relative prices of goods in two countries, adjusted for the exchange rate, are constant, we say there is ________________ .

5. The ________________ shows the response over time of imports to a devaluation.

True-False Questions

T F 1. An increase in the domestic price level improves the balance of trade.

T F 2. Sterilization operations break the link between the balance of payments and the money supply.

T F 3. Devaluation of the currency causes a recession.

T F 4. The long-run effect of an increase in the money supply is a proportional increase in the price level and the exchange rate.

T F 5. With perfect capital mobility, income must always be at the full-employment level.

T F 6. If purchasing power parity holds, differences in inflation rates between countries are offset by exchange rate changes.

Multiple-Choice Questions

1. If the typical German good costs 1000 marks and the typical Canadian good costs $250, and if the exchange rate is 25 cents, the terms of trade are
   - **(a)** 4 to 1
   - **(b)** 1 to 4
   - **(c)** 1 to 1
   - **(d)** 16 to 1

2. If German prices increase 10 percent while the Canadian dollar depreciates by 10 percent, constant Canadian prices would imply that relative prices
   - **(a)** increased 10 percent
   - **(b)** increased 20 percent
   - **(c)** remained constant
   - **(d)** fell 20 percent

3. With flexible prices, perfect capital mobility, and a flexible exchange rate, expansionary monetary policy will result in
   - **(a)** an increase in real income in the long run, but not in the short run
   - **(b)** an increase in real income in the short run, but not in the long run
   - **(c)** a decrease in the price level in the long run
   - **(d)** an appreciation of the nominal exchange rate in the long run

4. With flexible prices, perfect capital mobility, and a fixed exchange rate, expansionary fiscal policy will result in

(a) an increase in real income in the long run, but not in the short run

(b) no change in the real exchange rate in the long run

(c) a decrease in the price level in the long run

(d) an appreciation of the nominal exchange rate in the long run

5. If purchasing power parity always holds, if the current exchange rate is 25 cents per mark, and if the exchange rate in the next year is also expected to be 25 cents, German inflation over the year must be expected to be ________________ Canadian inflation.

(a) greater than

(b) the same as

(c) less than

(d) indeterminable because of insufficient information

6. Empirical evidence shows that following a devaluation, the dollar value of imports

(a) rises, then falls

(b) falls, then rises

(c) remains unchanged

(d) rises

PART 3 *Aggregate Demand and Stabilization Policy*

CHAPTER 10 *Consumption and Saving*

Focus of the Chapter

- Consumption is the largest sector of aggregate demand.
- Consumption this year depends not only on disposable income this year, but also on income in the past and expectations of future income.
- People try to spread their available lifetime resources over their entire lifetime. A transitory change in income makes little difference to lifetime resources and thus does not much affect consumption. A permanent change in income makes a great difference to lifetime resources and thus greatly affects consumption.

Section Summaries

10.1 The *life-cycle* theory is based on the notion that individuals plan in order to spread their available income over their entire lifetime. In particular, people save during their working lives in order to provide for retirement. Consumption is a function of wealth and of lifetime disposable income. Instead of simply stating a marginal propensity to consume, we can calculate the *MPC* on the basis of the number of years a person has remaining until retirement, and on the basis of life expectancy.

10.2 The *permanent-income* theory argues that people gear consumption to their long-term consumption opportunities. This is the same basic theme as the life-cycle theory, but it is made operational by assuming that, as a practical matter, people estimate their long-run opportunities by making a projection based on current and past income. This assumption suggests that a transitory change in income will have little lasting effect on consumption, and that a permanent change will have a large effect on consumption.

10.3 Researchers have found that household consumption systematically responds too much to changes in current household income, forcing macroeconomists to qualify the claim that consumers behave precisely according to the permanent-income/life-cycle hypothesis. This *excess sensitivity* may be the result of liquidity constraints on households, whereby households are unable to borrow or lend freely so as to smooth consumption over time. An alternative explanation for the sensitivity of consumption to current income is that consumers are myopic. In practice it is hard to distinguish this from the liquidity constraints hypothesis.

10.4 There is a large difference in international savings rates, with Japan having the highest rate and the United States the lowest over the period 1981–1987. Arguments have been made that policy measures to increase interest rates on savings will increase household saving, but empirical evidence suggests that changes in interest rates have little effect. The Barro-Ricardo hypothesis is the claim that a tax cut, matched by an increase in government borrowing to hold government expenditures constant, will have no effect on the interest rate. According to the Barro-Ricardo hypothesis, consumers view the increase in government debt as an increase in future taxes and, therefore, save their current tax cut for payment of future taxes.

10.5 The more sophisticated consumption function of this chapter can be put back in the *IS-LM* framework. The slope of the *IS* curve and the values of the fiscal policy and monetary policy multipliers now depend on the time frame of a policy action. Because the short-run *MPC* is less than the long-run *MPC*, the short-run multipliers are less than the long-run multipliers.

We can also see that a rise in the value of the stock market increases wealth and thus consumption, though the magnitude of this effect is fairly small.

Thinking Like an Economist

In Chapter 10 we noted that, with exception of Japan, national savings rates appear to be low. In this section we address two questions: first, Why does this matter? and second, Why do higher interest rates not appear to help?

In order to understand why low savings rates may be of concern, consider what happens to your money when you decide to save. Suppose that you decide to save more, and you buy a bond issued by some corporation. You buy this bond because it gives you some rate of return on your savings. However, the corporation does not offer you a rate of return because they are nice people, but rather because they are borrowing your money in order to make more money for themselves. How do they do this? They borrow money in order to build factories and machinery, so that they can produce products that consumers will purchase, and presumably the corporation will make a profit doing this. Therefore, your savings are going toward building the capital stock (which is the subject of investment theory, studied in detail in Chapter 11). An increased capital stock means that the consumption opportunities in the future will be larger. Therefore, if an economy chooses to save more, it is presumably choosing increased consumption possibilities in the future, while choosing to forgo some consumption today. Therefore, higher savings should mean more economic growth. (This concept will be studied in detail in the final chapter of the text.)

Given the above, why do higher interest rates not lead to more savings? Suppose that you are suddenly faced with higher interest rates. You can think of these higher interest rates as having two separate effects. First, every dollar that you save is worth more in the future, because of higher interest rates. Whether or not this will make you save more depends on your own preferences. For instance, you may only want to save enough so that you have a certain amount of money in the future. If interest rates increase in this instance, current savings would go down.

In order to understand the second effect, notice that increased savings is the same as giving up current consumption to receive more future consumption. The reward for doing this is an interest rate applied to your savings. Therefore, for every dollar of current consumption you are giving up the interest rate that you could have received for savings, which makes the interest rate the opportunity cost of current consumption. Therefore, increased interest rates increase the cost of current consumption. In this case increased interest rates generally increase savings.

The ultimate effect on savings of increased interest rates depends on how strong each of the two above effects are. If increased interest rates do not generally increase savings, as the empirical evidence appears to show, then ultimately individuals would appear to be choosing current consumption over increased future consumption.

Key Terms

Life-cycle hypothesis
Dissaving
Permanent income
Rational expectations
Liquidity constraints
Myopia
Dynamic multiplier
Excess sensitivity of consumption
Barro-Ricardo hypothesis

Graph It 10

This Graph It asks you to replicate one of the most important scientific investigations of postwar macroeconomics, the discovery of the life-cycle/permanent-income theory of consumption. As you know from Chapter 10, the marginal propensity to consume seems fairly low when we look at consumption over two or three years, but the *MPC* is quite high when looked at over decades. In this Graph It you will replicate this result.

Table 10-1 presents (made-up) consumption and income data for three groups of three years. Ignore for the moment all but the first group. Plot the three points on Chart 10-1. Draw a straight line that fits the three points as well as you can. What is

Table 10-1

	GDP	Consumption
Group 1	50	49
	60	54
	70	59
Group 2	10	13
	20	18
	30	23
Group 3	80	76
	90	81
	100	86

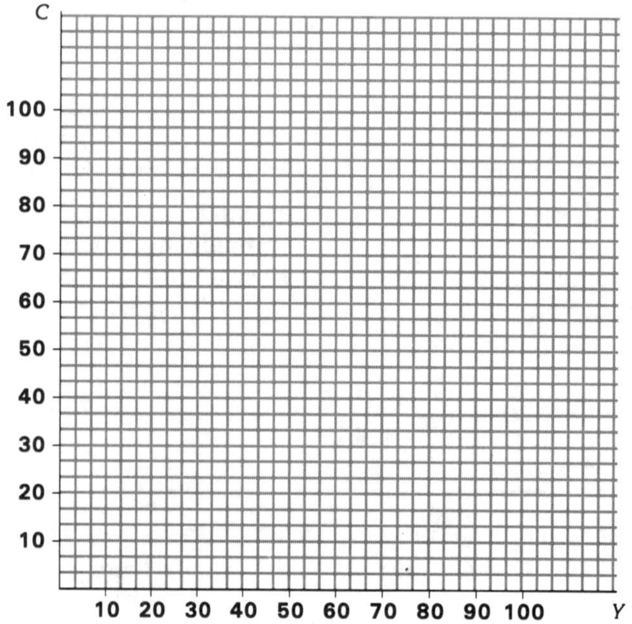

Chart 10-1

the slope (*MPC*) of the line? Now do the same for each of the two other groups. Do you get the same slope for each line? (You should.) Think of these as short-run consumption functions measured in three different decades.

Now draw a single consumption function line for all nine points. (It won't fit exactly, of course.) This represents a long-run consumption function. What's your estimate of the long-run *MPC*?

Fill-In Questions

1. The hypothesis that people plan consumption based on their wealth and all future income is called the ________________ theory.
2. Estimates of long-term consumption opportunities based on previous and current income are called ________________ income.
3. Using up wealth to provide for consumption is called ________________ .
4. The long-run average propensity to consume is about ________________ .
5. The long-run marginal propensity to consume is about ________________ .
6. The immediate response of GDP to a change in autonomous aggregate demand depends on the ________________ multiplier.
7. The eventual response of GDP to a change in autonomous aggregate demand depends on the ________________ multiplier.
8. The marginal propensity to consume depends on the number of ________________ years compared with the number of ________________ years.
9. The gradual adjustment of output to a shock illustrates a(n) ________________ lag.

True-False Questions

T F 1. The permanent-income theory suggests that the long-run marginal propensity to consume is less than the short-run marginal propensity to consume.

T F 2. Modern consumption theory suggests that consumption is proportional to long-run income.

T F **3.** A worker aged 20 who expects to retire at 65 and who has a life expectancy of 50 years should have a marginal propensity to consume out of income of 0.9.

T F **4.** A worker aged 20 who expects to retire at age 65 and who has a life expectancy of 50 years should have a marginal propensity to consume out of wealth of 0.02.

T F **5.** The long-run *MPC* and *APC* are approximately equal.

T F **6.** If a simple linear consumption function has a positive intercept, then the average propensity to consume falls as income rises.

T F **7.** Temporary changes in income produce relatively small changes in consumption.

T F **8.** The decision to leave an inheritance increases current consumption.

T F **9.** A growing population will have higher per capita savings than a static population.

T F **10.** The permanent-income theory and the life-cycle theory are fundamentally the same.

Multiple-Choice Questions

1. According to the life-cycle theory, an individual's marginal propensity to consume out of permanent labour income
- **(a)** rises over time
- **(b)** falls over time
- **(c)** remains constant
- **(d)** may be either **(a)**, **(b)**, or **(c)**, depending on circumstances

2. According to the life-cycle theory, an individual's marginal propensity to consume out of transitory labour income
- **(a)** rises over time
- **(b)** falls over time
- **(c)** remains constant
- **(d)** may be either **(a)**, **(b)**, or **(c)**, depending on circumstances

3. The weights used on income and all the lagged income to estimate permanent income should probably add up to
- **(a)** 0
- **(b)** between 0 and 1
- **(c)** 1
- **(d)** more than 1

4. If the marginal propensity to consume out of permanent income is 0.9 and the weight on current income in estimating permanent income is 2/3, the short-run simple Keynesian multiplier is
- **(a)** 1
- **(b)** 2.5
- **(c)** 3
- **(d)** 10

5. The life-cycle and permanent-income theories are associated with the
   - **(a)** Keynesian school
   - **(b)** monetarist school
   - **(c)** both
   - **(d)** neither

6. According to the life-cycle theory, wealth during the working years
   - **(a)** rises over time
   - **(b)** remains constant
   - **(c)** falls over time
   - **(d)** may either rise or fall, depending on the *MPC*

7. During a temporary recession, the average propensity to consume
   - **(a)** falls
   - **(b)** remains constant
   - **(c)** rises
   - **(d)** is neither **(a)**, **(b)**, nor **(c)**

8. During a temporary boom, the average propensity to save
   - **(a)** falls
   - **(b)** remains constant
   - **(c)** rises
   - **(d)** is neither **(a)**, **(b)**, nor **(c)**

9. The role of the stock market in determining consumption is shown most directly through the
   - **(a)** simple linear consumption function
   - **(b)** permanent-income theory
   - **(c)** life-cycle theory
   - **(d)** both **(b)** and **(c)**

10. When the expansionary effects of a permanent tax cut are compared with those of a temporary tax cut, the former tax cut
    - **(a)** is more expansionary
    - **(b)** has the same effect
    - **(c)** is less expansionary
    - **(d)** is either **(a)**, **(b)**, or **(c)**, depending on the *MPC*

Problems

1. Assume the typical consumer expects to work for 40 years and to live for 50. Assume consumers have perfect foresight. Disregarding any multiplier effects, how does consumption change this year as a result of a $100 annual tax cut on workers' income that

   (a) is permanent, and will begin immediately?

   (b) will last only for the current year?

   (c) is permanent, but will not go into effect until next year?

2. Assume that the typical consumer has a marginal propensity to consume of 0.8. Consumers must use historical information to estimate permanent income. Research has shown that they estimate permanent income by using a weight of 0.75 on current disposable income and 0.25 on lagged disposable income. Disregarding any multiplier effects, how does consumption change as a result of a $100 tax cut that

(a) is permanent? That is, how much the first year? How much the second year?

(b) is effective only for one year? That is, how much the first year? How much the second year?

CHAPTER 11 *Investment Spending*

Focus of the Chapter

- The second key sector of aggregate demand is investment spending.
- Investment is about 20 percent of GDP but investment is very volatile, and thus changes in investment account for much of the changes in GDP.
- Investment demand is especially important because it contains the main link through which monetary policy affects aggregate demand.
- Increased interest lowers investment because capital becomes more expensive.
- Decreases in expected sales lead manufacturers to reduce investment, thereby reducing aggregate demand.
- The three investment subsectors are *business fixed investment, residential construction*, and *inventory investment.*

Section Summaries

11.1 Unintended inventory accumulation occurs when sales fall unexpectedly. On the other hand, when sales are expected to fall, firms intentionally reduce inventories. This intentional reduction feeds back very quickly to accelerate movements in aggregate demand. This is the *inventory cycle*.

11.2 Businesses use machinery, equipment, and structures in the course of producing final output. These make up the *stock* of *business fixed capital.* We develop a theory of the *desired capital stock. Investment* is a *flow* that is the addition of new machinery to the existing capital stock. Investment closes the gap between the desired capital stock and the existing capital stock.

Manufacturers decide on how much capital they want by considering three factors: how much output they expect to sell; what the *marginal product of capital* is; and how much capital costs to use, or the *rental* or *user cost of capital.* The more output that must be produced, the more the required amount of capital. The higher the rental cost, the less capital will be used, since capital is more expensive. The most important component of the rental cost is the interest rate. Several other components are discussed below.

More capital always means that greater output can be made, but each additional unit of capital adds less and less additional production. However, each additional unit of capital costs as much to add as the previous unit. Thus, there is declining marginal product but constant marginal cost. The intelligent business manager adds just enough capital so that the last unit produces just as much as it costs.

Firms base their expectations of future sales on a period comparable to the life of the machinery. Current sales affect capital demand to the extent that they change expectations of sales over the life of the machinery.

The rental cost of capital is basically the market interest rate, since this is the opportunity cost of using funds to buy capital instead of "investing" in bonds. However, capital wears out over time. This depreciation cost must be covered in order to keep machines in working condition. If depreciation is d percent per year, then the cost of capital is

$$rc = i + d$$

In the presence of inflation, we distinguish the *real interest* rate from the *nominal interest* rate. The difference is the expected rate of inflation, denoted π^e. Since, on average, the price of goods produced will go up at the rate of inflation, the rental cost of capital properly depends on the real rate of interest. This leads to the following formula for the rental cost of capital:

$$rc \equiv r + d \equiv i - \pi^e + d$$

The rental cost of capital must be adjusted to account properly for taxes. Under the *investment tax credit*, the government pays some portion τ of the cost of new equip- ment to the firm in the form of a tax rebate. This rebate lowers the effective cost of equipment and therefore increases the demand for capital. The *corporate income tax* is essentially a proportional tax on corporate profits. Because of the complexities of the tax code, theory alone leaves the effects of the corporate income tax ambiguous.

The rate of investment depends on the difference between the desired and the actual capital stock. An important element of the way firms plan to adjust their capital stock is the gradual adjustment hypothesis. Each period firms close some portion of the gap between desired capital, K^*, and the capital available at the beginning of the period, K_{-1}. If the fraction of the gap closed each period is 1, then the investment function can be written

$$I = K - K_{-1} = \lambda (K^* - K_{-1})$$

The timing of investment with respect to changes in the investment tax credit is especially important. A temporary investment tax credit means that a firm gets a tax break on any investment done now, but none on any done in the future. It pays the firm to invest right away not only because capital is cheaper, but also because any investment planned for the future should be made immediately instead. This means that a temporary tax credit has a much larger effect on current investment than a permanent tax credit.

11.3 In practice, firms rarely think of calculating a desired capital stock as such. Rather, they use a *discounted cash flow analysis* to compare the cost of adding a machine with the present value of the flow of profits the machine will provide. High interest rates mean future profits have a lower value today, thus making adding an additional machine less desirable. Discounted cash flow analysis and computation of a desired capital stock are really just two different ways of looking at the same problem.

The *accelerator* model states that the desired capital stock is proportional to income and that investment is proportional to the change in income. The accelerator model is a special case of investment theory with instantaneous adjustment to the desired capital stock and a constant ratio of desired capital to income.

11.4 The price and quantity of housing depend on the supply and demand for homes. Investment in housing occurs when the demand for homes rises above the available stock. The demand for housing falls when interest rates, especially mortgage rates, rise. The ability of people to buy new homes depends on the availability of mortgage money, most of which is made available through financial institutions.

Appendix The chapter appendix explains the relation between coupon rates, yields, and the prices of bonds. On a *Consol*, or perpetual bond, the yield is the coupon payment divided by the price of the bond. More generally, the price of a bond is the present discounted value (*PDV*) of all the payments on the bond. The *PDV* is found by reducing the value of future payments according to the interest rate and the time when the payment is due.

Thinking Like an Economist

In Chapter 11 we introduced the crucial distinction between the nominal and real rates of interest. In this section we are going to look more closely at this distinction. It is important to understand that any interest rate, whether it be nominal or real, is a price, and a price is simply an exchange rate. All prices, or exchange rates, can be measured as nominal or real. Consider, for example, the price of scotch whiskey. If we say that the price of scotch whiskey is $20, then we are saying that $20 can be exchanged for one bottle of scotch. Because this is the *dollar* price of scotch, we label this the *nominal* price of scotch. A *real* price of scotch whiskey would be an exchange rate between scotch and another physical good or service. For instance, if rye whiskey cost $10 per bottle, the exchange rate between rye and scotch would be "two bottles of rye exchange for one bottle of scotch." This, then, would be the rye price of scotch (as opposed to the dollar price of scotch) and we would label this a real price, because it is denominated in goods rather than in money.

Now consider a nominal interest rate. Definitionally, a nominal interest rate is the rate of return on some financial instrument. Suppose that you buy a nominal asset, such as a bond, and the price of this bond at time t is A_t dollars, and that you sell this bond at time $t + 1$ for A_{t+1} dollars. The nominal interest rate on this bond is

$$i_t = \frac{A_{t+1} - A_t}{A_t}$$

This is a nominal interest rate because the rate of return is measured in dollars. Notice that it also a price, as it is the exchange rate of money over time. That is, if the nominal interest rate were 10 percent, you would exchange $100 for $110 tomorrow.

Now let's consider how to convert the nominal interest rate into a real interest rate. We know that A_t is the dollar value of the financial asset in period t. Suppose instead of buying the financial asset, you decided to purchase some amount of goods and services at time t. The amount of goods and services that you would be able to purchase with A_t dollars is given by A_t/P_t, where P_t is the general level of prices at time t. A_t/P_t is the real value of the nominal dollars A_t. (Notice the similarity between A_t/P_t, and the real money stock, M/P.)

Now recall that a real price is one that is denominated in goods and services. Therefore, the real interest rate should be the rate of return (which is the time price) denominated in goods and services. Accordingly, we can define the expected real rate of interest as

$$r_t^e = \frac{\dfrac{A_{t+1}}{P_{t+1}^e} - \dfrac{A_t}{P_t}}{\dfrac{A_t}{P_t}}$$

This is a very awkward formula; however, it highlights exactly what a real rate of interest is. A_{t+1}/P_{t+1}^e is the amount of goods and services that you *expect* to be able to purchase after you sell the bond, which A_t/P_t is the amount of goods and services that you could have purchased instead of buying the bond. Therefore, the expected real rate of interest is the rate of return on the bond measured in goods and services.

With a little algebraic manipulation, the above formula will look familiar. We can rewrite the above equation as

$$1 + r_t^e = \frac{\dfrac{A_{t+1}}{P_{t+1}^e}}{\dfrac{A_t}{P_t}}$$

Now bring the denominator to the top by inverting and multiplying:

$$1 + r_t^e = \frac{A_{t+1}}{P_{t+1}^e}\frac{P_t}{A_t}$$
$$= \frac{A_{t+1}}{A_t}\frac{P_t}{P_{t+1}^e}$$

From the definition of a nominal interest rate we can write

$$1 + i_t = \frac{A_{t+1}}{A_t}$$

We also know that expected inflation can be written as

$$\pi_t^e = \frac{P_{t+1}^e - P_t}{P_t}$$

or

$$1 + \pi_t^e = \frac{P_{t+1}^e}{P_t}$$

Therefore

$$\frac{1}{1+\pi_t^e} = \frac{P_t}{P_{t+1}^e}$$

Now substitute into the equation for the expected real rate of interest

$$1 + r_t^e = (1 + i_t)\left(\frac{1}{1+\pi_t^e}\right)$$

Multiplying out these terms we get

$$(1 + r_t^e)(1 + \pi_t^e) = 1 + i_t$$
$$1 + r_t^e + \pi_t^e + r_t^e\pi_t^e = 1 + i_t$$

Notice that inflation and interest rates are measured as decimals, i.e., 10 percent is 0.1. Therefore the last term on the left hand side is the product of two decimals, and we usually ignore it as being small. Rearranging terms, we arrive at the familiar equation for the expected real rate of interest used in the text:

$$r_t^e = i_t - \pi_t^e$$

Key Terms

Business fixed investment
Residential construction
Inventory investment
Desired capital stock
Marginal product of capital
Rental (user) cost of capital
Cobb-Douglas production function
Real interest rate
Gradual adjustment hypothesis
Discounted cash flow analysis
Accelerator model of investment
Inventory cycle
Present discounted value
q theory

Graph It 11

Chapter 11 explains that investment forms a relatively small part of aggregate demand, but that changes in investment are responsible for much of the changes in

Table 11-1

Year	GDP	I_t	$Y_t - Y_{t-1}$	$I_t - I_{t-1}$
1978	402.7	67.9		
1979	418.3	79.6	15.6	12.0
1980	424.5	77.7	______	______
1981	440.1	87.0	______	______
1982	426.0	64.1	______	______
1983	439.5	72.7	______	______
1984	467.2	81.5	______	______
1985	489.4	85.6	______	______
1986	505.7	91.6	______	______
1987	526.7	102.9	______	______
1988	551.4	112.9	______	______
1989	565.0	119.2	______	______
1990	567.5	108.9	______	______
1991	558.9	106.7	______	______

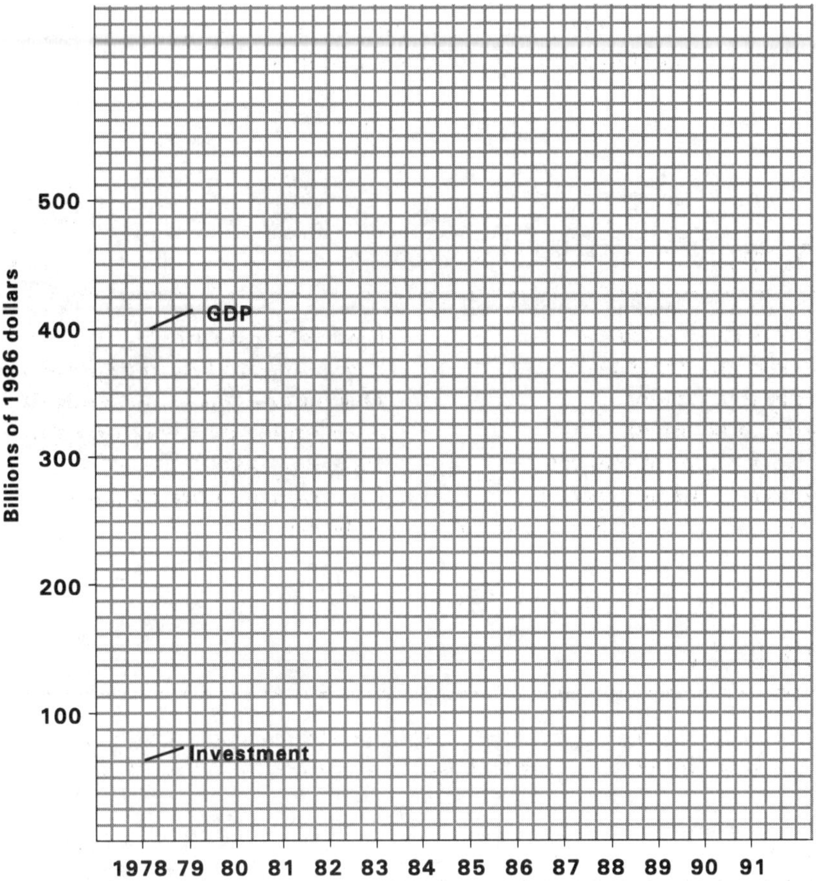

Chart 11-1

aggregate demand. Another way to say this is that investment is a small but volatile sector. In this Graph It, you are asked to demonstrate both parts of the relationship. In Chart 11-1, you are asked to plot Table 11-1, which plots 14 years of GDP and investment data. You will see from this graph that GDP and investment are related, but only moderately. In Chart 11-2, you are asked to plot the annual change in GDP and the annual change in investment. This second graph shows that the relation between investment volatility and aggregate demand volatility is very strong.

Table 11-1 provides data on GDP and gross investment. We've also left space for you to fill in the annual change data you'll need for plotting the second chart.

By the way, if you are also taking a statistics course, you might compare the correlation coefficients of GDP and investment versus the change in GDP and the change in investment.

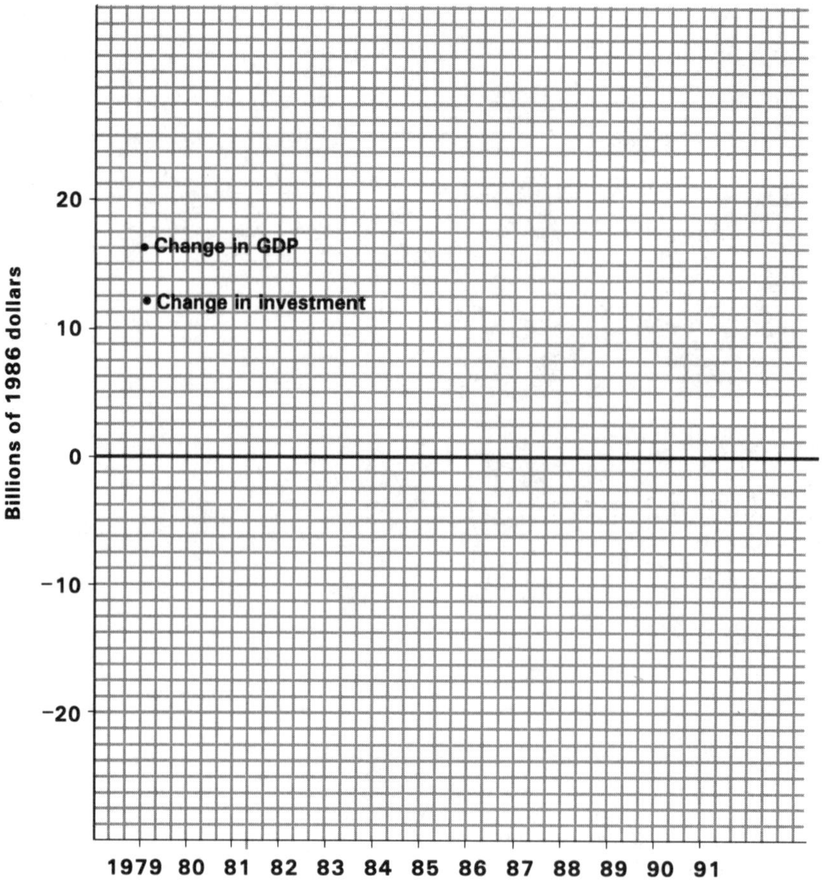

Chart 11-2

Fill-In Questions

1. The three principal investment sectors are ______________________, ______________________, and ______________________.
2. Investment is a(n) ______________________ devoted to maintaining the ______________________ of capital.
3. The contribution of an extra unit of capital to a firm's profits is the ______________________.
4. The cost of using capital for a year is the ______________________.

5. In planning how much capital to have, firms must estimate ________________ sales.

6. The government gives firms a rebate for new capital; it is called the ________________ .

7. The difference between gross and net investment is ________________ .

8. If sales fall below the level expected, the result is ________________ inventory investment.

9. The cycle of aggregate demand fluctuation that causes inventory fluctuation, causing more aggregate demand fluctuation, is called the ________________ .

True-False Questions

T F 1. Increased interest rates cause increased investment.

T F 2. Rising GDP causes increased investment.

T F 3. A permanent increase in the investment tax credit decreases current investment.

T F 4. High mortgage rates lead to increased investment.

T F 5. In the short run, the supply of housing is more or less fixed.

T F 6. A surprise sales boom leads to a drop in inventories.

T F 7. An expected sales boom leads to a drop in inventories.

T F 8. Changes in investment are directly proportional to income, according to the accelerator model.

T F 9. The actual capital stock adjusts gradually to the desired capital stock.

T F 10. Restrictive monetary policy decreases investment.

Multiple-Choice Questions

1. The effect of an increase of the corporate income tax on investment
   - **(a)** is an increase
   - **(b)** is a decrease
   - **(c)** is nonexistent
   - **(d)** theoretically is any of **(a)**, **(b)**, or **(c)**

2. Comparing the impact on current investment of a permanent versus a temporary increase in the investment tax credit, we find that a permanent increase is
   - **(a)** more effective
   - **(b)** less effective
   - **(c)** the same
   - **(d)** theoretically either **(a)**, **(b)**, or **(c)**

3. Empirically it has been found that an increase in the desired capital stock causes investment to
   - **(a)** rise instantly, then gradually drop off
   - **(b)** respond in an upside-down-U pattern
   - **(c)** rise, then return immediately to zero
   - **(d)** fall gradually

4. An increase in the depreciation rate causes net investment to
   - **(a)** rise
   - **(b)** remain the same
   - **(c)** fall
   - **(d)** theoretically do any of **(a)**, **(b)**, or **(c)**

5. An increase in the depreciation rate causes gross investment to
   - **(a)** rise
   - **(b)** remain the same
   - **(c)** fall
   - **(d)** theoretically do any of **(a)**, **(b)**, or **(c)**

6. If the nominal interest rate is 12 percent and the inflation rate is 6 percent, the real interest rate is
   - **(a)** 18 percent
   - **(b)** 2 percent
   - **(c)** 6 percent
   - **(d)** 8.4 percent

7. According to the simple accelerator model, the response of investment to a permanent increase in GDP is to
   - **(a)** rise, then return to zero
   - **(b)** rise gradually, then fall gradually
   - **(c)** rise to a new permanent level
   - **(d)** remain unchanged

8. Net investment is the change in the capital stock
   - **(a)** according to the flexible accelerator
   - **(b)** according to the simple accelerator
   - **(c)** always
   - **(d)** never

9. The response of the housing stock to economic conditions is
   - **(a)** very rapid
   - **(b)** quite slow
   - **(c)** slow during a boom, quick during a downturn
   - **(d)** quick during a boom, slow during a downturn

10. The response of the stock of inventories to economic conditions is
    - **(a)** very rapid
    - **(b)** quite slow
    - **(c)** slow during a boom, quick during a downturn
    - **(d)** quick during a boom, slow during a downturn

11. The price of a bond increases

(a) with the market interest rate
(b) with the coupon payment
(c) both
(d) neither one

Problems

1. Assume that the demand for capital is determined by the equation $K^* = 0.25\ Y/rc$. The nominal interest rate is 12 percent (that is, $i = 0.12$), the inflation rate is 6 percent, and capital depreciates at 10 percent per year.

(a) Initially, income is $16,000. What is the desired capital stock?

(b) Now income doubles. What is the new desired capital stock?

(c) Given the simple accelerator model of investment, what is the rate of net investment? Gross investment?

2. Suppose the desired capital stock jumps from $2000 to $3600. If companies close half the gap between existing and actual capital each year, and if depreciation is 10 percent, what are the values of gross and net investment for each of the three years following the change?

3. A friend offers to lend you $1000. You agree to pay him $220 in one year and to make a final payment in two years. The prevailing interest rate is 10 percent. You and your friend wish to agree on a fair final payment. How large should the final payment be?

CHAPTER 12 *The Demand for Money*

Focus of the Chapter

- We all hold money — either currency in our pockets or on deposit at a bank. In studying the demand for money, we try to discover exactly how much money a rational person will hold.
- Our basic goal is to find out how much money will be demanded for a known level of income and a known interest rate. (You will remember that we need this relation to form the *LM* curve, which we used in Chapter 4.)
- The evidence, both theoretical and empirical, is that higher income causes greater money demand and higher interest rates cause lower money demand.

Section Summaries

12.1 The most important characteristic of money is that we can use it directly to pay for things we buy. The assets in our economy that most closely fit this definition are cash and chequing accounts. Together, these form M1. Savings accounts are good substitutes for chequing accounts because you can get use of the savings deposit very quickly, even though you cannot actually make a payment by handing someone your savings passbook. Sometimes we use broader definitions of money that include savings accounts and other forms of deposits.

Money has traditionally been defined by four functions:

(a) Serving as a *medium of exchange* is far and away the most important function of money. When you buy something, you pay for it with money rather than barter with some other merchandise.

(b) Being a *store of value* means that money retains its value over time. You would hardly be willing to accept money in payment if you didn't think that someone else would accept the money from you tomorrow.

(c) Saying that money is the *unit of account* just means that prices are quoted in dollars and cents. (A grocery could post a sign showing that 3 apples cost 2 oranges.)

(d) *Standard of deferred payment* means that when someone owes a debt, the payment is specified in terms of money.

This section considers why people hold money. At first it seems strange to think that such a question ever needs to be asked. After all, we're all most happy to have money. The question we really need to answer is why people hold money instead of some better investment. Cash pays no interest at all, and chequing accounts usually pay less than is available in other safe investments. John Maynard Keynes gave three broad motives for holding money instead of some other investment:

- Transactions motive
- Precautionary motive
- Speculative motive

12.2 The *transactions motive* arises from the cost of cashing in part of an investment each time you make a purchase. For example, it's much more sensible to draw a week's worth of pocket money at a time rather than go to the bank each morning. The most famous transactions model is the *Baumol-Tobin* theory. The development of the theory has three steps.

(a) If we know how many times a month a person replenishes her cash, what will her average balance be? Suppose the person begins with $100 and is going to spend it at a steady rate. If she takes it all in cash on the first day and spends it down to zero by the end of the month, the average cash balance will be $50. Suppose, instead, she takes only $50 for the first half of the month and after using it up gets the other $50. The average will be $25. The pattern follows so that if the person begins with Y_N dollars and makes n transfers, the average cash balance is $\frac{1}{2}Y_N/n$. (The subscript N stands for "nominal.")

(b) Cash doesn't earn any interest, and so the opportunity cost lost by holding money is $i\frac{1}{2}Y_N/n$. In addition, the cost of each transfer is tc. So

$$\text{Total cost} = ntc + \frac{iY_N}{2n}$$

The more transfers, the higher the total costs of transactions and the less the interest lost. The better number of transfers is that which minimizes total costs. (The exact formula can be found by using calculus.)

(c) Once we know the right number of transfers, we can find the average cash balance directly. The famous square-root formula turns out to be

$$M* = \sqrt{\frac{tcY_N}{2i}}$$

This formula implies that the income elasticity of money demand is 1/2 and that the interest elasticity is –1/2.

12.3 The *precautionary motive* arises from the motion that we never know our spending plans exactly. It pays to keep a little extra money on hand in case the urge for a hot fudge sundae hits at a time when it's inconvenient to cash in an investment. The greater the uncertainty about our spending plans, the more money we would be wise to keep around just in case. Just as with the transactions motive, the higher the interest rate, the greater the cost of holding money.

The *speculative motive* states that a person might sometimes want to keep money in a savings account for investment purposes. Because other investments are risky, even though they offer higher average returns, people will hold some money as a hedge against risk. The speculative demand for money is actually a demand for a safe asset.

12.4 Empirical research has settled four key points about money demand:

(a) When the interest rate goes up, the demand for money goes down.

(b) When income goes up, the demand for money goes up, but less than proportionately.

(c) It takes time for money demand to adjust fully to changes in income and interest.

(d) If the price level doubles, the number of dollars of money demanded will double.

12.5 Sometimes, instead of discussing the money demand equation, economists look at *velocity*. Velocity is the ratio of income to money. (You can think of it as the number of times a dollar passes from hand to hand in a year.) Higher interest rates mean lower money demand and therefore higher velocity. Higher income increases money demand but by less than the increase in income, so that velocity increases with increased income.

Thinking Like an Economist

The quantity theory of money has been discussed at several points in the text. Basically, the quantity theory is simply a neutrality result: in the long run changes in the quantity of money should not change any *real* variables. It is, of course, hard to believe that the quantity theory holds in the short run. Indeed, this is what our short-run models tell us: the price level is at least sticky (Chapters 7 to 9), or perhaps even fixed (Chapters 1 to 6) in the short run. However, it is hard to believe that some form of the quantity theory does not hold in the long run. If you do not believe this, ask yourself the following question: If, as in the *IS-LM* model, expansionary monetary policy lowers interest rates and increases income, then why not shift out the *LM* curve forever? The answer is that the quantity theory can be viewed as a long-run constraint on this sort of policy: if you continue to excessively expand the money stock eventually you will get inflation.

If you are still doubtful that some form of neutrality holds in the long run, consider the following heuristic derivation of the quantity theory. Consider an economy that does not use money as a means of payment, but rather trades through barter. Individuals produce whatever kinds of goods that they have a comparative advantage in producing (that is, you do whatever you are good at). They bring these goods to the market where trade takes place through barter. Eventually a system of price (or exchange rates) emerges. For instance, two cows may trade for ten bushels of corn, etc. These exchange rates are *real* prices, as they are denominated in goods and services as opposed to money. (If this is not clear you should review Thinking Like and Economist in Chapter 11.) These prices arise from two fundamental sources: the ability of individuals to produce products and the demand for these products (that is, supply and demand).

Now consider the effects of introducing money as a medium of exchange in this economy. This clearly will make exchange more efficient, and will introduce a set of *nominal* prices into the economy. However, it is not likely to change your underlying ability to produce goods, or your underlying demand for certain goods. Therefore, the system of *real* prices should remain unaltered. Put another way, the introduction of money should have no real effects, only nominal effects, which is a statement of the quantity theory of money.

Key Terms

Real balances
Money illusion
M1
M2, M2+
Liquidity
Medium of exchange
Store of value
Unit of account
Standard of deferred payments
Transactions demand
Inventory-theoretic approach
Square-root formula
Precautionary demand
Speculative demand
Income velocity of money
Quantity equation
Quantity theory of money
Hyperinflation

Graph It 12

Most people find themselves ready for a relaxing exercise about halfway through the text. Graph It 12 asks you to demonstrate the essential principles of the precautionary demand for money by drawing some random wiggles on the graph provided. (Well, almost random.)

The idea behind the precautionary demand for money is that you want to hold enough money so that you rarely run out of money, but that you don't want to hold too much because of the opportunity cost. In Chart 12-1 we've drawn a solid wiggly line illustrating a random cash need. Now suppose your rule of thumb was that you wanted to run short of cash no more than twice during the period. We took a straightedge and drew a solid line as low as possible, but still consistent with the random wiggle peaking over the line only twice. The solid line shows the optimal precautionary demand for money.

Now you draw in a dashed line with the same number of wiggles, but with the cash needs generally having higher peaks. Then use a straightedge to draw in a new money demand line.

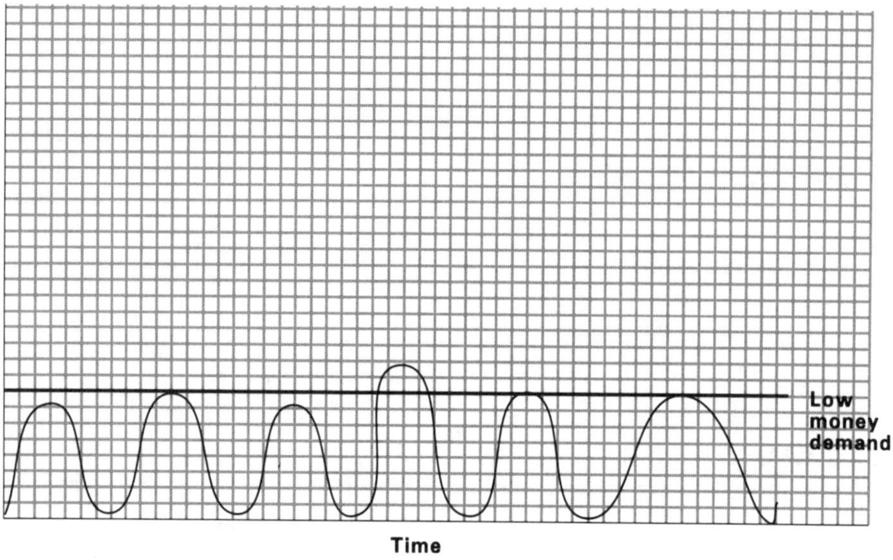

Chart 12-1

Fill-In Questions

1. The study of the demand for money is the study of the demand for __________________.

2. The assets forming M1 are ________________ .

3. The assets forming M2 are ________________ .

4. The Baumol-Tobin theory explains the ________________ motive for the demand for money.

5. The number of times a dollar is turned over per year is called ________________ .

6. The ratio of income to the money stock is ________________ .

7. The ________________ motive explains the need to hold money against unforeseen contingencies.

8. The need to hold money because it has a safe nominal value is called the ________________ motive.

9. The one motive that plays little role in explaining the demand for M1 is the ________________ motive.

10. In order to find the nominal demand for money, one multiplies the real demand for money by the ________________ .

True-False Questions

T F 1. If the number of dollars outstanding doubles and the price level goes up by 1/2, then real balances have increased by 1/3.

T F 2. If GDP and the money stock both fall by 50 percent, velocity remains constant.

T F 3. Higher inflation generally leads to higher velocity.

T F 4. High inflation is associated with high nominal interest rates.

T F 5. In certain circumstances, M2 may be smaller than M1.

T F 6. An individual who ignores changes in the price level so long as all real variables remain constant is said to suffer from money illusion.

T F 7. According to the Baumol-Tobin theory, money demand is proportional to GDP.

T F 8. Velocity increases with real income.

T F 9. A shift of assets from checking to savings accounts increases M2.

T F 10. According to the precautionary theory of money demand, greater uncertainty about spending plans results in higher money demand.

Multiple-Choice Questions

1. An increase in real income from 100 to 110 will, according to the Baumol-Tobin theory, cause money demand to change by a
   (a) 20 percent increase
   (b) 10 percent increase
   (c) 5 percent increase
   (d) 5 percent decrease

2. An increase in the interest rate from 5 percent per year to 6 percent per year will, according to the Baumol-Tobin theory, cause money demand to change by a
   (a) 0.5 percent decrease
   (b) 10 percent decrease
   (c) 20 percent decrease
   (d) 0.5 percent increase

3. A shift of $100 from a chequing account to a savings account means
   (a) M1 up, M2 up
   (b) M1 down, M2 up
   (c) M1 down, M2 unchanged
   (d) M1 down, M2 down

4. The most important function of money is as a
   (a) medium of exchange
   (b) store of value
   (c) unit of account
   (d) standard of deferred payment

5. The precautionary motive leads to people to hold more money when
   (a) the interest rate is high
   (b) uncertainty about expenses is high
   (c) both the rate and uncertainty are high
   (d) neither the rate nor uncertainty is high

6. The demand for money is a theory of the demand for
   (a) real balances
   (b) nominal balances
   (c) actual balances
   (d) frictional balances

7. The demand for money depends on
   (a) real income and real interest rates
   (b) real income and nominal interest rates
   (c) nominal income and real interest rates
   (d) nominal income and nominal interest rates

8. Empirical evidence indicates that the income elasticity of money demand is
   (a) greater than 1
   (b) between 1/2 and 1
   (c) between 0 and 1/2
   (d) less than 0

9. Empirical evidence indicates that the interest elasticity of money demand is
   (a) below –1
   (b) between –1/2 and –1
   (c) between 0 and –1/2
   (d) above 0

10. Money demand rises when
    (a) income rises
    (b) interest rates fall
    (c) both income rises and interest rates fall
    (d) neither income nor interest rates change

Problems

1. Assume that the Baumol-Tobin theory is true. If nominal GDP goes from $100 billion to $220 billion while the price level doubles, what is the increase in the real demand for money?

2. Suppose that we want to change the interest rate from 4 percent per year to 3 percent per year, while real GDP and the price level remain unchanged. By how much should we change the money stock if empirical investigation shows the interest elasticity to be –0.20?

CHAPTER 13 *The Money Supply Process*

Focus of the Chapter

- In previous chapters, the money supply has been taken to be exogenous. We now explore the process by which the Bank of Canada, the chartered banks, and the public interact in determining the stock of money.
- We also examine the way in which the Bank of Canada operates monetary policy.

Section Summaries

13.1 The sum of currency in circulation plus chartered bank deposits at the Bank of Canada (known as *reserves*) constitutes the *monetary base*, which is also known as high-powered money. The Bank of Canada controls the money supply indirectly by controlling the monetary base. High-powered money is the principal liability of the Bank of Canada. Its main asset is government bonds.

Three sectors play a role in determining the money supply: the non-bank public, the chartered banks, and the Bank of Canada. The Bank of Canada creates more money through an *open market purchase*, in which it buys bonds by writing a cheque on itself. The amount of the cheque is added to the total reserves available to the public and the banking system.

The federal government has bank accounts at the Bank of Canada and at the chartered banks. Transferring these deposits between the Bank of Canada and the chartered banks is an alternative to open market operations as a means of changing the monetary base.

13.2 The money supply multiplier is equal to the ratio of the money supply to the monetary base. The money supply multiplier depends on the *currency-deposit ratio* chosen by the public and by the *reserve-deposit ratio* of the chartered banks. We denote the currency-deposit ratio by cu and the reserve-deposit ratio as re. We can write the money supply multiplier as

$$\frac{M}{B} = \frac{cu + 1}{cu + re}$$

The smaller the reserve ratio, and the smaller the currency deposit ratio, the larger the money supply multiplier.

The currency-deposit ratio depends on the tastes and habits of the public. The reserve-deposit ratio depends on the level of *required cash reserves* and of *excess cash reserves*. Required cash reserves are determined by regulation. Banks hold excess cash reserves for reasons analogous to the consumer's precautionary demand for money. Excess reserves are available for making payments to other banks. In November 1991 the Bank of Canada announced that the required minimum reserve ratios were to be reduced to zero.

Banks are able to make credit available in the amount of their deposits minus reserves. When the base increases, banks are able to make more loans. These loans take the form of added deposits and more currency held by the public. The bank that receives the new deposits can then make more loans. This adjustment process describes the *multiple expansion of bank deposits* which, when added across all the banks in the economy, yields the money multiplier.

13.3 In November 1991, cash reserve requirements were eliminated, as they were deemed to be unnecessary for central bank control of the money supply.

The Bank of Canada implements monetary policy on a day-to-day basis through the daily cash setting. This refers to the setting of the supply of deposits at the Bank of Canada that are available to chartered banks and other financial institutions for the settlement of payments. These are known as settlement balances.

The *bank rate* is the rate of interest at which the Bank of Canada makes advances to the chartered banks. The major role of the bank rate has been as a signal of the Bank of Canada's views concerning the appropriate level of interest rates and its intentions with regard to monetary tightness or ease. The Bank of Canada uses a floating rate system under which the rate is automatically set each week at 1/4 of one percent above the interest rate on Treasury bills.

Equilibrium in the money market is determined by setting money supply equal to money demand. The Bank of Canada can control either the money supply or the interest rate, but not the two independently. The reason is that the money demand curve gives us a fixed relation between interest and the money stock.

Thinking Like an Economist

Students occasionally tend to overlook the fact that economists analyze the money market using the same supply and demand tools that we use in analyzing all other markets. In this section we are going to look at money supply and demand in order to expand on an important point made at the end of Chapter 13: the monetary authorities cannot control *both* the money supply and interest rates. Consider Figure 13-1(a).

The initial point of equilibrium in the money market, where supply equals demand, is at E. Assume that money demand increases to L' (perhaps because real income has increased). At the interest rate i_0, there is an excess demand for money. In any market, excess demand can be eliminated by either an increase in the price (which in this case is the interest rate), an increase in supply, or some combination of the two. In Figure 13-1(a), we have assumed that the money supply is *exogenous* (this is the assumption used in Chapter 4). Therefore the nominal interest rate must rise to i_1, because the money supply does not respond to changes that come from within the model (i.e., it is exogenous). In this case the interest rate is endogenous, as it is responding to changes that come from the model.

Suppose, however, that we are willing to make another assumption about the money supply. Assume that, for whatever reason, the monetary authorities do not like the kinds of interest rate changes that are implied by Figure 13-1(a). We know that the interest rate increased because there was an excess demand for money, and the money supply was held constant. The monetary authorities could, however, eradicate the excess demand for money by increasing the money supply. Suppose that they did this every time that demand for money changed, so that the interest rate would never change. This is illustrated in Figure 13-1(b).

In Figure 13-1(b), the money supply curve is now horizontal. This is because the money supply is no longer *exogenous*, but rather *endogenous*, because the money supply is now *responding to* changes in the model. Notice that in this situation the interest rate is now *exogenous*, because it is held fixed by the actions of the monetary authorities.

Therefore, in the case illustrated in Figure 13-1(a), the monetary authorities control the money supply, but not the interest rate. In the case illustrated in Figure 13-1(b), the monetary authorities are controlling the interest rate by keeping it constant. In order to do this they must allow the money supply to be at whatever level is needed so that there is never excess demand for money. Therefore, in this situation, they have lost control of the money supply.

This is not just a lesson concerning supply and demand in the money market, but rather it is a lesson concerning supply and demand in general. Either price *or* quantity can be controlled, *but not both*. If policy can keep a price constant in a market, then quantity must be endogenous, and if the government can somehow control quantity in a market, then price must be endogenous.

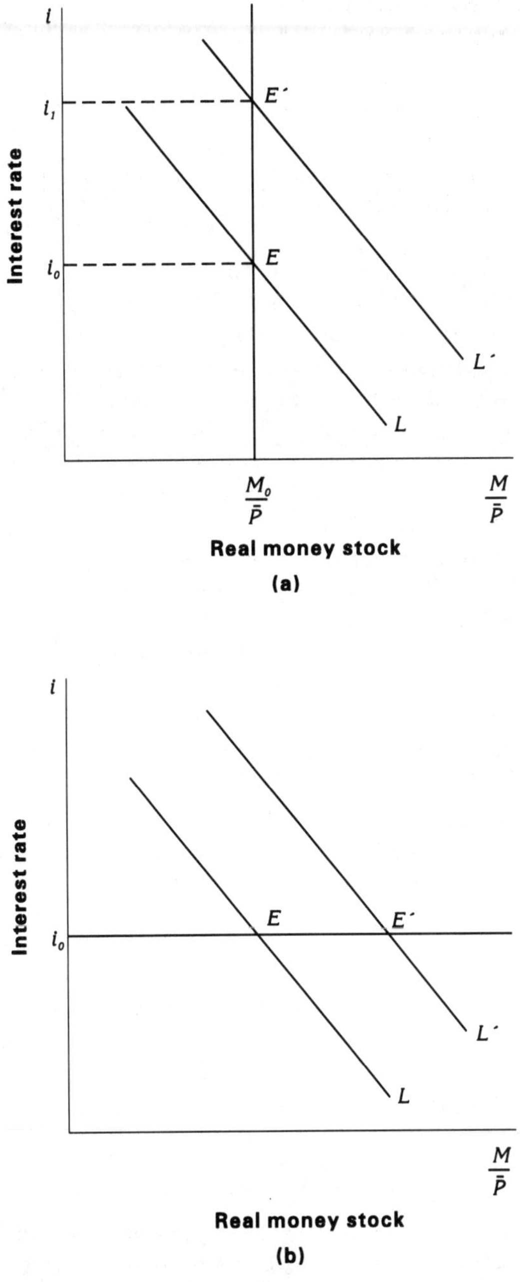
i
i_1
E´
Interest rate
i_0
E
L´
L
$\frac{M_0}{\bar{P}}$
$\frac{M}{\bar{P}}$
Real money stock
(a)
i
Interest rate
i_0
E
E´
L´
L
$\frac{M}{\bar{P}}$
Real money stock
(b)

Figure 13-1

Key Terms

Cash reserves
Clearing system
Canadian Payments Association
High-powered money (monetary base)
Money multiplier
Open market operation
Currency-deposit ratio
Excess cash reserves
Multiple expansion of bank deposits
Zero reserve requirements
Cash setting
Settlement balances
Bank rate

Graph It 13

Graph It 13 asks you to use balance sheets to illustrate the multiple expansion of deposits. We'll assume that there is only one bank and one person, Professor B. As the problem opens, Professor B has $200 on deposit. The bank is holding the $200 as reserves. The reserve requirement is 10 percent, and so $20 is required reserves and $180 is excess reserves. The first set of balance sheets follows.

Table 13-1 ***First Balance Sheet***

Professor B		Bank	
Assets	**Liabilities**	**Assets**	**Liabilities**
Deposit $200	None	Reserves $200 (Required 20) (Excess 180)	$200 Deposit
	$200 Net worth		
$200	$200	$200	$200

Professor B decides to borrow as much as possible from the bank, in order to finance advanced macroeconomic research. This being a worthy cause, the bank agrees to loan the entire $180 in excess reserves. Professor B signs the loan agreement, and the bank credits her account with the $180 dollars. Fill in the blanks in the second set of balance sheets.

Table 13-2 ***Second Balance Sheet***

Professor B				Bank			
Assets		Liabilities		Assets		Liabilities	
Deposit $_______		$180	Loan	Reserves $200		$_______	Deposit
				(Required _______)			
				(Excess _______)			
		$_______	Net worth	Loan		$_______	

Advanced macroeconomic research being as expensive as it is, Professor B decides to go for another loan. The bank again agrees to loan all its excess reserves. The bank increases the size of Professor B's loan balance and credits Professor B's account. Fill out the details in the third set of balance sheets.

Table 13-3 ***Third Balance Sheet***

Professor B				Bank			
Assets		Liabilities		Assets		Liabilities	
Deposit $_______		$_______	Loan	Reserves $_______		$_______	Deposit
				(Required _______)			
				(Excess _______)			
		$_______	Net worth	Loan _______			
$_______		$_______		$_______		$_______	

Table 13-4 ***Final Balance Sheet***

Professor B				Bank			
Assets		Liabilities		Assets		Liabilities	
Deposit $_______		$_______	Loan	Reserves $_______		$_______	Deposit
				(Required _______)			
				(Excess 0)			
		$_______	Net worth	Loan _______			
$_______		$_______		$_______		$_______	

Clearly, this process could go on for a long time. Using what you've learned about the money multiplier, fill out a final set of balance sheets reflecting the final multiple expansion of deposits and zero excess reserves.

Fill-In Questions

1. Currency plus bank reserves form ____________________, or ____________.
2. Total reserves of a bank are ____________________ reserves plus ____________ reserves.
3. The interest rate charged by the Bank of Canada to chartered banks is the ____________.
4. The Bank of Canada lowers its holdings of bonds and decreases the money supply through a(n) ____________.
5. The ratio of the money supply to high-powered money is the ____________.
6. The effects of bank rate changes on expectations are called ____________.
7. The Bank of Canada can exercise direct control over the expansion of bank loans through ____________.
8. Public portfolio preferences affect the money supply through changing the ____________.
9. The principal asset of the Bank of Canada is ____________.

True-False Questions

T F 1. An increase in high-powered money increases the money supply.

T F 2. An increase in the public's preferences for currency vis-à-vis deposits increases the money supply.

T F 3. An increase in reserve requirements increases the money supply.

T F 4. An increase in bank preferences for excess reserves increases the money supply.

T F 5. An increase in income increases the money supply.

T F **6.** Transfer of Government of Canada deposits from the Bank of Canada to the chartered banks increases the money supply.

T F **7.** Chartered bank demand for advances from the Bank of Canada has an important effect on the money supply.

T F **8.** An increase in high-powered money works through money demand to lower the interest rate.

T F **9.** An increase in chartered bank borrowing from the Bank of Canada increases the money supply.

T F **10.** Demand deposits are subject to a higher required cash reserve ratio than are notice deposits.

Multiple-Choice Questions

1. The money multiplier is
- **(a)** negative
- **(b)** between 0 and 1
- **(c)** exactly 1
- **(d)** greater than 1

2. An open market purchase increases
- **(a)** the monetary base
- **(b)** the money supply
- **(c)** bank credit
- **(d)** all of **(a)**, **(b)**, and **(c)**

3. Assets of the Bank of Canada include
- **(a)** deposits of the government
- **(b)** deposits of the chartered banks
- **(c)** government securities
- **(d)** all of **(a)**, **(b)**, and **(c)**

4. Liabilities of the chartered banks include
- **(a)** government securities
- **(b)** deposits at the Bank of Canada
- **(c)** demand deposits
- **(d)** all of **(a)**, **(b)**, and **(c)**

5. If the currency-deposit ratio is one-half and the reserve-deposit ratio is 10 percent, the money multiplier is
- **(a)** –0.75
- **(b)** 0.75
- **(c)** 1
- **(d)** 2.5

6. The money multiplier reaches a maximum when the currency-deposit ratio equals
- **(a)** 0
- **(b)** one-half
- **(c)** 1
- **(d)** infinity

7. The money multiplier reaches a maximum when the reserve-deposit ratio equals
- **(a)** 0
- **(b)** one-half
- **(c)** 1
- **(d)** infinity

8. The money multiplier reaches a maximum when excess reserves
   (a) equal required reserves
   (b) become negative
   (c) equal 0
   (d) approach infinity

9. An open market purchase from a chartered bank
   (a) has no direct effect on high-powered money
   (b) has no direct effect on the money supply
   (c) does not induce an expansion of deposits
   (d) has no effect on bank reserves

10. Bank credit will increase following an increase in
    (a) the reserve requirement
    (b) the monetary base
    (c) the bank rate
    (d) all of (a), (b), and (c)

Problems

1. Suppose that the only deposits requiring reserves are chequable deposits; that the reserve requirement on chequable deposits is 10 percent; and that people always hold 40 percent as much currency as they hold chequable deposits.

   (a) If high-powered money equals \$100 billion, what is the level of M1?

   (b) If high-powered money is increased by \$50 billion, by how much do chequable deposits increase?

2. Suppose that, in addition to the original conditions in problem 1, a 4 percent reserve requirement is put on savings deposits, and that consumers always hold 2 1/2 times as much in savings deposits as in chequable deposits.

   (a) What is the level of M2?

   (b) What is the level of M1?

3. The demand functions for currency and chequable deposits are given below. The reserve requirement on chequable deposits is 10 percent and no other assets require reserves. High-powered money equals \$1150; GDP equals \$2000. What is the interest rate?

$$CU = 0.5Y - 495i$$
$$D = Y - 50i$$

CHAPTER 14 *Problems of Stabilization Policy*

Focus of the Chapter

- Preceding chapters have developed a macroeconomic model that would appear to solve the problems of economic policy making. Once we know our national goals and all the appropriate policy multipliers, we need only perform a few calculations to discover the best economic policy. The world is far more complicated than this. In this chapter we discuss the three *handicaps of policy making:*

  1. *Lags* in the effects of policy
  2. The role of *expectations* in determining private sector responses to policy
  3. *Uncertainty* about the effects of policy

Section Summaries

14.1 The principal purpose of macroeconomic policy is to counteract the effects of *economic disturbances*. Anything that changes aggregate demand can move the economy away from full employment and/or change the price level. Thus anything that moves the *IS* or *LM* curve can be a source of disturbance. Anything that changes aggregate supply, such as the 1973–74 oil embargo, will also move the economy away from full employment and/or change the price level. It is often argued that policy makers may deliberately disturb the economy for political gain. This possibility gives rise to the *political business cycle*.

14.2 In order to combat economic disturbances, we need to know how much policy to use as well as what kind. *Econometric models* supply numerical estimates of multipliers. These models are also used to forecast GDP, interest rates, and inflation so that businesses may plan for the future.

14.3 The first difficulty in responding to a disturbance is determining whether the disturbance is permanent or temporary. If it is temporary, the disturbance will likely have passed before policy changes can become effective. If the timing of policy is poor, it may actually *destabilize* the economy.

Policy changes take time to become effective. This time is divided into the *inside lag*, the time necessary to undertake a policy change, and the *outside lag*, the time for the policy action to take effect. The inside lag is subdivided into the *recognition lag*, the *decision lag*, and the *action lag*. The recognition lag is the time required for policy makers to realize that a problem exists. The decision lag is the time spent between discovering the problem and deciding what to do about it. The action lag is the time needed to put decisions into effect. The recognition lag is the same for monetary and fiscal policy. Decision and action lags are generally much larger for fiscal than for monetary policy. Of course, *automatic stabilizers* have no inside lag at all.

The outside lag arises from the gradual response of the economy to policy changes. The *dynamic multipliers* of Chapter 10 are a prime example. The outside lag is a *distributed lag*: its effects are spread out over time. Fiscal policy generally has a shorter outside lag than does monetary policy.

14.4 *Expectations* of future economic conditions are critical in economic models. These expectations are extremely difficult to model accurately. Most econometric models approximate expectations with an average of past variables. This approach leads to serious errors when people know about the future impact of some event rather than having to rely solely on previous experience. In addition, expectations themselves depend on policy. Finding consistent models of expectations and policy rules is currently a major research problem. Lucas's *econometric policy critique* points out that many of today's macromodels lack this consistency.

14.5 There are three major sources of uncertainty in economic models. First, some events are unpredictable, such as natural disasters and simple changes in consumer tastes. Second, we recognize that we never know whether our models are exactly correct. Third, the true empirical values of the coefficients in our models are all uncertain.

14.6 Proponents of activist policy argue that we should use the tools of macroeconomics to reduce economic fluctuations. While some economists have argued against the use of activist policy entirely, active policy is appropriate so long as we recognize all the lags and uncertainty involved and are careful to be as modest as necessary in our attempts to offset disturbances.

14.7 The issue of money supply targets arises when we introduce unpredictable shifts in the *IS* and *LM* curves. The problem is illustrated in Figure 14-1 (text Figure 14-6).

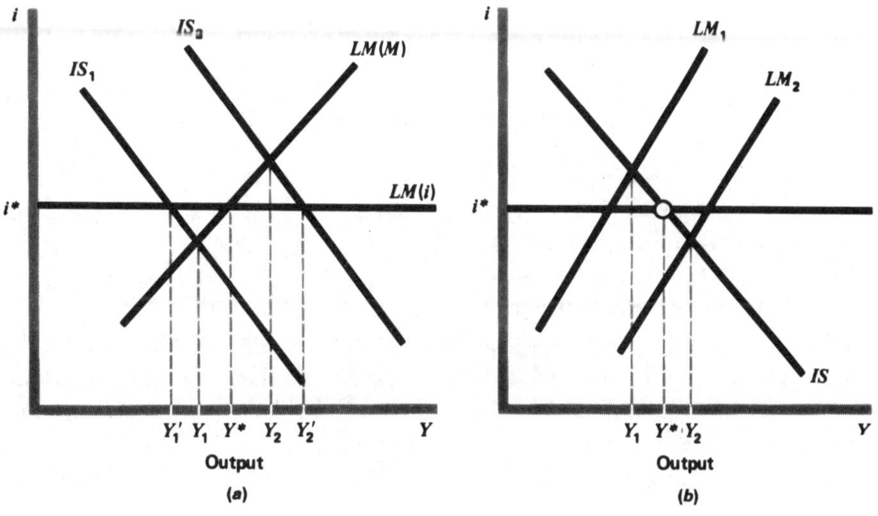

Figure 14-1

In part (a) we show a shifting *IS* curve. In this case the level of output stays closer to the target if the money supply is fixed so that we move along the *LM* curve *LM*(*M*). In part (b) it is the *LM* curve that is shifting and output can be maintained at the target level by holding the interest rate constant.

During the period 1975–81, the Bank of Canada operated monetary policy using target rates of growth of the money supply. The above analysis suggests that this is appropriate if the money market is stable and the goods market is subject to substantial disturbances.

Thinking Like an Economist

In this section we will look more closely at the possible effects of activist stabilization policy. Essentially we will give a concrete economic example of the Lucas econometric policy evaluation critique. In the 1960s and 1970s economists began to develop sophisticated, large-scale econometric models. We have seen in the text that an econometric model is a set of equations with numerical values for parameters, based on past behaviour of the economy, describing the behaviour of (perhaps) the economy as a whole.

Toward the end of the 1960s these econometric models were based on data from the 1950s and early 1960s. Inevitably, these models were used to answer questions such as: What would be the specific effects on the economy of, say, expansionary monetary policy? As a student of macroeconomics you know by now that the answer depends on whether you are asking about the short-run or the long-run effects. We have seen that in the short run expansionary monetary policy can increase *real* income, while in the long run expansionary monetary policy only brings about nominal changes.

What did the econometric models say? Recall that the models were based on data from the 1950s and 1960s. This period was characterized by almost zero inflation. (In fact, in the late 1950s the price level actually went down.) Therefore, when the policy question was addressed within the models, the models responded by predicting that real income would increase. However, because there was no inflation over the period that the models were estimated, the models were incapable of predicting the long-run inflationary consequences of expansionary monetary policy.

The reason that this happens is that the models were estimated over a period when there was no deliberate, that is, activist, monetary policy, and the estimated coefficients of the models reflected this. However, the policy experiment asked: *How will the economy react if policy is changed?* Notice that, because the model was estimated over the past, any experiment, such as a change in policy, is incapable of allowing agents to change their behaviour in response to the policy change. Therefore, the model can only tell you how agents would react *if they ignored the policy change.*

This point can also be made using the *AD/AS* model used in Chapters 7 and 8. Consider Figure 14-2.

Suppose that the short-run equilibrium of the economy is at point *E*, below full employment. We have seen that there are (at least) two ways to reach full employ-

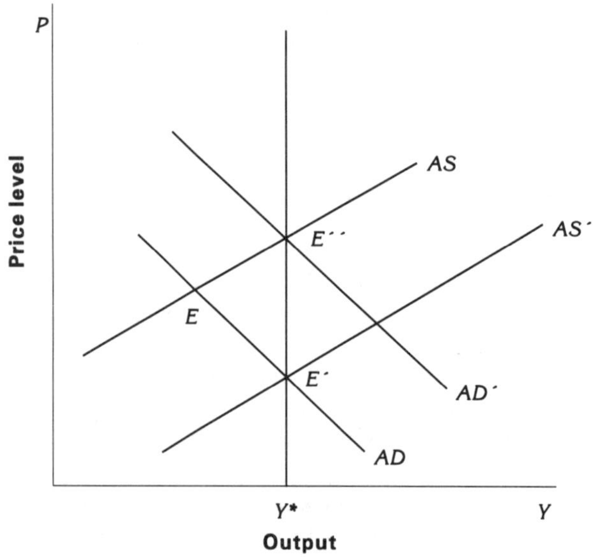

Figure 14-2

ment. First, the model has a self-correcting mechanism; if there is no policy intervention, eventually the *AS* curve will shift downward due to excess supply in the labour market, and the economy will reach a long-run equilibrium at E'. Or, activist policy could be used to shift the *AD* curve outward to reach a new equilibrium at point E''. By virtue of the adjustment assumptions in the model, the activist policy will reach equilibrium more quickly (recall that we have assumed sluggish labour market adjustment in the short run), and therefore activist policy would appear to be called for.

However, the Lucas critique would say that the *AD* and *AS* curves were estimated under a certain policy regime that was in place at the time. Any change in policy that attempts to shift the *AD* curve outward may change the way agents react to economic stimulus, and therefore, may not only cause the slopes of the curves to be different, but also probably make it impossible to predict how the change in policy will shift the *AD* curve. Therefore, it is possible that a change in policy may not be able to move the economy away from point *E*, because of a change in the policy stance causing agents to change their behaviour. What is even worse, activist policy could even have perverse effects, driving the economy away from equilibrium!

The lesson here is that activist policy, based on econometric models, could possibly be dangerous, because a lot of our models are incapable of predicting how agents' behaviour may change in response to the policy change.

Key Terms

Economic disturbances
Political business cycle
Econometric models
Inside lag
Recognition lag
Decision lag
Action lag
Outside lag
Econometric policy evaluation critique
Multiplier uncertainty
Activist policy
Fine-tuning
Rules versus discretion
Targets and instruments of monetary policy

Graph It 14

Economists make much of the distinction between stocks and flows. Capital, wealth, and the money supply are examples of stocks. Investment, GDP, and interest payments are examples of flows. A very much analogous distinction is made in business and in accounting between a balance sheet and an income statement. This Graph It gives you a balance sheet showing the stocks of assets and liabilities at a bank. You are then asked to prepare an income statement showing the bank's income and expense flows over the year and a new balance sheet showing the stocks at the beginning of the next year. The initial balance sheet appears below.

Table 14-1 ***Bank Balance Sheet 1***

Assets			Liabilities
Reserves	$ 200	$2000	Deposit
Treasury bills	400		
Loans	1600	200	Paid in capital
	$2200	$2200	

Assume that the bank receives no interest on reserves, 9.5 percent interest on Treasury bills, and 14 percent interest on loans. The bank pays 5.5 percent on deposits and pays a 20 percent dividend. Any profits left over after paying dividends are called retained earnings and are added to the paid in capital account. Fill in the details of the income and expense statement.

Table 14-2 ***Bank Income Statement***

Income			Expenses
Interest on reserves	$ 0	$ ______	Deposit interest
Interest on T-bills	______	______	Stockholders' dividends
Interest on loans	______	______	Retained earnings
	$ ______	$ ______	

Assume that the bank invests its profits entirely in Treasury bills and that depositors withdraw all their interest. Show how the balance sheet looks at the beginning of the second year.

Table 14-3 ***Bank Balance Sheet 2***

Assets			Liabilities
Reserves	$ ______	$ ______	Deposit
Treasury bills	______	______	Paid in capital
Loans	______		
	$ ______	$ ______	

Fill-In Questions

1. The time required for policy makers to counteract an economic disturbance is the ____________________ .
2. The time required for a new policy to produce a change in the economy is the ____________________ .
3. The three handicaps of policy making are ____________________ , ____________________ , and ____________________ .
4. The ____________________ is the period between the point when a new policy is chosen and the point when the policy is first put into effect.
5. The time required for an economic disturbance to be discovered is the ____________________ .
6. The time necessary for policy makers to choose a new policy is called the ____________________ .
7. A policy that requires no direct action on the part of policy makers is called a(n) ____________________ .
8. Economists who believe policy should be used to counteract economic disturbances are called ____________________ .
9. The ____________________ lag is much longer for fiscal than for monetary policy.
10. The ____________________ lag is shorter for fiscal than for monetary policy.

True-False Questions

T F **1.** Activist policies are ones that are designed to minimize government involvement.

T F **2.** Disturbances are shifts in aggregate demand or supply that cause output, interest rates, or the price level to diverge from their target paths.

T F **3.** The recognition lag is the lag between a policy decision and its implementation.

T F **4.** Built-in stabilizers have an inside lag of zero.

T F **5.** Fine-tuning is a policy which is used in the case of major disturbances to the economy.

Multiple-Choice Questions

1. The historical record of the unemployment rate shows
   - **(a)** that stabilization policy appears to have been effective
   - **(b)** that stabilization policy appears to have been not very effective
   - **(c)** that economic performance over the past 60 years has been very good
   - **(d)** that fluctuations in the unemployment rate are very small

2. Handicaps of policy making are
   - **(a)** lags in the effects of policy
   - **(b)** the role of expectations in determining private sector responses to policy
   - **(c)** uncertainty about the effects of policy
   - **(d)** all of the above

3. The decision lag is
   - **(a)** the delay between the recognition of the need for action and the policy decision
   - **(b)** the delay between the policy decision and its implementation
   - **(c)** the delay between the time a disturbance occurs and the decision that action is needed
   - **(d)** none of the above

4. If output deviates from its equilibrium value mainly because of shifts in the *IS* curve
   - **(a)** then output is stabilized by keeping the money stock constant
   - **(b)** then output is stabilized by keeping the interest rate constant
   - **(c)** then neither policy can stabilize output
   - **(d)** then fiscal policy will stabilize output

CHAPTER 15 *Fiscal Policy and Public Finance*

Focus of the Chapter

- The *Great Depression* of the 1930s left an indelible mark on economic history and led to the development of Keynesian economics. (The depression in Britain, where Keynes developed his theories, had begun in the 1920s.)
- During the Great Depression, unemployment reached nearly one-fifth of the work force, prices fell by 20 percent, and the bottom dropped out of the stock market.
- The 1950s and 1960s were a time of prosperity and rapid growth. Keynesian theory was put into practice to move the economy to full employment by increasing aggregate demand.
- The difference between government spending and tax receipts is the *budget deficit*.
- Government debt used to finance the deficit accumulates over time to build up the *national debt*.

Section Summaries

15.1 Along with most of the rest of the industrialized world, the economy of Canada collapsed between 1929 and 1933. GNP fell by 30 percent, unemployment rose nearly to 20 percent, prices fell 20 percent, and the value of stocks dropped 70 percent.

15.2 It is now generally agreed that the Great Depression could have been avoided and that it is unlikely to happen again. Two camps of thought exist with respect to what caused the depression.

1. An autonomous decline in aggregate demand, in either investment or consumption

2. A monetary contraction

15.3 Since World War II the federal government has been regarded as having a responsibility to maintain high and stable levels of employment. In comparison with earlier eras, the 1950s and 1960s were years of prosperity and steady growth, although there was a prolonged slump during the period 1958–61. Inflationary forces became entrenched in the second half of the 1960s, and stagflation became the major policy dilemma of the 1970s and 1980s.

15.4 Since 1975 the federal budget has been in a substantial deficit position. Provincial and municipal governments as a whole were close to budget balance from 1975 to 1980, but this represented the net effect of a substantial surplus generated by natural resource revenues in Alberta, British Columbia, and Saskatchewan, and a substantial deficit in the remaining provinces. In the early 1980s, all governments suffered a marked deterioration in their budgetary position as a result of the low level of economic activity.

15.5 The *budget deficit* is the difference between government spending and tax receipts. The government can finance the deficit in either of two ways:

1. It can sell government bonds to the public.

2. It can borrow from the central bank by selling bonds to the Bank of Canada.

When the government borrows from the Bank of Canada, the bank lends newly "printed" high-powered money. Deficit finance through sales of bonds to the public does not affect the money stock. Financing through borrowing from the central bank increases high-powered money by the amount borrowed. For this reason, deficit finance through sales of the debt to the central bank is called *monetizing the debt*. The Bank of Canada independently decides on how much of the national debt it wishes to buy up so that there is no necessary connection between the government deficit and the money supply.

15.6 The primary deficit is defined as the total deficit less interest payments on the public debt. If there is a primary deficit, then the total deficit will keep growing as more debt is issued and interest payments rise. The ratio of debt to income is more likely to rise, the higher the primary deficit, the lower the output, and the higher the interest rate. A rising debt-to-income ratio cannot continue indefinitely.

15.7 In recent years the persistence of large deficits and associated rapid growth of the national debt have raised concern about the implications for the future. With the exception of debt held by foreigners, the national debt is not a burden, since we owe it to ourselves. However, the debt may be a burden in the long run because it leads to a decline in the capital stock.

Thinking Like an Economist

This chapter is a bit different from other chapters in that there is no specific model that is constructed in order to address the issues raised. However, it may be helpful to look at government deficits in a supply and demand framework. When a government runs a deficit, the shortfall of expenditures over revenues must be paid for. Raising taxes is one method of increasing revenue. However, over the past ten years federal government deficits have become too large to be covered by raising taxes. This means that the government must borrow money to pay for their shortfall, the same way that you and I must take out a bank loan if we wish to spend more than we earn. The government borrows by issuing bonds, and this is a demand for funds. Of course, private corporations are also issuing bonds and demanding funds.

The supply of funds comes from individuals who buy these bonds as savings vehicles. Recall, from Chapter 10 of this *Study Guide*, that increased savings, in the long run, can be viewed as a desire on the part of an economy for increased future consumption. That is, your savings dollars eventually work their way into increases in the capital stock, which increase the productive capacity of the economy.

However, what if you choose to buy a government bond instead of the bond of a private corporation? To the extent that the government is running large deficits, it may be dominating the demand side. Also, the government may be borrowing to pay the interest on past debt that it has issued, and therefore your savings dollars are not going to increase the capital stock. Therefore, in this sense large government deficits could impede economic growth, as they may divert the supply of funds away from productive uses.

Key Terms

Structural deficit
Debt finance
Money finance
Monetizing the debt
Debt-income ratio
Government budget constraint
National debt
Primary deficit
Burden of the debt
Barro-Ricardo equivalence

Graph It 15

The federal government entered the 1980s with huge deficits. Since the economy was also in a terrible recession, we know that a large part of the deficit represented cyclical factors. In this Graph It, we made some "back of the envelope" calculations to see the difference between the cyclical and the structural deficit.

Table 15-1

(1) Estimate of potential GDP, 1982	380	390	400
(2) Actual GDP, 1982	345	345	345
(3) Gap [(1) – (2)]	________	________	________
(4) Cyclical deficit [1/3 × (3)]	________	________	________
(5) Actual deficit, 1982	20.3	20.3	20.3
(6) Structural deficit [(5) – (4)]	________	________	________

Both government revenues and government transfer spending vary with the state of the economy. We know that taxes are about 18 percent of GDP. Total transfers are around half of government spending, but not all transfers vary cyclically. Let's guess that transfers minus taxes rises about 1 dollar for every 3 dollars GDP rises. In Table 15-1, you are asked to split the budget into cyclical and structural components using three different assumptions about the natural rate of unemployment. Government estimates use far more detailed figures and therefore can be more accurate, but it's not hard to get a rough idea of how much of any given budget deficit is due to a recession and how much to longer-run fiscal policy.

Fill-In Questions

1. The __________________ is the difference between government expenditures and receipts.
2. The __________________ is the net accumulation over the years of the difference between government expenditures and receipts.
3. Sale of government bonds by the government to the central bank is called __________________ .
4. The method of government financing through sales of debt to the public is called __________________ .
5. The method of government financing through sales of debt to the central bank is called __________________ .
6. The part of the deficit not including interest payments is called the __________________ .

True-False Questions

T F 1. The Great Depression was accompanied by a sharp increase in prices.

T F **2.** The Great Depression was primarily an American experience.

T F **3.** A budget surplus is a negative budget deficit.

T F **4.** The government budget deficit is a flow.

T F **5.** The national debt is a stock.

T F **6.** A deficit necessarily leads to an increase in the money supply.

Multiple-Choice Questions

1. The 1960s were primarily a period of
- **(a)** high growth and stable prices
- **(b)** slow growth and stable prices
- **(c)** high growth and gradually increasing inflation
- **(d)** slow growth and gradually increasing inflation

2. The deficit is $35 billion per year with an initial national debt of $700 billion. If no money is printed, what will the level of the national debt be in three years?
- **(a)** $105 billion
- **(b)** $700 billion
- **(c)** $735 billion
- **(d)** $805 billion

3. During the second half of the 1970s
- **(a)** the federal government ran substantial deficits
- **(b)** provinces with large natural resource revenues had surpluses
- **(c)** other provinces ran deficits
- **(d)** all of **(a)**, **(b)**, and **(c)**

4. If the budget surplus is $100 billion and the government sells $10 billion in bonds to the public, high-powered money
- **(a)** increases by $100 billion
- **(b)** remains constant
- **(c)** falls by $100 billion
- **(d)** falls by $110 billion

PART 4 *Unemployment, Inflation, and Growth*

CHAPTER 16 *The Rate of Inflation in the Short and Long Run*

Focus of the Chapter

- Modified to take account of inflationary expectations, the Phillips curve becomes a dynamic aggregate supply curve. When the expected inflation rate is equal to the actual inflation rate, output is at its full-employment level. For a *given* rate of expected inflation, the dynamic aggregate supply curve implies a tradeoff between output and inflation. In the long run, the tradeoff cannot persist because inflationary expectations will "catch up" with the actual inflation rate.
- Together with the dynamic aggregate supply curve, the dynamic aggregate demand curve determines the equilibrium level of output and inflation. In the short run, adaptive expectations imply that output may deviate from full employment as a result of monetary, fiscal, and other forms of shocks. In the long run, inflation is mainly a monetary phenomenon. Rational inflationary expectations imply that anticipated monetary and fiscal policy has no real effects.

Section Summaries

16.1 The aggregate supply curve

$$P = P_{-1}\left[1 + \lambda(Y - Y^*)\right]$$

is derived by combining the Phillips curve, the inverse relationship between the unemployment rate and the level of output, and the markup pricing rule of firms.

An implication of markup pricing is that firms pass wage increases on to consumers directly. Thus, in our model, wages and prices always rise or fall at the same rate.

We define the rate of wage inflation, g_w, as

$$g_w = \frac{w - w_{-1}}{w_{-1}}$$

Using the aggregate supply curve, we can write the wage Phillips curve as

$$g_w = \lambda(Y - Y^*)$$

Friedman and Phelps argued that the simple wage Phillips curve incorrectly ignores the effect of expected inflation on wage rates. At the very least, workers will demand periodic wage increases to compensate for expected inflation. Workers care about real wages, not nominal wages. To take account of the role of expected (price) inflation on wage changes, we write the expectations-augmented wage Phillips curve

$$g_w = \pi^e + \lambda(Y - Y^*)$$

When Y is equal to Y^*, wages rise at the expected rate of inflation. When Y is below (above) Y^*, wages rise at a rate below (above) the expected rate of inflation.

Since π, the actual inflation rate, is equal to w, the rate of wage inflation, we can substitute into the expectations-augmented wage Phillips curve to derive the dynamic aggregate supply curve

$$\pi = \pi^e + \lambda(Y - Y^*)$$

16.2 There is a short-run (dynamic) aggregate supply curve corresponding to every level of expected inflation. Consider Figure 16-1 (text Figure 16-1).

At an expected inflation rate of 5 percent, the dynamic aggregate supply curve is *SAS*. At $Y = Y^*$, the actual inflation rate equals the expected inflation rate (5 percent), as should be the case. If expected inflation were to jump to 10 percent, the new short-run aggregate supply curve would be *SAS′*. Along each short-run aggregate supply curve there is a tradeoff between inflation and unemployment.

The short-run dynamic aggregate supply curve appeared to shift in the late 1960s as the public began to expect higher inflation rates. Higher actual inflation rates became associated with each level of GDP.

If the actual inflation rate remains stable for a long period of time, the public will begin to anticipate that particular level of inflation. The only level of output consistent with $\pi = \pi^e$ is full employment. When the economy is resting at full employment, prices and wages are rising at the rate expected by the public; the long-run aggregate supply curve is vertical.

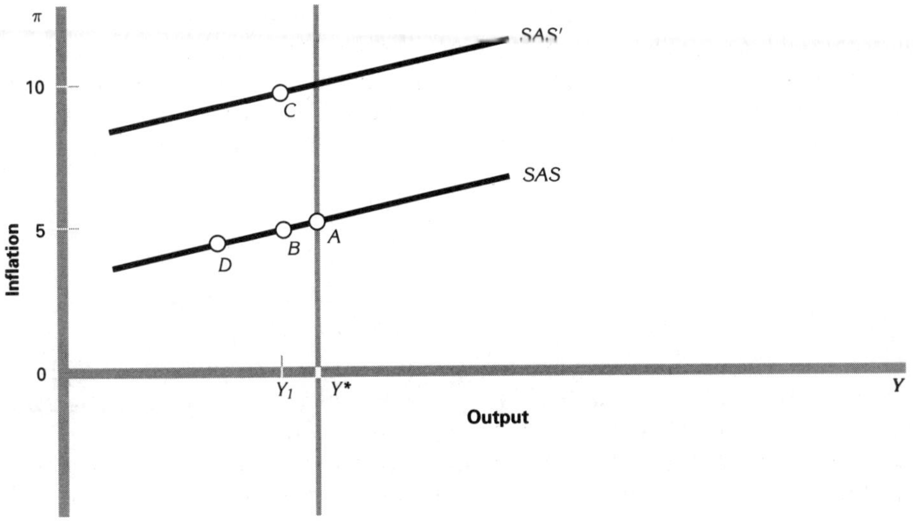

Figure 16-1

16.3 It is not clear whether wage adjustments required by labour contracts reflect compensation for past inflation or expectations of current and future inflation. The fact that many adjustments are based on last period's inflation rate gives wage changes the appearance of being compensation for past inflation.

If wage adjustments are based on last period's inflation rate, wages and prices change only gradually over time.

Anticipated inflation based on the past behaviour of inflation is called *adaptive expectations*. For example, inflationary expectations are adaptive when

$$\pi^e = \pi_{-1}$$

According to the rational expectations hypothesis, people use all the relevant and (economically) available information to forecast the future behaviour of the price level. The rational expectations hypothesis implies that the public does not make systematic mistakes in forecasting the inflation rate.

The dynamic aggregate supply curve under the adaptive expectations hypothesis is

$$\pi = \pi_{-1} + \lambda(Y - Y^*)$$

16.4 The dynamic aggregate demand curve shows the relationship between the rate of inflation and the rate of change in aggregate demand for a fixed level of nominal money supply growth and a fixed rate of fiscal expansion. It is

$$Y = Y_{-1} + \psi(m - \pi) + \sigma \cdot f$$

where ψ and σ are positive constants, $m - \pi$ is the rate of change of real money balances, and f is the rate of fiscal expansion. The dynamic aggregate demand curve says that the rate of change in aggregate demand, $Y - Y_{-1}$, is positively related to the growth of real money balances and fiscal expansion.

We rewrite the dynamic aggregate demand curve (derived from a simplified *IS-LM* model) as

$$\pi = m - \frac{1}{\psi}(Y - Y_{-1})$$

to highlight the relationship between actual inflation, the rate of growth of the nominal money stock, and the change in aggregate demand (assuming, for simplicity, that f is zero). Plotting π against Y (for a given m and Y_{-1}), the dynamic aggregate demand curve is downward-sloping, as in Figure 16-2 (text Figure 16-3).

Holding the rate of growth of the nominal money stock fixed, a reduction in π causes real balances to grow more rapidly and spending to increase.

An increase (decrease) in the nominal growth rate of money causes the dynamic aggregate demand curve to shift up (down).

16.5 The equilibrium inflation rate and level of output are determined by the intersection of the dynamic aggregate supply curve with the dynamic aggregate demand curve.

In the short run, holding the expected inflation rate constant, an increase in the growth rate of the nominal money stock will shift the dynamic aggregate demand

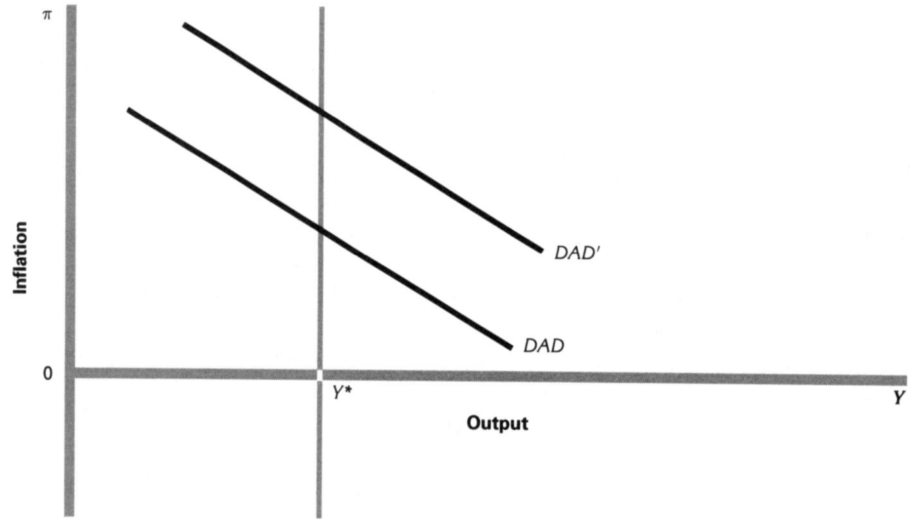

Figure 16-2

curve rightward, raising the level of output. The inflation rate will increase, but not by as much as the growth rate of the money stock.

An exogenous increase in expected inflation will reduce output in the short run. Actual inflation will rise, but not by as much as the expected inflation rate.

When the economy is resting at full employment and the nominal money stock is growing at a positive rate (assumed to be zero), the expected inflation rate, the actual inflation rate, and the growth rate of the nominal money stock are all equal. In the long run ("steady state"), the inflation rate is determined solely by the growth rate of the money stock.

In reality, the economy never reaches a steady state. However, over a long period of time, macroeconomists would expect the average behaviour of the economy to approximate the steady-state behaviour predicted by our model.

16.6 We consider the dynamic adjustment of the inflation rate and the level of output to a permanent increase in the growth rate of the money stock under the assumption that inflationary expectations are adaptive.

The economy is initially at point *E* in Figure 16-3 (text Figure 16-5), where money growth rate is m_0 and inflation rate π_0. An increase in the growth rate of money to m_1

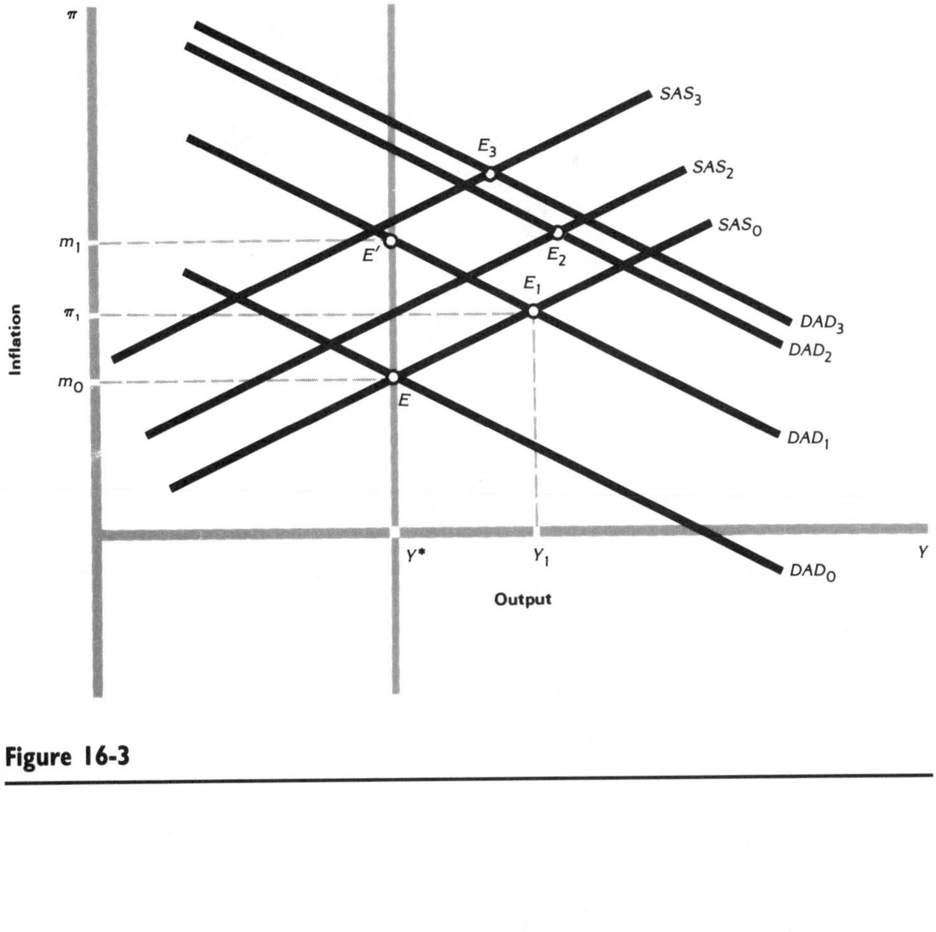

Figure 16-3

shifts the aggregate demand curve upward; the inflation rate is now π_1 and the level of output is Y_1 (point E_1). Expected inflation is still last period's actual level of inflation, π_0.

Because output has increased from its initial level, the dynamic aggregate demand curve shifts again. The aggregate supply curve shifts up now as expected inflation rises to π_1; the economy moves to point E_2. The actual inflation rate has already risen above its eventual steady-state level, π_1. At some point during the adjustment process the inflation rate must fall, but this can only happen if the economy suffers a period of falling output, that is, a recession. The economy will go through a cycle, as shown in Figure 16-4 (text Figure 16-6). During the process of adjustment to an increase in the growth rate of money, the economy exhibits a period of stagflation and overshooting.

With perfect-foresight inflationary expectations — the equivalent of rational expectations when there is no uncertainty —

$$\pi = \pi^e$$

and the economy is at full employment always. Under rational expectations, unexpected changes in the growth rate of the money supply may cause temporary

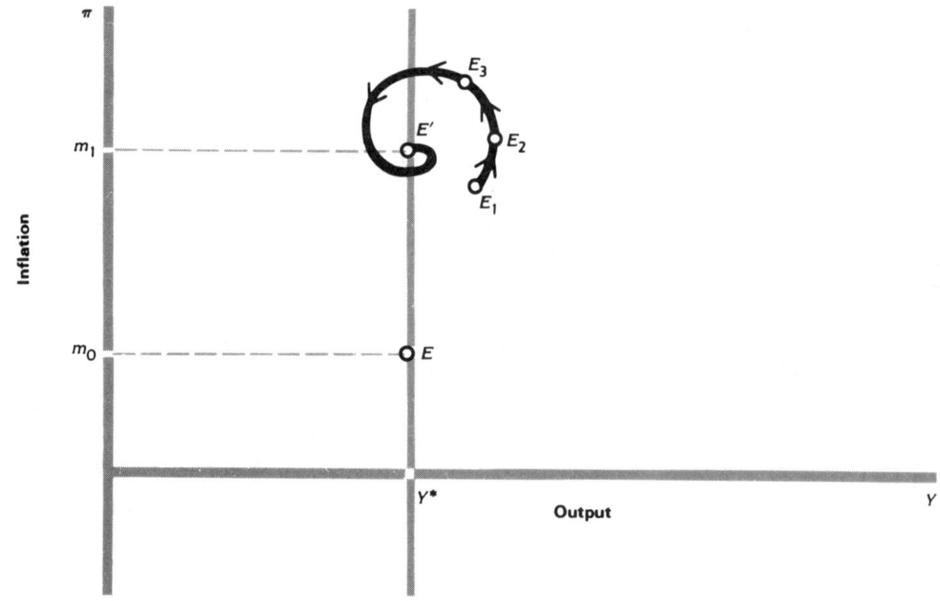

Figure 16-4

deviations of output from its full-employment level, but adjustment back to full employment will occur within one period.

16.7 A permanent fiscal expansion will temporarily raise output and increase the inflation rate. With an unchanged money supply growth rate, the economy must eventually return to its initial equilibrium, where Y equals Y^*, and $\pi = m_0$. During the adjustment process the economy exhibits overshooting — a recession — and since government spending exceeds its old level in the new equilibrium, some private spending has been permanently crowded out.

16.8 In fighting inflation, we choose between *gradualism*, in which we have a small recession for a long time, and *cold turkey policies*, where we have a shorter, deeper recession. The choice is difficult. However, the cold turkey policies have the advantage of being *credible*. If people really believe the government is going to reduce inflation, then π^e falls. For every point π^e falls, we get rid of one point of inflation without having to pay the unemployment price.

Thinking Like an Economist

Students sometimes find this chapter to be more difficult than other chapters in the book. However, if you have mastered Chapter 8, you can understand this chapter, as the model is basically the same, only more dynamic. In Chapters 8 and 16, the aggregate demand curve is based on the *IS-LM* model, and the aggregate supply curve is based on sticky wage and price adjustment.

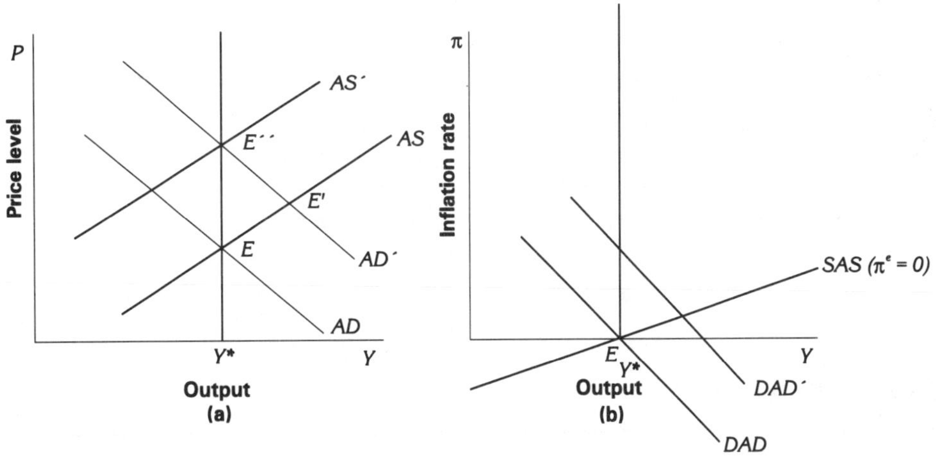

Figure 16-5

To see how the models in the two chapters are related, consider Figure 16-5. Figure 16-5(a) reproduces the model used in Chapter 8. The initial equilibrium is at point *E*. Figure 16-5(b) shows the model used in Chapter 16, assuming that inflationary expectations are zero. Point *E* in this figure is the same as point *E* in the left-hand panel. This is because at point *E* in each panel, actual and expected inflation are zero, as is the rate of growth on the nominal money stock.

Now suppose that there is a one-time increase in the level of the nominal money stock. (This was how expansionary monetary policy was described in Chapter 8.) In the left-hand panel, the *AD* curve shifts to *AD′*, and there is a temporary equilibrium at point *E′*. In the right-hand panel, *DAD* shifts out, because, for one period, there is an increase in the rate of growth of money.

In the left-hand panel, we know that, because the economy is beyond full employment, wages and prices begin to rise and the *AS* curve shifts upward until the economy reaches a new long-run equilibrium at point *E″*.

During the transition from *E* to *E″*, the price level has been rising, and therefore there has been inflation. Remember that we are assuming that inflationary expectations were zero, and therefore, in the right-hand panel *SAS* never shifts. The *DAD′* curve shifts back to its original position, because the *rate of growth* of the nominal money stock is zero, as the level only changed once. Therefore in the right-hand panel *E* and *E″* are the same point. That is, the economy moved out along the *SAS* curve and then back down along the *SAS* curve.

In long-run equilibrium, the rate of growth of the nominal money stock, inflation, and inflationary expectations are all zero, and the two models are the same. However, the two models are only the same under the special case that inflation and inflationary expectations are zero in long-run equilibrium.

Key Terms

Expectations-augmented aggregate supply curve
Short-run aggregate supply curve
Long-run aggregate supply curve
Adaptive expectations
Rational expectations
Stagflation
Overshooting
Gradualism
Cold turkey
Credibility

Graph It 16

Graph It 16 asks you to calculate the opportunity cost differences between money, bonds, and capital. The purpose of this exercise is to see when you should look at the nominal interest rate and when you should look at the real interest rate.

Assume that money pays no interest. Bonds pay the nominal interest rate. Capital takes the form of seed corn. Every bushel of seed corn you have at the beginning of

Table 16-1

Asset	Beginning Value	End Dollar Value	End Real Value	Dollar Difference	Real Difference
Money	$100	$100	$ 98.04	$7	________
Bonds	$100	$107	________	________	________
Corn	$100	$112.2	$110.0		

Table 16-2

Asset	Beginning Value	End Dollar Value	End Real Value	Dollar Difference	Real Difference
Money	$100	________	________	________	________
Bonds	$100	________	________	________	________
Corn	$100	________	________	________	________

the year grows into 1.1 bushels by the end of the year. Initially, the general price level equals 1.0, and a bushel of corn costs $1. You start with $100 in money, $100 in bonds, and 100 bushels of corn.

Fill out Table 16-1 on the basis of the assumption that the price level, of corn and everything else, rises to 1.02 by the end of the year and that the nominal interest rate is 7 percent.

Fill out Table 16-2 on the basis of the new assumptions that the price level rises to 1.12 by the end of the year and that the nominal interest rate is 17 percent.

You should be able to see that in both tables the opportunity cost of money (versus bonds) is approximately the nominal interest rate — whether the cost is measured by the real difference or the dollar difference. The opportunity cost of capital (seed corn) is approximately the real interest rate in both cases. At low inflation rates (such as in Table 16-1), the real and nominal interest rates are approximately the same, so it doesn't matter terribly much which one we look at. At high inflation rates (such as in Table 16-2), the difference is crucial.

Fill-In Questions

1. ____________________ occurs when the inflation rate rises above or below its steady-state level during the adjustment to a disturbance.

2. So long as people do not make systematic errors in predicting the future of the economy, they are said to have ________________ .
3. In order to explain inflation, the ________________ curve takes into account not only the current state of the economy but also people's expectations about future price changes.
4. The theory that in the long run the economy must return to full employment is shown by the long-run ________________ curve.
5. Simultaneous high inflation and high unemployment is called ________________ .
6. A(n) ________________ government policy pronouncement is one that the public believes the government will act upon.
7. People are said to have ________________ expectations when there is no uncertainty and they know the actual inflation rate precisely.
8. Simultaneous high inflation and high unemployment is called ________________ .

True-False Questions

T F 1. Rational expectations theory says that GDP always equals potential GDP.

T F 2. If output is above full employment, the short-run aggregate supply curve will shift upward.

T F 3. When wages and prices are rising by the same amount, the real wage is falling.

T F 4. Along the short-run aggregate supply curve the expected rate of inflation is constant.

T F 5. We can think of the Phillips curve being vertical when expected inflation and actual inflation are equal.

T F 6. Inflation is increased by high expectations of inflation.

Multiple-Choice Questions

1. Initially the general price level is 100. If six months later the general price level is 102, the annual inflation rate has been
   - **(a)** 2 percent
   - **(b)** 4 percent
   - **(c)** 5 percent
   - **(d)** 12 percent

2. If expected inflation rises one percentage point, the short-run aggregate supply curve
   - (a) shifts down by one point
   - (b) shifts up by one point
   - (c) remains in the same position
   - (d) rotates about full-employment output

3. If output is held above full employment, the short-run aggregate supply curve
   - (a) shifts down
   - (b) shifts up
   - (c) remains in the same position
   - (d) rotates about full-employment output

4. An increase of 1 percent per year in the rate of growth of the money supply will increase inflation in the long run by
   - (a) 0
   - (b) 0.5 percent
   - (c) 1 percent
   - (d) more than 1 percent

5. A permanent increase in the rate of growth of money of 1 percent will permanently increase GDP by
   - (a) 0
   - (b) 0.5 percent
   - (c) 1 percent
   - (d) more than 1 percent

6. A permanent increase in government spending will generate
   - (a) temporarily increased inflation
   - (b) permanently increased inflation
   - (c) no change in inflation
   - (d) temporarily decreased inflation

7. A permanent increase in the level of money stock, with no change in the rate of growth, will generate
   - (a) temporarily increased inflation
   - (b) permanently increased inflation
   - (c) no change in inflation
   - (d) temporarily decreased inflation

Problems

Use the following equations for each of the questions below:

$$Y = Y_{-1} + 2f + 2000(m_{-1} - \pi_{-1}) + 1000\,\Delta\pi^e$$ *Dynamic aggregate demand*

$$\pi = \pi^e + 0.8$$ *Expectations-augmented Phillips curve*

$$\pi^e = \pi - 1$$ *Inflationary expectations*

Initially, GDP equals 4000, as does potential GDP. Initial $\overline{A}(f = 0)$ is 1000, and both inflation and inflationary expectations have been zero for some time. The rate of growth of the money supply, m, is also initially zero.

1. Suppose the government permanently increases spending by 500. What is the level of GDP in the year of the increase? What is the inflation rate? What inflation rate will people expect for the next year? What actually happens to GDP and inflation the following year? The year after?

2. Suppose, instead, that the money supply is permanently increased by one-half, so that m equals 0.5 and then returns to 0 in the following year. Obviously, aggregate demand is not changed the first year, since money only affects income with a lag. What happens to GDP and inflation the next year? The year after? The year after that?

3. Suppose the government lets the money supply grow at 50 percent per year permanently. What happens to GDP and inflation in years 2, 3, 4, and 5 of the new policy?

CHAPTER 17 *Inflation and Unemployment*

Focus of the Chapter

- We study the *anatomy of unemployment*, its distribution among different groups in society, and the determination of the natural rate.
- We then look at the costs of inflation, with special emphasis on the difference between *anticipated* and *unanticipated inflation*.
- We conclude with a look at alternative strategies for reducing the rate of inflation.

Section Summaries

17.1 There are three central facts about unemployment. These facts help us to understand who bears the cost of unemployment.

(a) There are substantial flows in and out of unemployment each month, and most people who become unemployed return to work very quickly.

(b) Much of the total number of unemployed persons is made up of people who are unemployed for long periods.

(c) Different groups in society have very different unemployment rates. Unemployment is higher in the 15–24 age group and, across regions, the Atlantic provinces have experienced the highest unemployment rates.

17.2 The *natural rate of unemployment*, also called the full-employment level of unemployment, or the nonaccelerating inflation rate of unemployment (NAIRU), is the unemployment rate at which flows in and out of unemployment just balance *and* at which expectations about prices and wages are correct. The natural rate of unemployment changes over time. Since the overall natural rate is a weighted average of natural rates of different groups in society, the natural rate has risen as groups with higher unemployment have become a larger part of the labour force.

17.3 The burden of unemployment is not spread evenly over society since most of it is borne by the individuals who find themselves out of work. Some unemployment is a good thing. For example, people leaving school often spend some time "unemployed" while searching for a first job.

17.4 In determining the costs of inflation, we made a critical distinction between *perfectly anticipated* and *imperfectly anticipated* inflation. If everyone knew how much inflation there would be, all agreements and contracts would be written to reflect this inflation. The only costs of anticipated inflation arise because the interest rate on currency cannot be adjusted to inflation (since there is no interest on currency) and because people have to spend a lot of time remarking price tags. Both costs are trivial. When inflation is *unanticipated* or *imperfectly anticipated*, people who owe nominal debts repay them with cheaper dollars and people who are creditors are paid off in cheaper dollars. Thus debtors benefit and creditors lose. Of course, most people are both debtors and creditors. Unanticipated inflation helps some individuals and hurts others. The effect of unanticipated inflation is mostly *distributional*.

17.5 A policy that has been suggested to reduce inflation without paying an unemployment price is an *incomes policy*. Incomes policy means either formal or informal wage or price controls. This policy faces two problems. First, relative price changes are necessary for efficient allocation of economic resources, and controls greatly interfere with the market's ability to change prices. Second, governments try to use these policies instead of controlling aggregate demand. However, these controls will not work unless accompanied by appropriate aggregate demand changes.

Thinking Like an Economist

Toward the end of 1992, the federal government introduced legislation designed to make it harder for certain individuals to qualify for UIC benefits, and to generally "tighten up" the UIC system. The motivation behind this legislation was the belief that some individuals were taking advantage of the system by collecting UIC benefits when they could have been working. In this section we are going to look at the labour supply decision of individuals when they are faced with the possibility of receiving UIC benefits.

First we will look at labour supply in a classical long-run framework where, if you wish to work, there are jobs available. That is there is no *involuntary* unemployment.

Consider what motivates an individual to work. Clearly, you need to receive an income in order to be able to consume goods and services. However, this must be balanced against the demand for leisure time (beyond the need for sleep). When you are faced with a real wage rate in the marketplace, you must decide whether it is high enough so that you can buy the goods and services that you demand, and still have enough leisure time available. If the real wage offer is not high enough, then you could choose not to work. In this situation, because you have chosen not to work (and therefore, have chosen to consume more leisure), you are not counted as being unemployed. Accordingly, in this long-run classical world, because an individual can never be involuntarily unemployed, there is no need for unemployment insurance.

Now consider a short-run world, where it is not always true that if you wish to work, there is a job available. For instance, you may get laid off in a recession, and become involuntarily unemployed. The philosophy behind the UIC system is to protect these type of workers who face a probability of becoming temporarily, involuntarily unemployed.

Now suppose that you are an individual who likes to consume a lot of leisure time. Suppose further, that UIC rules allowed you to quit your job (versus being laid off), and still be eligible for UIC benefits. This would provide an incentive for you to work just long enough to qualify for UIC benefits, and quit your job. In this situation, the unemployment rate would be higher than it would have been in the absence of a UIC system. Some of the UIC changes that were introduced in 1992 were aimed at deterring this type of behaviour.

In the above situation, the individual who voluntarily quit work in order to collect UIC benefits was simply responding to the incentives created by the original UIC system. There is a very important lesson to be learned here. That is, in order for any government policy to have its desired results, it must be designed in a manner such that it creates the proper incentives for individuals to behave in a manner that brings forth the desired economic results of the policy. Economists call these types of policies incentive-compatible policies. The above example of an individual being able to go in and out of the labour force *voluntarily*, and still receive UIC benefits, is an example of an incentive-*incompatible* policy. The 1992 changes are designed to make the UIC system more incentive-compatible. Another suggestion along these lines is to make the UIC system into true insurance, where the premium that you pay is based on your probability of becoming unemployed.

Key Terms

Unemployment pool
Duration of unemployment
Natural rate of unemployment
Structural unemployment
Perfectly anticipated inflation
Nonaccelerating inflation rate of unemployment (NAIRU)
Wage indexation
Incomes policy

Table 17-1 *"The Old Days"*

	Unemployment Rate	Number in Labour Force	Number Employed
Male	3.00	1000	970
Female	7.00	200	186
Total	3.67	1200	1156

Table 17-2 *"The New Days"*

	Unemployment Rate	Number in Labour Force	Number Employed
Male	2.80	1000	________
Female	5.50	800	________
Total	________	________	________

Graph It 17

As you know, statistics can be misleading. When a statistic is a weighted average of underlying data, changes in the weights can easily lead us to guess wrong about what is going on in the economy. Graph It 17 illustrates this by looking at changes in the natural rate of unemployment.

The underlying formation for Table 17-1 is the unemployment rate for men and women and the number of men and women in the labour force. From these figures we calculated the number employed. Then we added up the total labour force and the total employed and worked backward to get the overall unemployment rate, 3.67 percent [3.67 = 1 – (1156/1200)].

Now you fill in Table 17-2 and answer the following two questions. Has the overall unemployment rate risen? If so, what group is unemployed more?

Fill-In Questions

1. The problem of stabilization policy concerns the tradeoff between ________________ and ________________.

2. The ________________ is the permanently sustainable rate of unemployment.
3. Contracts can be adjusted in advance for ________________ inflation.
4. Unforeseen inflation is called ________________ or ________________.
5. The effects of unforeseen inflation are mostly ________________.
6. An unforeseen increase in prices benefits ________________.
7. This group benefits at the expense of ________________.

True-False Questions

T F 1. The natural rate of employment is determined by long-run aggregate demand policies.

T F 2. The effects of unanticipated unemployment are mostly distributional.

T F 3. The effects of unanticipated inflation are mostly distributional.

T F 4. The effects of anticipated unemployment are very large.

T F 5. The effects of anticipated inflation are trivial.

T F 6. Most people who become unemployed return to work quickly.

T F 7. Most unemployment is accounted for by people who are only briefly unemployed.

T F 8. Optimally, the unemployment rate would be zero.

T F 9. The natural rate of unemployment cannot be changed by government economic policies.

T F 10. Aggregate demand policies cannot be used to change inflation in the long run.

Multiple-Choice Questions

1. The natural rate of unemployment is currently estimated at around
   - **(a)** 0
   - **(b)** 2 to 3 percent
   - **(c)** 6 to 7 percent
   - **(d)** 9 to 10 percent

2. In recent years the lowest unemployment rates have been experienced in
   - **(a)** Ontario
   - **(b)** Quebec
   - **(c)** western Canada
   - **(d)** the Atlantic provinces

3. During the 1970s the fastest-growing group in the labour force was
   (a) men aged 15–24
   (b) women aged 15–24
   (c) men aged 25 and over
   (d) women aged 25 and over

4. The natural rate of unemployment is the level at which
   (a) entry and exit from the unemployment pool balance
   (b) expectations about wages and prices are correct
   (c) neither **(a)** nor **(b)** occurs
   (d) both **(a)** and **(b)** occur

5. The natural rate of unemployment changes in response to
   (a) labour market policies
   (b) the composition of the labour force
   (c) neither **(a)** nor **(b)**
   (d) both **(a)** and **(b)**

6. Inflation could be brought to an abrupt halt by
   (a) a deep, short recession
   (b) a shallow, short recession
   (c) a big boom
   (d) neither **(a)**, **(b)**, nor **(c)**

7. Inflation could be brought to a gradual halt by
   (a) a deep, long recession
   (b) a shallow, long recession
   (c) a big boom
   (d) neither **(a)**, **(b)**, nor **(c)**

8. If the government commands total credibility and prices and wages are fully flexible, inflation
   (a) can be stopped instantly, but with high unemployment
   (b) can be stopped instantly, with no unemployment
   (c) can be stopped gradually, with no unemployment
   (d) cannot be stopped

9. Anticipated inflation largely transfers wealth from
   (a) debtors to creditors
   (b) creditors to debtors
   (c) poor to rich
   (d) none of **(a)**, **(b)**, or **(c)**

10. Unanticipated inflation largely transfers wealth from
   (a) young to old
   (b) poor to rich
   (c) creditors to debtors
   (d) none of **(a)**, **(b)**, or **(c)**

Problems

1. Suppose that the natural rate of unemployment is 5 percent for men and 8 percent for women. If women are 40 percent of the labour force, what is the overall natural rate? What would the natural rate be if the number of working women increased until women made up 50 percent of the labour force? Would full-employment GDP be higher or lower at this new natural rate?

2. Suppose that in a typical month, four people out of every hundred leave their jobs. If two of these people are out of work for one month, one is out of work for two months, and one is out of work for a year, what is the average duration of unemployment? What is the employment rate?

3. Assume you buy a one-year bond at $100 with a 7 percent nominal interest rate and that over the year the inflation rate is 10 percent. What is your real gain over the year?

4. Assume people expect the inflation rate to be 10 percent. What nominal intérest rate will they charge to obtain a 2 percent real return?

5. Suppose you own a piece of real estate that is gaining in value at 2 percent per year plus the inflation rate. If the inflation rate is 10 percent and the capital gains tax rate is 25 percent, what is your real after-tax return if you well after two years?

CHAPTER 18 *Money, Deficits, and Inflation*

Focus of the Chapter

- Very high inflation rates are due primarily to excessive money growth, but the link between money and inflation at low inflation rates is much weaker.
- We look at whether money growth raises or lowers interest rates.
- Financing of government spending by money creation can be viewed as an inflation tax.
- We examine the relationship between hyperinflations and money growth.

Section Summaries

18.1 The monetarists claim that monetary growth affects the inflation rate, but not real variables, is essentially correct in the long run. In the short run, monetary and nonmonetary forces influence both the inflation rate and real variables.

In the model developed in Chapter 16, we found that growth in aggregate demand, $\Delta Y = Y - Y_{-1}$, depends on the rate of growth of real money balances, and that the rate of growth of real money balances equals the difference between nominal money growth and inflation.

$$\Delta Y = (m - \pi)$$

Aggregated demand rises (falls) when nominal money growth is greater (less) than inflation. These scenarios are graphed in Figure 18-1(a) [text Figure 18-1(a)], where arrows indicate the direction in which aggregate demand is changing at the specified inflation rate.

The aggregate supply curve is

$$\pi = \pi^e + \lambda(Y - Y^*)$$

If we assume adaptive expectations, such as $\pi^e = \pi_{-1}$, then

$$\pi - \pi^e \equiv \pi - \pi_{-1} \equiv \Delta\pi = \lambda(Y - Y^*)$$

The inflation rate will be rising if the level of output, Y, exceeds the full-employment rate of output, Y*, and will be falling if the opposite is true. These scenarios are pictured in Figure 18-1(b) [text Figure 18-1 (b)], where the arrows indicate the direction in which the inflation rate is moving at the specified level of output.

The upper portion of Figure 18-2 [upper portion of text Figure 18-2] combines aggregate demand [Figure 18-1 (a)] and aggregate supply [Figure 18-1 (b)] into one figure that describes the dynamics of inflation and output. In region I, output and inflation are both rising; in region II, inflation is rising and output is falling; in region III, inflation and output are both falling; and in region IV, output is rising and inflation is falling.

In the lower portion of Figure 18-2 [text Figure 18-2], we graph the *IS* schedule for a given level of autonomous spending. The upper and lower portions of Figure 18-2 permit us to keep track of the real interest rate, the actual inflation rate and level of output, and the dynamics of inflation and output, all at once.

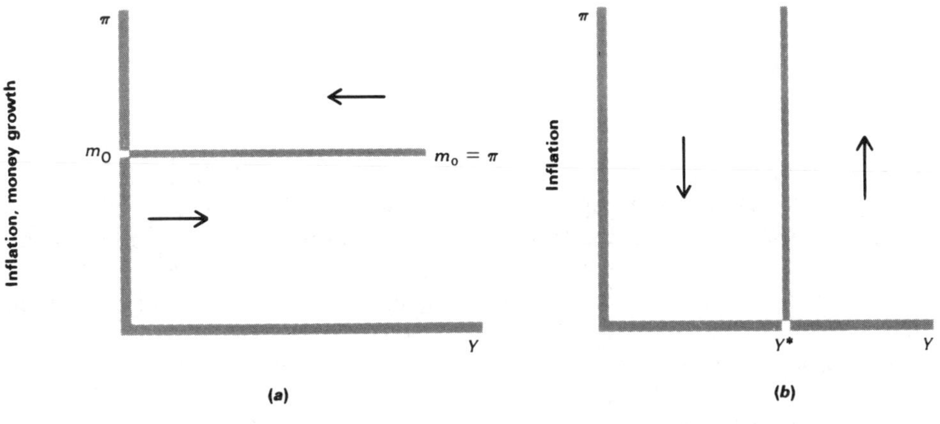

Figure 18-1

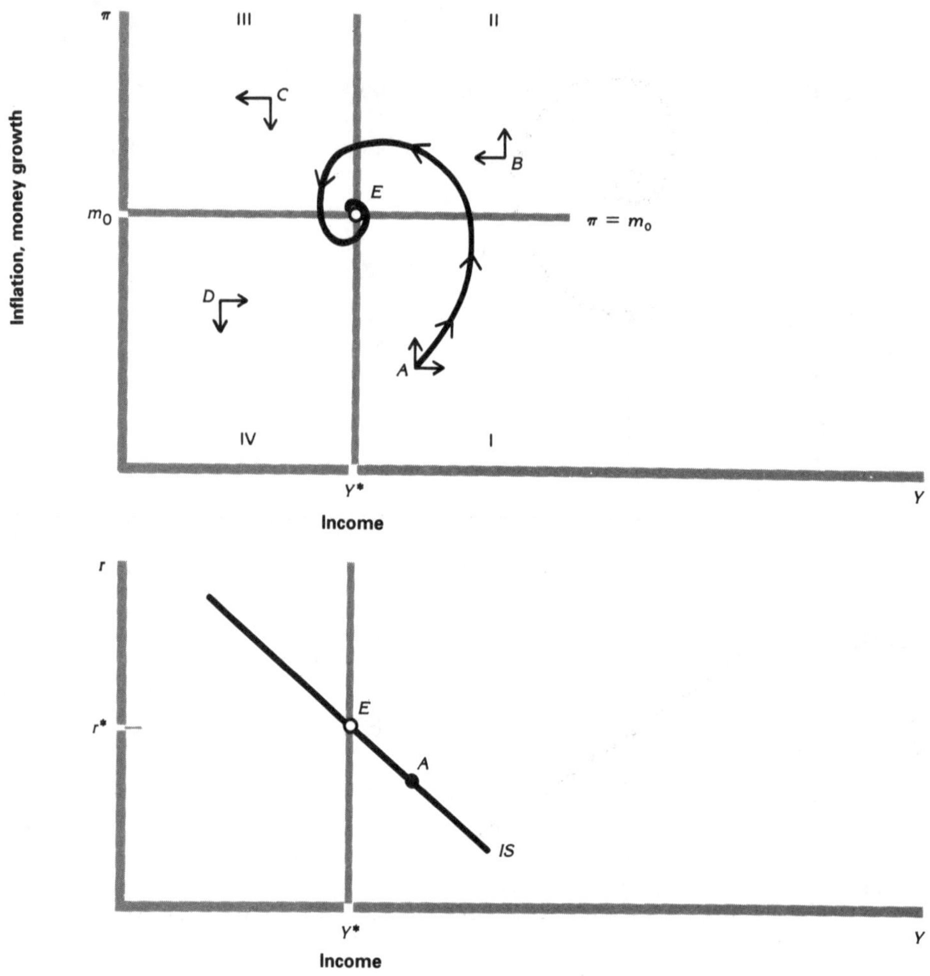

Figure 18-2

A permanent increase in the growth rate of the money stock shifts the $\pi = m$ schedule upward as in the upper portion of Figure 18-3 [text Figure 18-3]. With adaptive expectations the expected inflation rate is last period's inflation rate, so the equilibrium real interest rate initially falls. With output above its full-employment level, the inflation rate is rising. Output eventually returns to Y^*, the real interest rate returns to r^*, and the inflation rate rises to its new level, m', which is the new growth rate of the money stock. The adjustment path looks something like the path drawn in the upper portion of Figure 18-3.

In contrast, with the assumption of rational expectations, the economy will immediately jump to the new $\pi = m$ point at full employment.

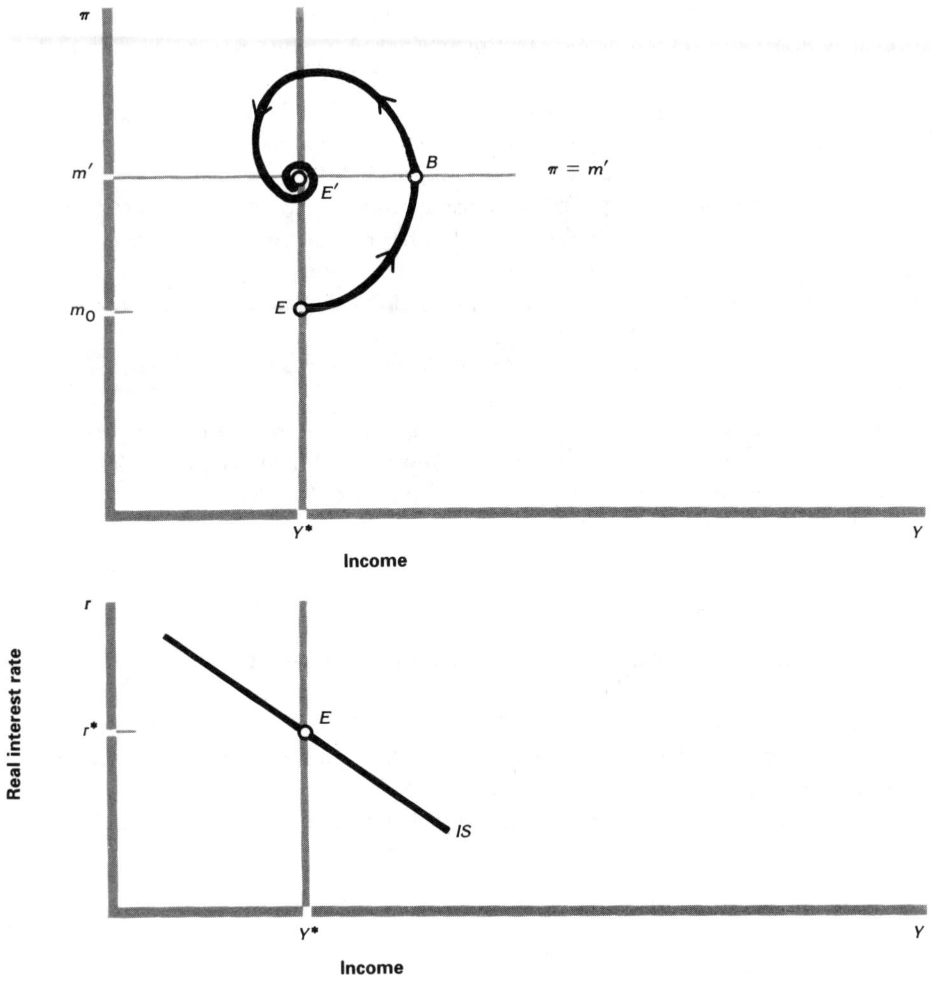

Figure 18-3

The Fisher equation

$$r^* = i - \pi^*$$

helps us track the nominal interest rate during the adjustment of the economy to a new equilibrium. If inflationary expectations are adaptive, the nominal interest rate adjusts slowly to changes in the growth rate of the money stock. If, for example, there is a permanent increase in the growth rate of the money, the nominal interest rate will initially fall by the same amount as the initial decline in the real rate, but eventually rise above its initial level by the amount of the increase in the steady-state inflation rate.

The declining phase of the nominal interest rate adjustment path is called the *liquidity effect* to denote the impact of increased real balances on the interest rate. The income effect — which causes the nominal and real interest rates to begin to rise — results from the fact that increased nominal income causes the real demand for money to rise. The Fisher or expectations effect denotes the adjustment of the nominal interest rate to changing inflationary expectations.

A sustained increase in the growth rate of the money stock must eventually reduce real money balances. In order for this to occur, there must be a period during the adjustment to the increase in which the price level rises more rapidly than the money stock.

18.2 Empirical evidence suggests that changes in the monetary growth rate are associated with changes in the inflation rate, though with a lag. The length of the lag is not constant but may range anywhere from a few months to several years.

For a given, stable money demand function, we have

$$\pi = m - \eta g^*$$

where η is the elasticity of real money demand with respect to output and g^* is the growth rate of real GDP. Data for different countries indicate that π does not follow the relationship above precisely. In all likelihood, shifts in the position of the money demand function have played an important role in determining the relationship between π and m.

By definition, the real interest rate is the difference between the nominal interest rate and the inflation rate.

$$r \equiv i - \pi$$

The *Fisher effect* suggests that, in the long run, an increase in the inflation rate increases the nominal interest rate one for one and does not change the real interest rate.

In Chapter 9 we introduced the interest parity condition which states that the domestic nominal interest rate (i) equals the foreign nominal interest rate (i^*) plus the expected rate of depreciation of the domestic currency (x):

$$i = i^* + x$$

In the long run we would expect differences in inflation rates between two countries to be the major determinant of movements in the nominal exchange rate between the two countries. Denoting the domestic and foreign inflation rates by π and π^* respectively, we can write

$$x = \pi - \pi^*$$

Therefore,

$$i = i^* + \pi - \pi^*$$

or,

$$i - \pi = i^* - \pi$$

Therefore, in the long run, nominal interest rates will differ across countries according to the differences in inflation rates, and real interest rates will be equalized by interest parity.

18.3 The creation of high-powered money serves as an alternative to taxation in financing a deficit. "Tax" revenue obtained by money creation is known as *seigniorage*. The government collects seigniorage by creating high-powered money that is used to pay for the government's expenditure on goods and services.

The amount collected through the inflation tax is

$$\text{Inflation tax revenue} = \text{inflation rate} \times \text{real money base}$$

The government cannot collect inflation tax revenue at arbitrarily high rates of inflation. Eventually, as the money growth rate becomes large, the real money stock will fall to zero. In practice, the amount of inflation tax revenue collected by governments in developed countries is small, although there have been examples where as much as 10 percent of GDP was collected through seigniorage.

It is possible that debt-financing of a deficit may be more inflationary than money financing, as when a government finances a current deficit through debt, it incurs an obligation to pay interest on that debt in the future. If the national debt is growing relative to GDP, then ultimately the government will have to raise taxes or raise the inflation rate to meet its debt obligations.

Increasing nominal interest rates increases the size of the measured deficit, but the measured deficit gives a distorted picture of its true size. A better measure is the inflation-corrected deficit, which accounts for the fact that the real value of the government's outstanding debt falls with inflation.

18.4 A rough characterization of a hyperinflation economy would be one for which the annual inflation rate was 1000 percent per year or more.

All hyperinflating economies suffer from large budget deficits and rapid monetary growth. Usually the tax collecting system has broken down, and the government has resorted to the collection of seigniorage. Countries that have been able to stop a hyperinflation have done so by balancing the government budget and (eventually) reducing the growth rate of the money supply.

Thinking Like an Economist

In this section we are going to take a closer look at the real rate of interest and the *Fisher effect*. The Fisher effect is a classical proposition concerning the long-run relationship between the inflation rate and the real interest rate. Classical macroeconomics teaches us that a change in the rate of growth of the nominal money stock will lead to an equal change in the rate of price inflation (if real income remains constant). The Fisher effect states that this increase in price inflation will lead to a one-for-one increase in the nominal interest rate, leaving the real interest rate unaltered.

In order to see how the effect may come about, let us consider it from the point of view of the individual economic agent. Consider the following scenario. You have \$100 today and you are considering buying a good whose price today is \$1 per unit. Therefore, you could purchase 100 units of the good. Instead of buying the good, you could purchase a nominal bond today. If the bond bears a 10% rate of return you will have \$110 next period. Suppose that you decide that you would rather purchase the bond because you wish to be able to purchase 10 more units of the good next period. However, you can only purchase 110 units of the good next period if the price of the good remains at \$1. If the price of the good increases while you are holding the bond, you will only be able to purchase less than 110 units of the good. For instance, if the good costs \$1.15 next period, and you have \$110, you are only able to buy approximately 95 units of the good, and you are actually worse off having bought the bond.

The above example illustrates the real rate of interest, measured in units of goods (of course, all real variables are measured in units of goods). One hundred units of the good could have been purchased instead of buying the bond, and 95 units of the good could be purchased because you bought the bond and received a 10% nominal rate of return. Therefore, the real rate of interest equals 95 – 100 = –5 units of the good. We would get the same answer using the formula in the text:

$$r = i - \pi$$

Substituting in the numbers from the above example, $i = 10$, $\pi = 15$ and therefore, $r = -5$, thus showing that you are 5 units of real goods worse off.

The Fisher effect proposes that the inflation rate cannot lower (or raise) the real interest rate in the long run. The reason is that rational agents would not buy a bond that bears a nominal rate of return that is less than the required real return (that is the equilibrium real interest rate) plus full compensation for expected inflation. In the above example, if you knew with certainty that the inflation rate was going to be 15%, you would not purchase the bond.

Our macroeconomic models tell us that in long-run equilibrium, expected inflation equals actual inflation. Therefore, in the long run agents will not have their real returns lowered by a known increase in the inflation rate, and accordingly the nominal interest rate must increase so that the real interest rate does not change.

Key Terms

Fisher effect
Liquidity effect
Expectations effect
Hyperinflation
Inflation tax
Seigniorage
Inflation-corrected deficit

Graph It 18

In the 1980s, interest payments on the national debt became a substantial portion of federal government spending. Because a large part of the nominal interest payments go to cover inflation, rather than the real cost of interest, it can be hard to see how big the debt really is. Graph It 18 asks you to do a little inflation accounting to get a handle on this problem.

Tables 18-1 and 18-2 track the debt using five rows of information. The row "Spending deficit" shows how much the government spent on goods and services in excess of its revenues. (Assume the government does all its spending on the first day

Table 18-1

Year	1	2	3	4	5
Spending deficit	100.00	100.00	100.00	100.00	100.00
Beginning debt	100.00	202.00	_____	_____	_____
Interest	2.00	4.04	_____	_____	_____
Price level, end of year	1.00	1.00	_____	_____	_____
Real debt, end of year	102.00	206.04	_____	_____	_____

Table 18-2

Year	1	2	3	4	5
Spending deficit	100.00	110.00	121.00	133.00	146.41
Beginning debt	100.00	222.00	_____	_____	_____
Interest	12.00	26.64	_____	_____	_____
Price level, end of year	1.10	1.21	_____	_____	_____
Real debt, end of year	101.82	205.49	_____	_____	_____

of the year.) The row "Beginning debt" is last year's beginning debt plus last year's interest plus this year's spending deficit. The "Interest" row shows the interest due on the beginning debt plus the spending deficit. "Price level" records the price at the end of the year. "Real debt" equals the spending deficit plus beginning debt plus interest, all deflated by the price level.

We want to know what difference inflation makes. Fill out the remainder of Table 18-1, which is based on zero inflation and a 2 percent interest rate. Then fill out Table 18-2, which is based on 10 percent inflation and a 12 percent interest rate. (Notice that the real spending deficit is the same in both cases.) What is the dollar difference in what the government owes by the end of year 5? How large is the real difference?

Fill-In Questions

1. An extremely rapid inflation is called a(n) ________________ .
2. Government revenue from printing money results in what is sometimes called an ________________ .
3. The revenue the government receives from printing money is also known as ________________ .
4. Official deficit figures can be adjusted for the drop in the value of the national debt due to inflation to obtain the ________________ .
5. The ________________ describes the connection between the nominal interest rate, the real interest rate, and the expected inflation rate.
6. An increase in the money supply moves the *LM* curve and thus initially lowers the interest rate through the ________________ .
7. As nominal income starts to rise, interest rates start to rise because of the ________________ .
8. Another name for the Fisher effect is the ________________ .

True-False Questions

T F 1. In the long run, growth of the money supply has a major effect on the inflation rate.

T F 2. In the long run, growth of the money supply has a major effect on real output.

T F 3. In the long run, growth of the money supply has a major effect on nominal GDP.

T F **4.** In the long run, growth of the money supply has a major effect on the nominal interest rate.

T F **5.** In the long run, growth of the money supply has a major effect on the real interest rate.

T F **6.** Hyperinflations are always caused by very rapid money growth.

T F **7.** Hyperinflations are usually accompanied by very large budget deficits.

T F **8.** The economy responds to a change in money growth with a lag of uncertain length.

T F **9.** The nominal interest rate and the inflation rate are tightly linked.

Multiple-Choice Questions

1. If the nominal money supply is growing at 6 percent a year while the real money supply is constant at $100 billion, then the "inflation tax" is
- **(a)** $100 billion
- **(b)** $60 billion
- **(c)** $6 billion
- **(d)** 0

2. When the rate of inflation is greater than the rate of money growth, the real money supply
- **(a)** rises
- **(b)** falls
- **(c)** remains constant
- **(d)** may do any of **(a)**, **(b)**, or **(c)**

3. A hyperinflation usually ends with
- **(a)** a reduction of the budget deficit
- **(b)** a reduction in the growth in the money supply
- **(c)** a currency reform
- **(d)** all the above

4. An increase in the rate of growth of the money supply
- **(a)** raises interest rates
- **(b)** lowers interest rates
- **(c)** first lowers, then raises interest rates
- **(d)** first raises, then lowers interest rates

5. If expected inflation rises by one percentage point, in the long run the nominal interest rate will
- **(a)** remain constant
- **(b)** rise by less than one point
- **(c)** rise by one point
- **(d)** rise by more than one point

6. If expected inflation rises by one percentage point, in the short run the expected real interest rate will
- **(a)** remain constant
- **(b)** fall by less than one point
- **(c)** fall by one point
- **(d)** fall by more than one point

7. If expected inflation rises by one percentage point, in the long run the expected real interest rate will
   (a) remain constant
   (b) fall by less than one point
   (c) fall by one point
   (d) fall by more than one point

8. As the inflation rate rises, the revenue from the "inflation tax"
   (a) rises
   (b) falls
   (c) rises, but eventually starts to fall
   (d) falls, but eventually starts to rise

9. An increase in the rate of the money growth will eventually cause the real money supply to
   (a) be higher
   (b) be lower
   (c) remain constant
   (d) do any of **(a)**, **(b)**, or **(c)**, depending on the country

10. Compared with the speed of movement of the economy under adaptive expectations, the speed under rational expectations is
    (a) faster
    (b) slower
    (c) faster, but adjustment is incomplete
    (d) slower, but adjustment is more complete

Problems

1. What rate of money growth can Canada sustain without any inflation?

2. If the annual rate of inflation is 1000 percent, what is the monthly rate of inflation? If the annual rate of inflation is 19,000 percent, what is the daily rate of inflation?

3. Suppose that the nominal interest rate is 50 percent per year and the inflation rate is 48 percent per year. If you invest $100 today, what will be the real value of your investment in ten years?

CHAPTER 19 *Monetarism and the Fight Against Inflation in Canada*

Focus of the Chapter

- The Great Depression of the 1930s gave rise to Keynesian economics, which remained the mainstream until inflation became a major problem in the 1960s. During the early 1970s, *monetarist* views were influential in the formulation of policy.
- We begin this chapter with a description of monetarism and its influence on Bank of Canada policy. This is followed by a discussion of anti-inflationary policy in Canada from the mid-1970s to the early 1990s.

Section Summaries

19.1 *Monetarism*, whose foremost spokesman is Milton Friedman, has the central tenet that the money supply is the most important determinant of prices and of economic activity. Friedman has summarized monetarism by saying:

> *I regard the description of our position as "money is all that matters for changes in nominal income and for* short-run *changes in real income" as an exaggeration but one that gives the right flavor of our conclusions.**

Friedman has also argued that there are "long and variable lags" in the connection between the money supply and economic activity. He suggests that because the money supply is so important but its effects so hard to predict, we should use a *monetary rule*. For example, the money supply ought to be increased 4 percent every year without regard to the current state of the economy.

Monetarists have further argued that the central bank should use a *money supply target* rather than an interest rate target. The three themes which seem to best distinguish a monetarist are:

(a) Emphasis on the growth rate of the money stock

(b) Arguments against fine-tuning

(c) A relatively greater weight on the costs of inflation than on the costs of unemployment

Many of Friedman's basic propositions are now accepted by mainstream economists.

19.2 In the mid-1970s the Bank of Canada shifted to a monetarist policy involving target ranges for the growth rate of narrowly defined money (M1). A gradualist strategy was implemented through successive reductions in the target range.

19.3 The success of the Bank of Canada's policy during the period 1975–80 was hindered by three problems:

(a) Supply shocks in the form of oil price increases exacerbated inflation.

(b) The Bank's policy may have been too gradual. Indeed, this strategy was abandoned in 1981 when there was a severe tightening of monetary policy.

(c) Instability in the demand for money impaired the usefulness of money supply targets. For this reason the setting of targets was discontinued in 1982.

In 1987 John Crow, the new Governor of the Bank of Canada, announced a renewed fight against inflation. In early 1991 the Governor and the Minister of Finance jointly announced declining target rates of inflation. In response to a tightening of monetary policy in 1990, the economy fell into a recession and the inflation rate fell below 3 percent in 1991. In early 1992 the target of 2 percent inflation by the end of 1995 had already been met.

---

* "A Theoretical Framework for Monetary Analysis," *Journal of Political Economy*, March/April 1970, p. 217.

Thinking Like an Economist

In the text we quoted Franco Modigliani who said "We are all monetarists now." Professor Modigliani was referring to the fact that we (almost) all believe in the importance of money in the macro economy. One exception would be the adherents to real business cycle theory who believe that money is endogenous, and therefore changes in money are a *result of* macro activity rather than *causing* macroeconomic changes.

Even if most economists do believe in the importance of money, it is not true that we all agree on how money is important and why money is important. Consider first Keynesian economists, a great deal of whom have a belief that, because markets do not necessarily clear in the short run, then short-run adjustment is extremely important. This group believes that, for instance, if you decrease the rate of growth of the nominal money stock, nominal and real interest rates will increase, and real economic activity will decrease. Because these effects are predictable, monetary policy is a powerful stabilization tool in the short run. These economists also believe that eventually (that is, in the long run) money is neutral, but that the long run may be so far off that it is not important.

Now consider an adherent to Friedman's point of view. Friedman would agree that changes in the nominal money stock will have important real effects in the short run. However, Friedman argues that, because the lags in the effects of monetary policy are long and variable, we cannot predict the short-run effects of monetary policy. Friedman argues that we do understand the long-run effects of monetary policy, that is, the neutrality of money, and therefore, monetary policy should not be used as a short-run stabilization tool, but rather be aimed at the long-run goal of achieving some steady-state inflation rate.

Finally consider the New Classical school. These economists agree with Friedman, in that they believe that we know the long-run effects of monetary policy, and therefore monetary policy should be aimed at the long-run inflation rate. However, they believe this, not because monetary policy has powerful short-run effects, but rather because all markets clear and therefore, there are no real effects associated with monetary policy (except of course for temporary misperceptions, as in the Lucas model).

Of course, not all economists fall neatly into these three camps, but most can be categorized according to whether they think that we should pay close attention to the short run, or it is the long run that matters. Therefore, we are (mostly) all monetarists, but monetarists with different emphases.

Key Terms

Monetary rule
Anti-Inflation Board (AIB)
Monetarism

Graph It 19

Table 19-1 provides quarterly data on the unemployment rate and the inflation rate during the 1981–82 recession. Use this data to plot the short-run Phillips curve for this period.

Table 19-1

Year & Quarter		Unemployment Rate (%)	Inflation Rate (%)
1981	3	7.4	13.2
	4	8.3	13.7
1982	1	8.9	13.1
	2	10.4	12.4
	3	12.2	11.5
	4	12.7	10.4

Chart 19-1

Fill-In Questions

1. The school of economic thought "led" by Milton Friedman is the ________________ school.

2. An example of a(n) ____________________ is that the nominal money supply should grow at a strict 4 percent a year.

3. Monetarists argue that the effects on GDP of a change in the growth rate of money occur with ____________________ and ____________________ lags.

4. Monetarists believe that monetary policy should not be aimed at ____________________ targets, but rather at ____________________ targets.

5. In the mid-1970s the Bank of Canada adopted a policy of ____________________ ____________________.

6. In early 1991 the Governor of the Bank of Canada and the Minister of Finance jointly announced declining target ____________________ ____________________ ____________________.

True-False Questions

T F 1. Monetarists believe that the private sector is inherently unstable.

T F 2. Monetarists believe in the importance of the money supply for determining real economic activity.

T F 3. Monetarists believe that the money supply is the primary determinant of nominal GDP in the long run.

T F 4. Monetarists believe that the money supply is the primary determinant of real GDP in the long run.

T F 5. Monetarists emphasize the use of a money supply target instead of an interest rate target.

T F 6. Monetarists believe that in the short run monetary policy can have real effects.

Multiple-Choice Questions

1. Friedman has argued that monetary policy should be conducted according to
   - **(a)** a nominal interest rate rule
   - **(b)** a money supply rule
   - **(c)** a policy of fine-tuning
   - **(d)** none of the above

2. A high nominal interest rate, together with a high inflation rate, means
   - **(a)** a high real interest rate
   - **(b)** a low real interest rate
   - **(c)** restrictive monetary policy
   - **(d)** money is neutral

3. The Bank of Canada had to abandon monetary targeting because
   - (a) of financial innovation
   - (b) of excessive gradualism
   - (c) the M1 demand function became unstable
   - (d) all of the above

4. Monetarists believe that
   - (a) the private sector is inherently unstable
   - (b) the private sector in inherently stable
   - (c) the private sector may be stable, but needs government intervention
   - (d) monetary policy will stabilize the private sector

5. Monetarists place a greater weight on
   - (a) the costs of inflation relative to unemployment
   - (b) the costs of unemployment relative to inflation
   - (c) the long-run destabilizing effects of monetary policy
   - (d) the importance of the nominal interest rate

Problems

1. In the early 1980s the Bank of Canada was faced with large amount of innovation in financial markets and the instability of the M1 money demand function. Discuss how these two events are related.
2. Discuss whether you think that the financial innovation was caused by the Bank of Canada policy or whether it was exogenous to policy.

CHAPTER 20 *Current Issues in Macro-economic Policy*

Focus of the Chapter

- The lack of success in reducing inflation in the 1970s led to a reconsideration of the premises of macroeconomics and the development of the *rational expectations* approach.
- The rational expectations/equilibrium approach suggests that markets clear, that most policy is ineffective, and that the economy is, at least in a sense, efficient. New ideas — such as efficiency wage theory and small menu cost theory — have arisen to explain why policy might indeed be effective and why the economy may not always be efficient.
- These ideas gave rise to the New Keynesian school of thought. It is an attempt to combine the Keynesian recognition that the economy does not adjust instantly and smoothly to shocks, with an insistence on building their models on micro-economic foundations.

Section Summaries

20.1 The rational expectations/equilibrium approach to macroeconomics emphasizes the ideas that

(a) Individuals use information efficiently and do not (systematically) make forecasting errors.

(b) Individuals maximize utility, firms maximize profits, and markets are in equilibrium.

As a theory of expectations, the rational expectations assumption implies that effective policy cannot be based on attempts to systematically "fool" the public.

Members of the rational expectations/equilibrium school have attempted to explain business cycles while adhering to the notion that all markets clear.

One story offered is the following. Suppose the economy is composed of many markets. A supplier in market i knows the price of his or her own product, but not the aggregate price level. Each supplier's output is an increasing function of the supplier's price relative to the expected aggregate price level.

Shocks to the economy take two forms: shocks to relative prices, which sum to zero across markets, and shocks to the aggregate price level, which affect all prices in the same proportion. An anticipated increase in the money supply is known (by producers) to increase all prices in the same proportion and cannot lead to an increase in output. However, an unanticipated increase in the money supply will raise output in all markets because every producer mistakenly believes that the relative price of his or her product has increased.

Robert Lucas has used such a model to produce a Phillips curve type of relationship between output and inflation. The key feature of Lucas's work is that only unanticipated changes in the money stock (and, thus, the price level) produce variation in output.

20.2 Consider the model used in Chapter 16:

$$\text{Supply: } \pi = \pi^e + \lambda(y - y^*) + u$$
$$\text{Demand: } y = y_{-1} + \varphi(m - \pi) + v$$

Where u and v represent unpredictable shocks to the supply and demand curves. Using the Keynesian assumption of adaptive expectations, there are two sources of variation in income: the unsystematic disturbances caused by u and v, and the systematic disturbances generated by the structure of the model. The unsystematic disturbances can never be offset by deliberate policy measures.

Consider a countercyclical monetary policy rule based on knowledge of past behaviour of income and the inflation rate:

$$m = \pi_{-1} + \varphi(y_{-1} - y^*) + w$$

Using this rule, it can be shown that the systematic deviations of income from full employment can be eliminated. This supports the extreme Keynesian position that fine-tuning of the economy is possible.

Once the assumption of adaptive expectations is replaced with the assumption of rational expectations, the basic New Classical results of Chapters 8 and 16 can be shown to hold: changes in the money supply only affect output if they are unanticipated. More generally, under rational expectations, the variation in income is entirely unsystematic. This is because, using the above model, the only systematic variation in income arises from systematic mistakes in expectations formation, and this is eliminated under rational expectations. It follows that, under rational expectations, income is independent of the choice of policy rule. This is known as the *policy ineffectiveness proposition*.

Rational expectations/equilibrium theorists stress that policy will be more effective the more credible it is. They also adopt the view that since the public eventually catches onto the nature of changes in monetary and fiscal policy, the best policies are stable policies. The rational expectations school argues that stable policy is ensured by effective institutional reform.

20.3 Equilibrium real business cycle theory takes the view that business cycles are mainly a consequence of real shocks such as shifts in labour productivity and government spending. Equilibrium business cycle theorists believe that business cycles are propagated by large swings in the supply of labour over time, a phenomenon which is known as the "intertemporal substitution of labour supply." According to real business cycle theorists, changes in the money supply are correlated with movements in output because the central bank accommodates movements in GDP. Changes in the money supply are not the cause of, but rather are caused by, changes in GDP.

20.4 New Keynesians are similar to classical economists in that they believe models should be built that are based on micro foundations of individual behaviour, but are similar to old-style Keynesians in that they believe that markets do not always clear quickly in response to a shock.

New Keynesianism is built on three main micro foundations: efficiency wage theory, imperfect competition, and imperfect information in financial markets. Efficiency wage theory argues that firms may pay above-market wages to attract more efficient workers. In combination with small menu costs and imperfect competition, efficiency wage theory can account for sticky wages and prices as well as unemployment. In this case, an increase in the nominal money stock will lead to an increase in output.

Thinking Like an Economist

Throughout this *Study Guide* we have attempted to show that macroeconomics can generally be divided into two schools of thought. First, there are economists who take a long-run view of macroeconomic events, and second, there are those who think that the short run is important.

Generally speaking, those who adhere to the long-run view could be labelled "classical" economists. They believe that markets clear and that countercyclical policy could actually be destabilizing. Pre-Keynesian classical economists are an example of this school of thought, and it is the thinking of these economists that gives us the vertical long-run aggregate supply curve that we have seen throughout the text. As well, New Classical economists belong to this group, as they are basically pre-Keynesian classical economist who believe that not only do expectations matter, but that expectations are formed in a rational manner.

Milton Friedman and the original monetarists also believe in long-run analysis, but for a different reason than above. They believe that markets do not always clear in the short run, but that the short-run response of an economy to monetary policy is variable and unpredictable. Therefore, the long run is the only thing that we understand well, and accordingly, we should concentrate on the long-run response of the economy. In this sense the monetarists are closer to the classical school.

The other school of thought comprises those who think that some markets — especially those for wages and prices — are very slow to adjust in the short run. In this situation, policy can be beneficial in that it can help to speed up adjustment of the economy in response to shocks. This group is essentially what we have been labelling as Keynesian throughout the text.

It may seem as if we have different models to describe the economy when we are discussing the different schools of thought. However, this is not true. Economists can always agree that it is supply and demand which are important, and in macroeconomics it is aggregate supply and aggregate demand. The basic aggregate supply aggregate demand model is shown in Figure 20-1.

Suppose that the economy is in an initial equilibrium at *E*. Assume that the monetary authorities pursue expansionary monetary policy so that the *DAD* curve shifts out to *DAD′*. Individuals in each school of thought would agree that the new long-run equilibrium is at *E″*. The disagreement arises in discussing the path to equilibrium. A pre-Keynesian classical economist would say that you go directly, and instantly, to *E″*, as all markets always clear. Notice then, that this implies that *SAS* does not exist, which must be true for a classical economist, as the derivation of *SAS* was built on sluggish adjustment of wages and prices. A New Classical economist would say that you may possibly go to *E′ for one period* if there are misperceptions of the inflation rate. However, if there were another nominal shock after the economy had reached equilibrium at *E″*, rational expectations would dictate that the economy would never go to the same *E′* again, as rational agents would not make the same mistake twice. This implies that *SAS may* exist, but it cannot be exploited for policy purposes. A Keynesian economist would say that, not only would you go to *E′* in response to a policy shock, but the adjustment to *E″* would be long and involve overshooting and stagflation. Further, the Keynesian economist would say that a similar path would be followed each time there was a nominal shock. Notice, finally, that Friedman would say that you would go to *E′* and *eventually* to *E″*, but because the short-run effects of a nominal shock are unpredictable, another nominal shock

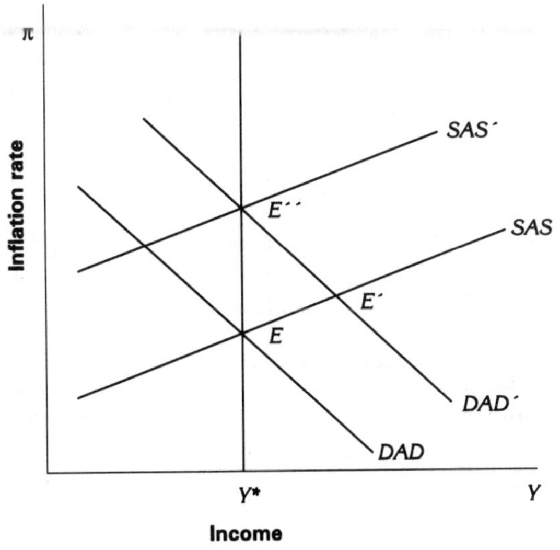

Figure 20-1

would not necessarily drive the economy to E', nor would the economy follow the same path to E''.

Therefore, you can see that there is not so much disagreement as differing emphasis on the path to long-run equilibrium.

Key Terms

New Classical macroeconomics
Rational expectations/equilibrium approach
Lucas supply curve
Imperfect information
Real business cycles
Propagation mechanism
Intertemporal substitution of leisure
Productivity shock
Efficiency wage
Small menu costs
New Keynesianism
Policy ineffectiveness proposition

Graph It 20

Table 20-1 provides quarterly data on the unemployment rate and the inflation rate during the period 1990 quarter 4 to 1992 quarter 1. In a manner similar to that of Graph It 19, use this data to plot the short-run Phillips curve for this period.

Table 20-1

Year & Quarter		Unemployment Rate (%)	Inflation Rate (%)
1990	4	9.3	5.0
1991	1	11.7	6.2
	2	9.8	5.8
	3	9.3	5.4
	4	10.2	3.8
1992	1	12.5	1.7

Chart 20-1

Fill-In Questions

1. The relatively new school of economic thought that holds the belief that only unanticipated changes in policy have any real effect is the ________________ school.

2. ________________ theory suggests that economic fluctuations have nothing to do with money, but rather arise from shocks to productivity and aggregate supply changes.

3. Recent alternatives to the rational expectations school include ________________ theory . . .

4. . . . and the idea of ________________ .

5. The amount by which temporary wage fluctuations affect how much people work depends on the ________________ .

6. New Keynesians believe in the theory of ________________ wages.

True-False Questions

T F 1. Keynesians believe that anticipated changes in the money supply are a major determinant of economic activity.

T F 2. *Rational expectations theorists* believe that anticipated changes in the money supply are a major determinant of economic activity.

T F 3. Real business cycle theory teaches that the nominal money supply is exogenous.

T F 4. In the rational expectations equilibrium approach, money is always neutral.

T F 5. With adaptive expectations, monetary policy is capable of reducing the systematic variance in output.

Multiple-Choice Questions

1. Rational expectations theory suggests that
   - **(a)** only unexpected changes in the stock of money affect the price level
   - **(b)** only unexpected changes in the stock of money affect the level of output
   - **(c)** only expected changes in the stock of money affect the price level
   - **(d)** only expected changes in the stock of money affect the level of output

2. The idea that surprise increases in the money supply increase GDP is associated with
   - **(a)** Keynesians
   - **(b)** monetarists
   - **(c)** rational expectations theory
   - **(d)** all the above

3. The idea that small menu costs are important is associated with
   - **(a)** New Classical economics
   - **(b)** Keynesian economics
   - **(c)** Classical economics
   - **(d)** New Keynesian economics

4. The policy ineffectiveness proposition is associated with
   - **(a)** New Classical economics
   - **(b)** Keynesian economics
   - **(c)** Classical economics
   - **(d)** New Keynesian economics

5. Which of the following attempts to build models based on microeconomic foundations?
   (a) Classical economics
   (b) New Classical economics
   (c) New Keynesian economics
   (d) all of the above

Problems

1. In the short run, we know that expansionary monetary policy lowers the nominal interest rate, yet in the long run expansionary monetary policy (an increase in the growth rate of money) increases the nominal interest rate. Discuss how you reconcile these two views.

CHAPTER 21 *Long-Term Growth and Productivity*

Focus of the Chapter

- We study here two related topics.
  1. *Potential output*:
     Potential output is determined by *factor inputs* and the state of *technology*. Technology is described by a *production function*.
  2. *Long-term growth*:
     By studying how factor inputs change over time, in particular how saving leads to the accumulation of capital, we can predict how potential output will change in the future.
- *In this chapter we always assume that GDP equals potential GDP.* We allow no role for aggregate demand and no role for incorrect expectations.

Section Summaries

21.1 Output depends on factor input and on the technology applied to that input. The *production function* relates output to input. Using Y to represent output and K and N to represent capital input and labour input, respectively, we can write a production function as

$$Y = AF(K, N)$$

The rate of growth of output can be written as

$$\frac{\Delta Y}{Y} = (1 - \theta)\frac{\Delta N}{N} + \theta\frac{\Delta K}{K} + \frac{\Delta A}{A}$$

where θ is capital's share in income, and A represents the level of technology. Thus the three sources of growth are more labour, more capital, and improved technology.

21.2 The growth rate in Canadian per capita output declined markedly after 1973. This decline in productivity growth has been attributed to a fall in the growth of the capital/labour ratio and to a decline in productivity in the oil and gas industry.

21.3 Supply-side economists argue that potential GDP can be increased by improving incentives to supply labour or to invest in new capital. While such effects clearly exist, they are fairly small and unlikely to have much short-run significance. They may be of greater importance in terms of very long-run economic well-being.

21.4 Growth theory is the study of the growth of factor inputs and the resultant growth in output. We assume that population grows at a constant percentage rate, $\Delta N/N \equiv n$. We also assume no technological change.

It is sometimes more convenient to think about output per capita. (*Per capita* is Latin for "by head," that is, per person.) We write output per capita as $x \equiv Y/N$ and capital per worker, also called the capital/labour ratio, as $k \equiv K/N$. We assume that the production function has *constant returns to scale.*

The *steady state* of the economy is the position in which capital per worker is constant. Just enough is saved to replace machinery that has worn out and to provide machines for new workers. Output per head is constant whenever capital grows as fast as population.

$$\frac{\Delta K}{K} = n$$

The change in capital is the difference between saving and depreciation. We assume that people save a constant fraction s of their income and that depreciation is a constant percentage d of the existing capital stock.

$$\Delta K = \text{saving} - \text{depreciation}$$
$$\Delta K = sY - dK$$

Dividing both sides by K and subtracting n from both sides,

$$\frac{\Delta K}{K} - n = \frac{sY}{K} - n - d$$

Recognizing that the rate of growth of capital minus the rate of growth of labour is the rate of growth of capital per head and that the ratio of output to capital is the same as the ratio of per capita output to per capita machinery,

$$\frac{\Delta k}{k} = \frac{sx}{k}(n + d)$$

$$\Delta k = sx - (n + d)k$$

This final formula looks formidable. All it says is that the amount of capital each worker has available rises when saving goes up and falls when depreciation rises or when capital must be spread out among more workers.

The growth process can be studied in terms of Figure 21-1 (text Figure 21-4). The x curve gives the level of output per head as a function of the capital/labour ratio. This is a graph of the production function. This sx curve shows the amount saved. The $(n + d)k$ line is the investment requirement, the amount needed to prevent capital per worker from falling.

To the left of point C, saving is above the investment requirement, so capital per worker is growing. To the right of point C, saving is less than required investment, so capital is falling. Point C is the steady state of the economy, the point at which the capital/labour ratio is neither rising nor falling. Steady-state per capita output is found by reading x off the production function directly above point C. Note that while C shows the long-run equilibrium of the economy, nothing prevents the economy from being away from steady-state equilibrium most of the time.

An increase in the saving rate increases steady-state per capita GDP. It does not change the growth rate of per capita GDP permanently. In the steady state, per capita

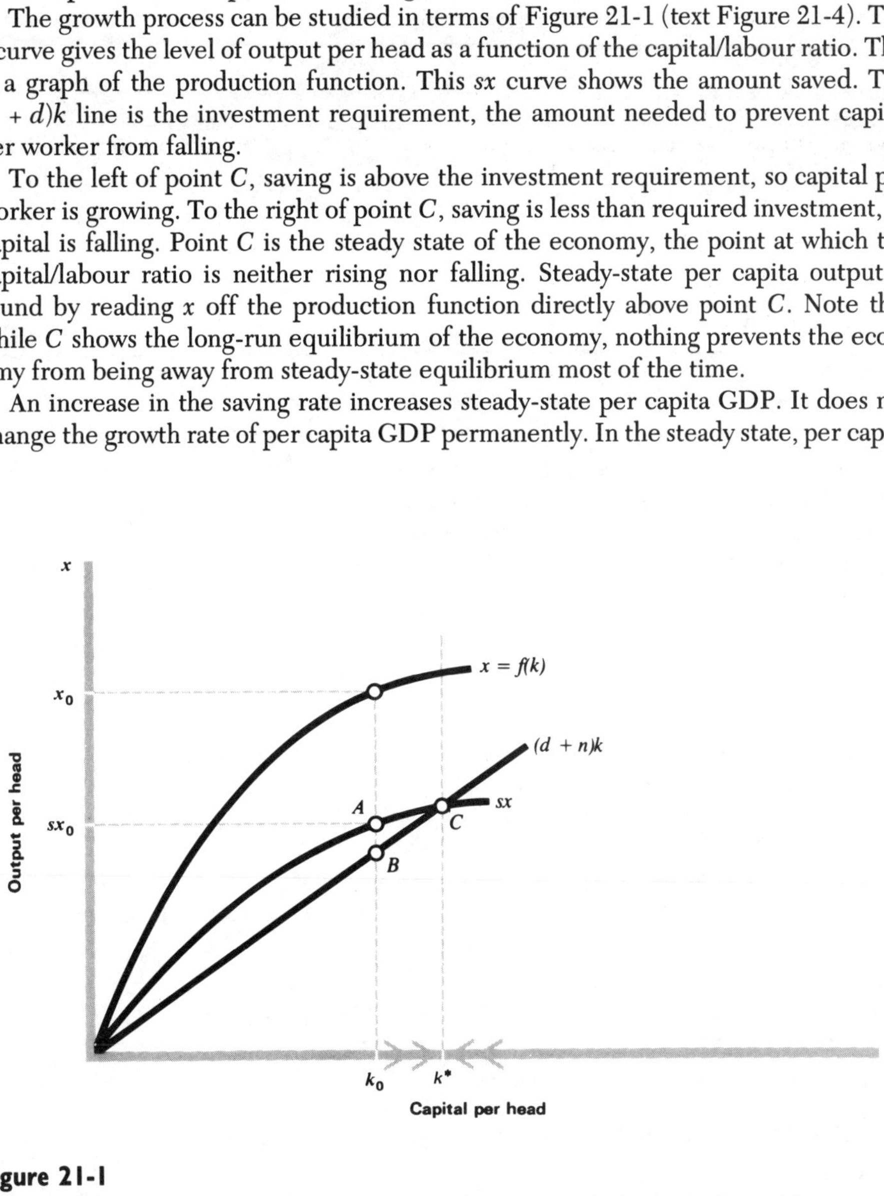

Figure 21-1

GDP is constant, so its growth rate is zero. Faster population growth reduces per capita GDP in the steady state. Even though GDP grows faster with higher population growth, it does not grow rapidly enough to keep up with the increasing population. Thus, faster population growth means a lower steady-state per capita GDP.

Key Terms

Potential output
Production function
Growth accounting
Sources of growth
Labour productivity
Technical progress
Growth of total factor productivity
Supply-side economics
Steady state
Limits of growth

Graph It 21

We know that an increase in investment increases both aggregate demand and aggregate supply. Aggregate demand rises because of the increase in I in the $C + I + G$, and aggregate supply rises because of the increase in the capital stock. How do the two effects compare? We'll use 1979 as a base year, because 1979 was the most recent year in which the economy was approximately at full employment. Assume that we could increase investment spending by 20 percent and that the aggregate demand multiplier on investment is 2.0.

Fill out Table 21-1. Notice that this table is headed "Short- and Long-Run . . ." If we permanently increase investment, we permanently increase aggregate demand. In other words, aggregate demand goes to a new, higher level and stays there, but it doesn't keep increasing.

In Table 21-2 we try to figure out the increase in aggregate supply. Aggregate supply goes up because increased investment increases the capital stock. Suppose that a 1 percent increase in the capital stock increases output by about one-fourth of 1 percent and that the capital stock is three times GDP. Using these facts, fill in Table 21-2 to calculate the supply side of the impact of a 1-year and a 5-year increase in investment. (Use the same annual investment increase as in Table 21-1.)

Table 21-1 ***Short- and Long-Run Increase in Aggregate Demand***

(1) 1979 investment (billions of 1981 dollars)	61
(2) 20% increase	______
(3) Increase in GDP [2 × (2)]	______
(4) Actual 1979 GDP	338

Table 21-2 *Short- and Long-Run Decrease in Aggregate Supply*

	1 Year	5 Years
(1) Increase in annual investment	______	______
(2) Cumulative increase in capital	______	______
(3) Total capital (roughly 3 × GDP)	______	______
(4) As percentage of capital	______	______
(5) Relative increase in production [1/4 × (4)]	______	______
(6) Increase in *AS* [GDP times (5)]	______	______
(7) As fraction of *AD* increase [100 × (6)/(3) above]	______ %	______ %

Fill-In Questions

1. When all factors of production are fully employed, we say that the economy is producing ______________ GDP.
2. Total output divided by the number of people is ______________ GDP.
3. Output per worker is a measure of labour ______________ .
4. The technological relation between output and inputs is described by the ______________ .
5. The addition of one unit of capital, with other inputs fixed, increases output by the ______________ .
6. Payment to capital as a fraction of GDP is called ______________ .
7. Technology is said to have ______________ when a proportional increase in all inputs results in a proportional increase in output.
8. GDP per person is constant in the ______________ .
9. Continuing growth of GDP per person is due to ______________ .

True-False Questions

T F 1. An exogenous addition to the capital stock leads to an immediate increase in per capita GDP.

T F 2. An exogenous addition to the capital stock leads to an increase in steady-state per capita GDP.

T F 3. An increase in the saving rate leads to an immediate increase in per capita GDP.

T F 4. An increase in the saving rate leads to an increase in steady-state GDP.

T F 5. An increase in the saving rate leads to an increase in the steady-state rate of growth of GDP.

T F 6. An increase in the rate of population growth leads to an immediate drop in GDP per capita.

T F 7. An increase in the rate of population growth leads to a drop in steady-state per capita GDP.

T F 8. An increase in the rate of population growth leads to a drop in steady-state GDP.

T F 9. A higher depreciation rate leads to lower steady-state capital.

T F 10. A higher depreciation rate leads to lower steady-state GDP.

Multiple-Choice Questions

1. The most important factor responsible for growth in per capita output in Canada has been
   (a) population growth
   (b) technological change
   (c) capital accumulation
   (d) stimulative government spending

2. Growth in real income per head
   (a) will necessarily come to a halt in the near future
   (b) will definitely continue in the future
   (c) may continue in the future because of technical progress
   (d) cannot be limited by the growth of factor supplies

3. Over the past 100 years, per capita output has grown about
   (a) 0.5 percent per year
   (b) 2 percent per year
   (c) 6 percent per year
   (d) 8 percent per year

4. Productivity growth in Canada
   (a) has been close to zero since World War II
   (b) slowed down markedly after 1973
   (c) slowed down markedly in the mid-1960s
   (d) has been steady since World War II

5. Assuming everyone is in the labour force, an increase in population causes
   (a) an immediate increase in GDP
   (b) an immediate increase in GDP per capita
   (c) immediate increases in both
   (d) no increases in either

6. A 15 percent increase in the capital stock leads to an increase in GDP of
(a) 0 percent **(c)** 15 percent
(b) between 0 and 15 percent **(d)** more than 15 percent

7. Labour's share of GDP in Canada is approximately
(a) 2 percent **(c)** 70 percent
(b) 25 percent **(d)** 98 percent

8. If the capital stock increases 15 percent while the labour force increases 7 percent, the capital/labour ratio increases approximately
(a) 2 percent **(c)** 8 percent
(b) 4 percent **(d)** 15 percent

9. If half the capital in the economy were to be destroyed, per capita GDP would drop
(a) not at all **(c)** to one-half its original level
(b) by less than half **(d)** by more than one-half

10. If population were suddenly to double, per capita GDP would
(a) remain unchanged **(c)** drop by less than one-half
(b) double **(d)** drop by more than one-half

Problems

The Cobb-Douglas production function is

$$Y = AKaN^{1-a}$$

1. Find the function that gives per capita GDP based on capital per person, using the Cobb-Douglas production function above.

2. Prove that if $a = 0.25$, labour's share of GDP will be 75 percent.

3. Assume that labour's share of GDP is 75 percent and capital's share is 25 percent. If the labour supply increases by 10 percent and the supply of capital increases by 20 percent, by how much does GDP increase? GDP per capita?

4. Assume the economy is initially in long-run equilibrium. Suppose half the capital of society is destroyed. Show the time path of per capita GDP.

5. Assume the economy is initially in long-run equilibrium. Suppose that the saving rate increases. Show the time path of per capita GDP.

ANSWERS *To Study Guide Questions and Problems*

Chapter 1

Graph It 1

Table 1-1

Year	GDP	Percentage Change from Previous Year
1971	287.0	—
1972	303.5	5.7
1973	326.9	7.7
1974	341.2	4.4
1975	350.1	2.6
1976	371.7	6.1
1977	385.1	3.6
1978	402.7	4.6
1979	418.3	3.9

Table 1-1 (continued)

Year	GDP	Percentage Change from Previous Year
1980	424.5	1.5
1981	440.1	3.7
1982	426.0	–3.2
1983	439.5	3.2
1984	467.2	6.3
1985	489.4	4.7
1986	505.7	3.3
1987	526.7	4.2
1988	551.4	4.7
1989	565.0	2.5
1990	567.5	0.4
1991	558.9	–0.2

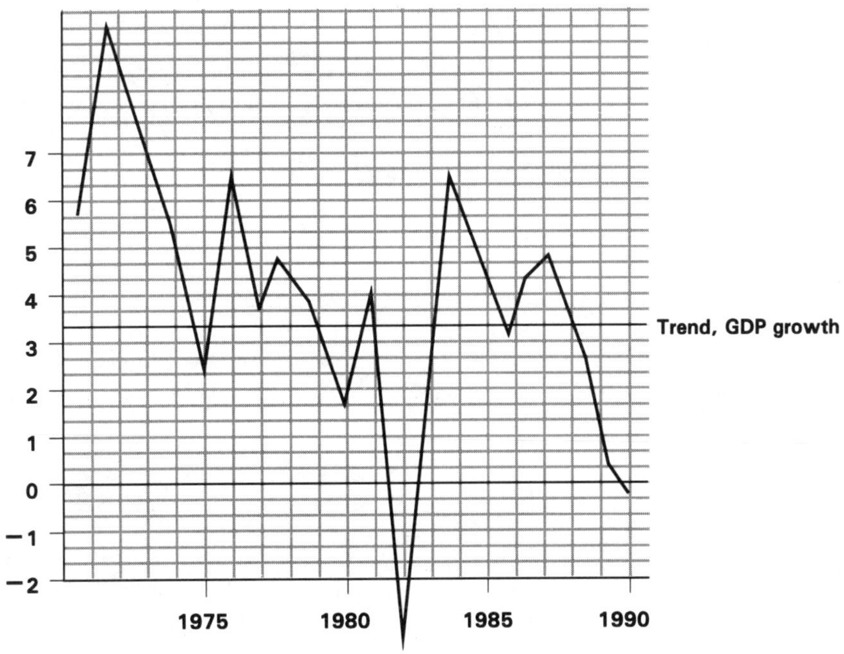

Chart 1-1

Fill-In Questions

1. potential output
2. output gap
3. trough
4. fiscal
5. monetary
6. stabilization policies
7. Okun's Law
8. recovery or expansion
9. recessions
10. rational
11. government intervention

True-False Questions

1. False. Okun's Law says that when GDP goes up, unemployment goes down.
2. True.

Chapter 2

Graph It 2

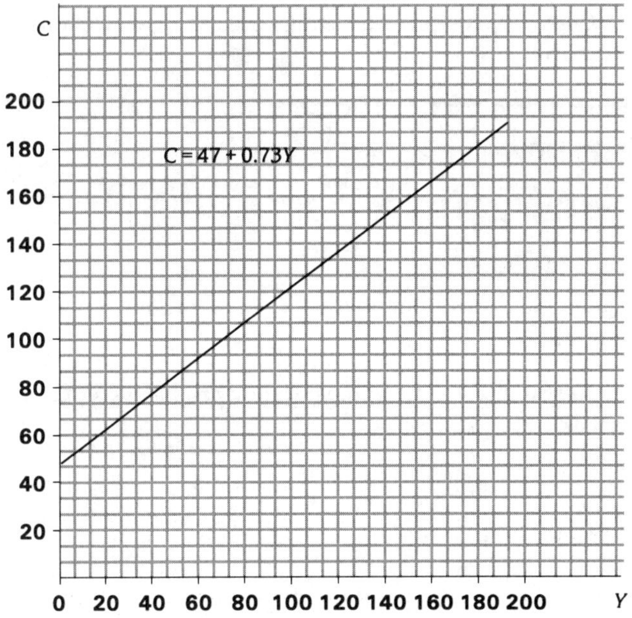

Chart 2-2

Fill-In Questions

1. gross domestic product (GDP)
2. depreciation (capital consumption allowance)
3. Canadian and nonresident
4. consumed, saved
5. transfers, taxes
6. nominal, real
7. GDP deflator
8. consumer price index (CPI)

9. the budget deficit, the foreign trade surplus
10. exports, imports

True-False Questions

1. False. Investment equals private savings plus the government budget surplus minus net exports.
2. False. Sale of a home just transfers assets from one person to another. No *new* production is added.
3. True.
4. True.
5. False. An individual can't spend that part of production needed to replace worn-out machines.
6. False. By "investment" we mean buying new productive equipment, not financial investment.
7. True.
8. True.
9. True.
10. True.

Multiple-Choice Questions

1. (b) **2.** (c) **3.** (b) **4.** (a) **5.** (d) **6.** (a) **7.** (d) **8.** (d) **9.** (c) **10.** (b)

Worked-Out Problems

1. $BD = G + TR - TA = 0$; therefore $G = TA - TR = 300$.
   $YD = C + S = 1000 + 100 = 1100$
   $YD = Y - TA + TR = 1100 = Y - 300$
   Therefore, GDP equals \$1400.

2. $TA - TR - G = I - S + NX$
   $-50 = I - 200 - 10$
   $I = \$160$

Chapter 3

Graph It 3

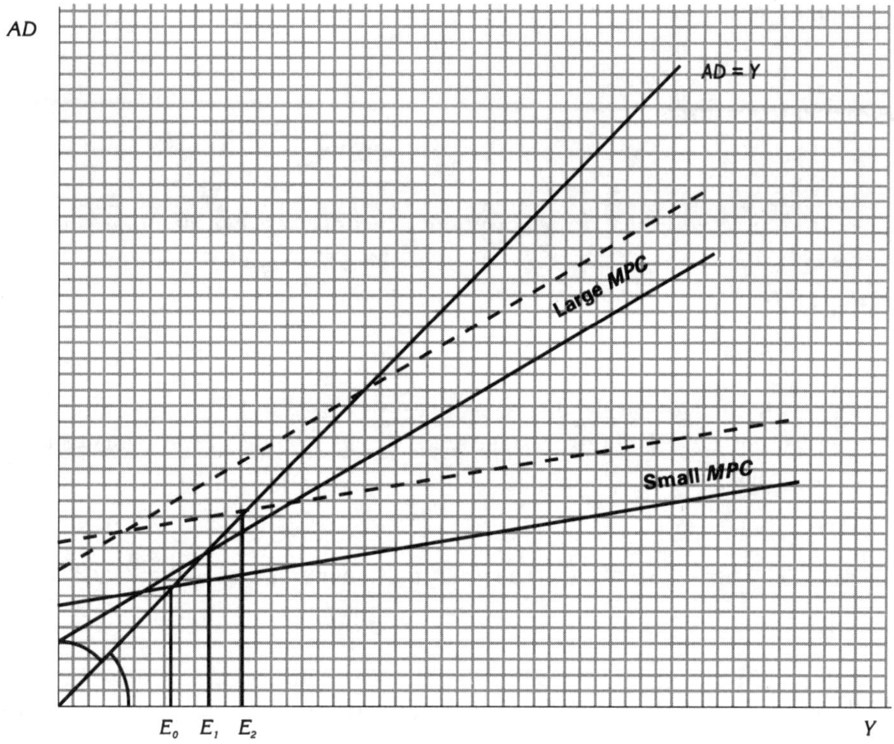

Chart 3-1

Fill-In Questions

1. equilibrium
2. the consumption function
3. marginal propensity to consume (*MPC*)
4. marginal propensity to save (*MPS*)
5. multiplier

6. budget deficit (BD)
7. automatic stabilizer
8. full-employment budget surplus (BS^*)
9. 1
10. planned saving, actual investment

True-False Questions

1. True.
2. False. More taxes mean lower disposable income, less consumption, and thus lower GDP.
3. True.
4. True.
5. False. The budget surplus increases because GDP, and thus taxes, rise. However, potential GDP doesn't change, and so the *full-employment* budget surplus doesn't change.
6. True.
7. False. The higher MPC means a larger multiplier and thus higher GDP.
8. True.
9. False. GDP will go up by $1/[1 - c(1 - t)] \cdot \Delta G$ because of the increase in G and down by $c/[1 - c(1 - t)] \cdot \Delta G$ because of the drop in TR. Thus the net effect is an increase of $(1 - c)/(1 - c + ct) \cdot \Delta G$.
10. False. This is just the opposite of having a high MPC.

Multiple-Choice Questions

1. (c) **2.** (a) **3.** (b) **4.** (b) **5.** (a) **6.** (b) **7.** (c) **8.** (a) **9.** (d) **10.** (b)

Worked-Out Problems

1. $C = \overline{C} + cYD$
   $Y_d = Y - TA$, combining these two equations
   $C = \overline{C} + c(Y - TA)$
   $Y \equiv C + I + G$, combining these two equations
   $Y = \overline{C} + c(Y - TA) + I + G$

$$Y - cY = \overline{C} - cTA + I + G$$

$$Y = \frac{1}{1-c}(C + I + G) - \frac{c}{1-c}TA$$

$$Y = \frac{1}{1-0.9}(100 + 200 + 500) - \frac{0.9}{1-0.9}400$$

$$Y = \$4400$$

2. First, we need to calculate the appropriate multiplier. The income tax is $TA = tY$. Disposable income is $Y - tY$ or $(1 - t)Y$. Thus the consumption function is

$$C = \overline{C} + c(1 - t)Y$$

Combining this with the aggregate demand identity gives

$$Y = \overline{C} + c(1 - t)Y + I + G$$
$$Y(1 - c(1 - t)) = C + I + G$$

$$Y = \frac{1}{1 - c(1 - t)}(C + I + G)$$

Since autonomous consumption and investment do not change in this problem, we can rewrite the equation as

$$\Delta Y = \frac{1}{1 - c(1 - t)}\Delta G$$

The value of the multiplier is $\frac{1}{1 - 09.9(2/3)} = \frac{1}{1 - 0.6} = 2.5$

$$\Delta Y = 2.5\Delta G$$
$$750 = 2.5\Delta G$$
$$\Delta G = 750/2.5 = \$300$$

The change in the budget deficit is the change in government spending minus the change in tax collections. Government spending goes up \$300. Since income goes up \$750 and the marginal tax rate is 1/3, tax collections go up by \$250. The budget deficit goes up by \$50.

3. This problem essentially needs to be worked backward. We start by analyzing the sources of change in the budget deficit:

$$BD = G - TA$$
$$\Delta BD = \Delta G - \Delta TA$$

In part (a), investment changes. This changes income and tax collections. Government spending does not change.

$\Delta BD = 0 - \Delta TA$
$TA = tY$, so $\Delta TA = \Delta tY = t\Delta Y$
$\Delta BD = -t\Delta Y$
$15 = -(1/3)Y$

We see that a \$15 increase in the budget deficit implies that GDP fell by \$45. The only remaining step is to see how large a change in investment would cause a \$45 drop in income. From the previous problem, we know that the multiplier on investment is 2.5. Therefore, the change in investment must have been –45/2.5. Investment dropped by \$18.

In part (b), government spending and tax collections are both changing.

$\Delta BD = \Delta G - t\Delta Y$

We know from the preceding problem that $\Delta Y = 2.5\Delta G$.

$\Delta BD = \Delta G - (1/3)2.5\Delta G = (1 - (1/3)2.5)\Delta G = (1/6)\Delta G$
$\Delta G = 6\Delta BD = 6(15) = \$90$

This illustrates one of the fundamental findings of macroeconomics. An increase in the budget deficit can result from either a dropoff in economic activity or an increase in government spending.

Chapter 4

Graph It 4

(See next page.)

Fill-In Questions

1. income, interest rate
2. goods
3. assets or money
4. open market purchase
5. demand for
6. liquidity trap
7. classical case
8. investment
9. real balances
10. transmission mechanism

True-False Questions

1. True.
2. True.
3. True.
4. False. The *IS* curve has a negative slope.
5. False. Monetary policy has the largest possible effect. See the Graph It.
6. False. Monetary policy has no effect. See the Graph It.
7. True.
8. False. Interest rates go up, and so investment goes down.
9. False. Transfers change *A* by less than government purchases change *A*, so the *IS* curve is moved farther to the right by *G* than by *TR*.
10. False. Tax rates enter the multiplier and thus affect the slope of the *IS* curve.

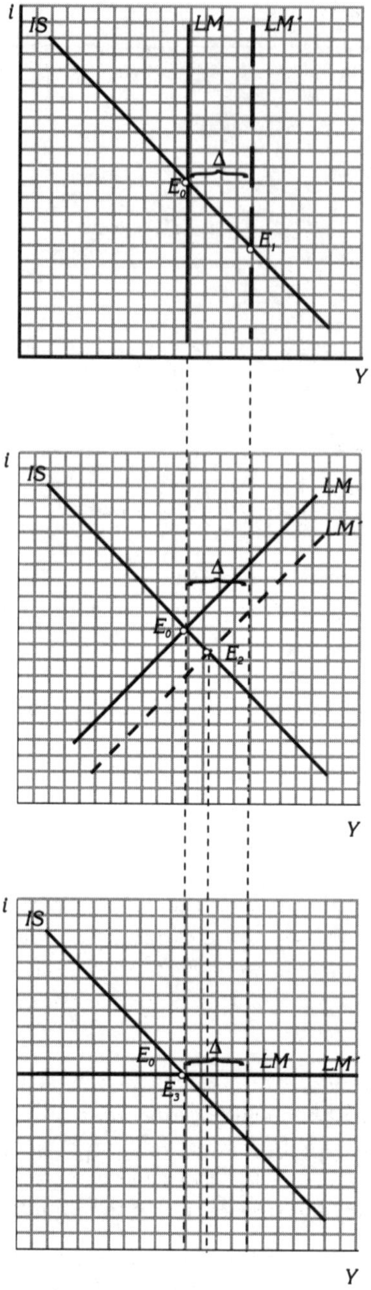

***Note*: E_0 and E_3 are the same.**

Chart 4-1

Multiple-Choice Questions

1. (c) **2.** (b) **3.** (b) **4.** (a) **5.** (c) **6.** (b) **7.** (c) **8.** (b) **9.** (b) **10.** (a)

Worked-Out Problems

1. (a) IS: $Y = 100 + 0.8(Y - 500) + \bar{I} - 1000i + 550$
$Y(1 - 0.8) = 250 + \bar{I} - 1000i$
$Y = 1250 + 5\bar{I} - 5000i$

(Note that we use $\bar{I}$ in place of 200 because autonomous investment changes in part (c).)

LM: $M/P = Y - 1000i$

(b) Substituting the *IS* curve into the *LM* curve,

$M/P = 1250 + 5\bar{I} - 5000i - 10\,000i$
$i = (1250 + 5\bar{I} - M/P)/15\,000$
$i = 0.09$

Substituting the equation for the interest rate back in the *IS* curve,

$Y = 1250 + 5\bar{I} - 5000(1250 + 5\bar{I} - M/P)/15\,000$
$Y = (2/3)(1250 + 5\bar{I}) + (M/P)/3$
$Y = \$1800$

Disposable income equals \$1800 – \$500, or \$1300. Inserting this into the consumption function, we can calculate that consumption is \$1140. Putting the interest rate into the investment function, we find that investment is 110. Note that we now have a check on our calculations. $C + I + G = 1100 + 110 + 550 = 1800 = Y$, as it should.

(c) Using the formulas derived in solving part (b), we see the fiscal policy multiplier is 10/3. Therefore, GDP drops by \$300. The interest rate multiplier of autonomous spending is 1/3000, and so the interest rate drops by 3 percent. This increases investment by \$30. The induced increase of \$30 plus the autonomous drop of \$90 means that overall investment drops by \$60.

(d) We need to increase Y by \$300. The monetary policy multiplier is 1/3. Therefore, we need to increase the money supply by \$900. Using the equation for the interest rate, we see that this will decrease the interest rate by an additional 6 percent.

(e) See Figures (a), (b), (c).

2. (a) The consumption function is

$$C = 100 + 0.9(Y - Y/3) = 100 + 0.6Y$$

The *IS* curve is

$$Y = 2500 - 2500i$$

The equilibrium equations for interest and income are

$$i = 0.20 - 0.00008\ (M/P)$$
$$Y = 2000 + 0.2\ (M/P)$$

The initial interest rate is 16 percent. Putting this into the investment function, we find investment equals \$40 and GDP equals \$2100. Taxes are one-third of income, and so tax collections come to \$700. Since government spending is \$710, the budget deficit is \$10.

(b) In order to balance the budget, tax collections would have to rise by \$10. This implies GDP would have to rise by \$30. Since the monetary policy multiplier is 0.2, the money supply must increase by \$150.

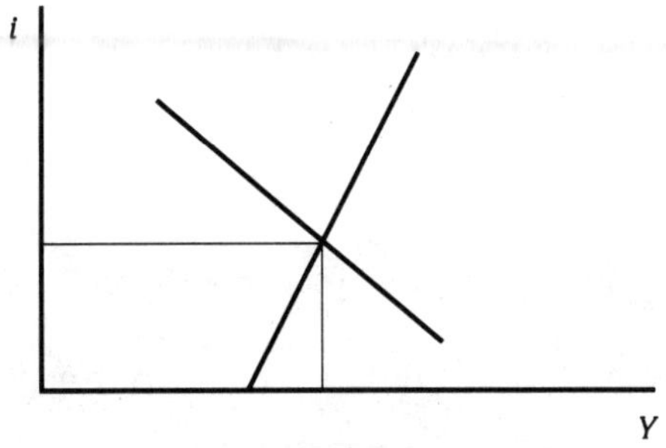

(a)

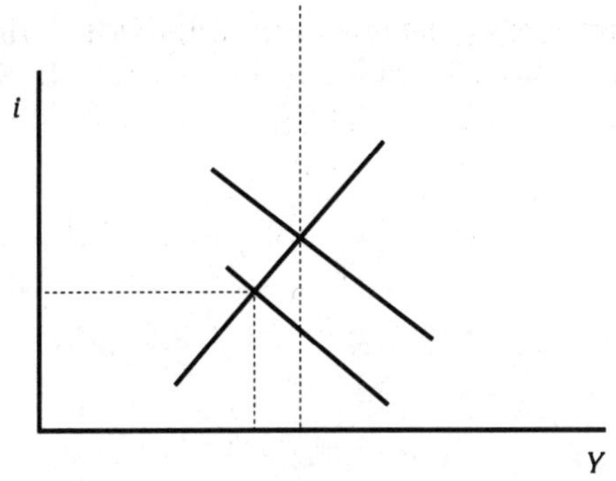

(b)

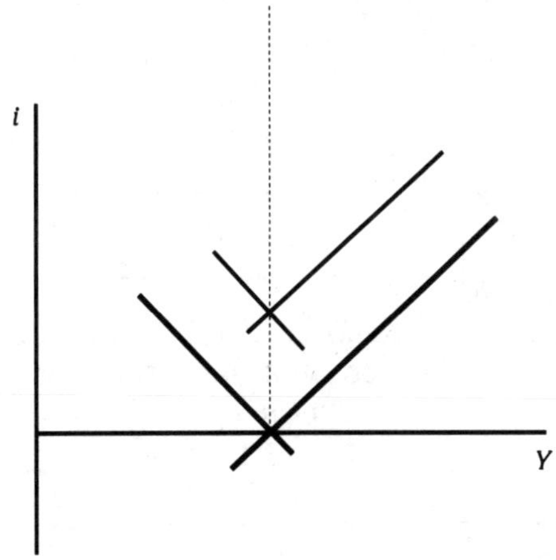

(c)

Figures (a), (b), (c)

Chapter 5

Graph It 5

Substituting for exports and imports, we obtain the aggregate demand line as follows:

$$AD = 0.6Y + 200 + X - Q = 0.5Y + 250$$

This line has an intercept of 250 and crosses the 45° line at $Y = 500$.

The import function can be plotted using the intercept of 25 and the value of 75 (equal to exports) when $Y = 500$.

An increase in exports of 100 increases income by 200 and therefore increases imports by 0.1(100) = 10. Thus the trade surplus increases by 90.

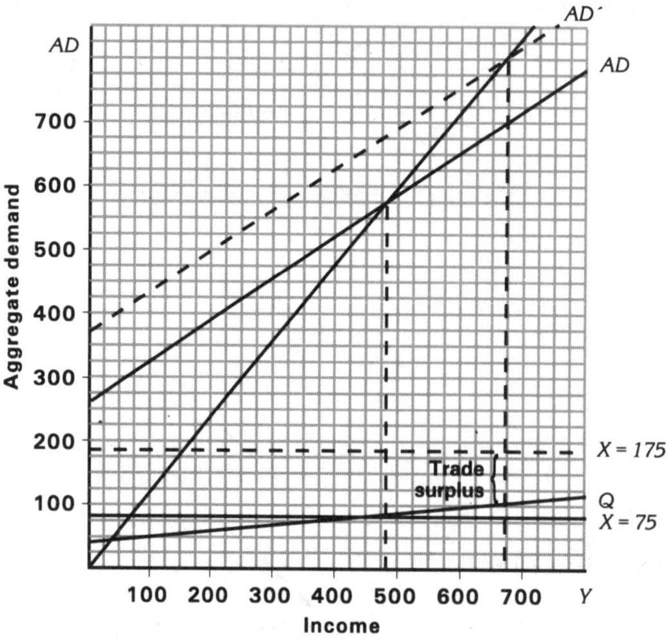

Chart 5-1

Fill-In Questions

1. exchange rate
2. current account

3. capital account
4. balance of payments
5. fixed exchange rate regime
6. floating exchange rate regime
7. dirty or managed floating
8. depreciation
9. devaluation
10. expenditure switching policy
11. real exchange rate

True-False Questions

1. False. Expansionary policy increases imports, increasing the trade deficit.
2. False. Interest rates are lower, and so capital leaves the country.
3. True.
4. True.
5. True.
6. False.
7. False.
8. False
9. True.

Multiple-Choice Questions

1. (b) **2.** (a) **3.** (a) **4.** (c) **5.** (a) **6.** (b) **7.** (a) **8.** (a) **9. (a)**

Worked-Out Problems

1. Initially, there are 4 marks to the dollar. A 50 percent devaluation leaves 2 marks to the dollar. Another 20 percent leaves 1.6 marks per dollar. One mark is now worth 62.5 cents.
2. $Y = C + I + G + NX = \overline{C} + 0.9Y + \overline{I} + G + \overline{X} - (\overline{Q} + 0.1Y)$
   $Y(1 - 0.9 + 0.1) = (\overline{C} + \overline{I} + G + \overline{X} - \overline{Q})$

The multiplier is thus 1/(1 – 0.9 + 0.1) = 1/0.2 = 5.

3. The essential thing is to recognize that our imports are German exports and vice versa. Variables without subscript are for Canada.

$$Y = C + I + G + NX$$
$$= \overline{C} + 0.9Y + \overline{I} + G + (\overline{Q}_G + 0.2Y_G) - (\overline{Q} + 0.1Y)$$
$$Y(1 - 0.9 + 0.1) = (\overline{C} + \overline{I} + G + \overline{Q}_G - \overline{Q}) + 0.2Y_G$$
$$Y = 5(\overline{C} + \overline{I} + G + \overline{Q}_G - \overline{Q}) + Y_G$$
$$Y_G = C_G + I_G + G_G + NX_G$$
$$= \overline{C} + 0.8Y_G + \overline{I}_G + \overline{G}_G + (\overline{Q} + 0.1Y) - (\overline{Q}_G + 0.2Y_G)$$
$$Y_G(1 - 0.8 + 0.2) = (\overline{C}_G + \overline{I}_G + \overline{G}_G + \overline{Q} - \overline{Q}_G) + 0.1Y$$
$$Y_G = 2.5(\overline{C}_G + \overline{I}_G + \overline{G}_G + \overline{Q} - \overline{Q}_G) + 0.25Y$$

To conserve on notation, call autonomous Canadian and German spending A and A_G, respectively. Thus several substitutions show

$$Y = 5\overline{A} + Y_G$$
$$Y_G = 2.5\overline{A}_G + 0.25Y$$
$$Y = 5\overline{A} + 2.5\overline{A} + 0.25Y$$
$$Y(1 - 0.25) = 5\overline{A} + 2.5\overline{A}_G$$
$$Y = (4/3)(5\overline{A} + 2.5\overline{A}_G)$$

and also that

$$Y_G = 2.5\overline{A}_G + 0.25(4/3)(5\overline{A} + 2.5\overline{A}_G) = (5/3)\overline{A} + (10/3)\overline{A}_G$$

So, the multiplier of the Canadian government's spending on Canadian GDP is 20/3 and the multiplier on German GDP is 5/3. Notice that, including all repercussion effects, the estimate of the multiplier rose from question 2 to question 3 from 5.0 to 6 2/3.

Chapter 6

Graph It 6

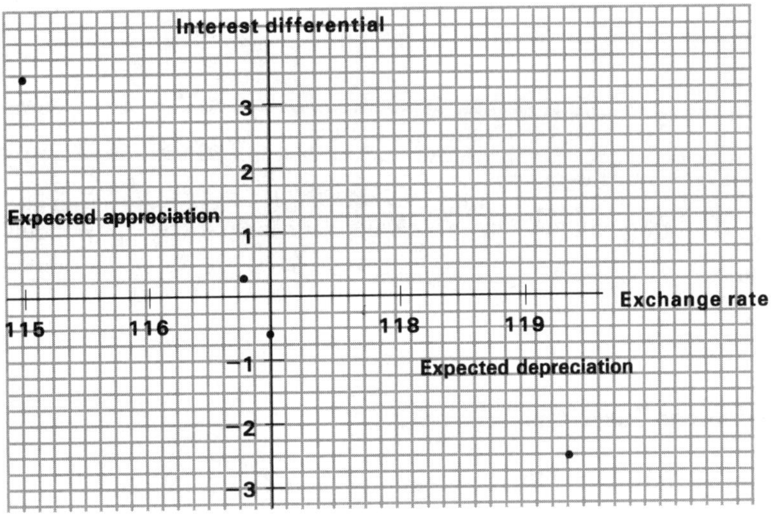

Chart 6-1

Fill-In Questions

1. competitiveness
2. perfect capital mobility
3. imperfect capital mobility
4. beggar-thy-neighbour
5. flexible (or floating)
6. interest parity condition
7. depreciation
8. depreciation

True-False Questions

1. False.
2. False.
3. True.
4. False. It is the *BP* curve that is horizontal.
5. True.
6. False. There is an appreciation and complete crowding out.
7. False. Net exports decrease.
8. False. This is true under a fixed exchange rate and perfect capital mobility.
9. True.
10. True.

Multiple-Choice Questions

1. (a) **2.** (a) **3.** (a) **4.** (c) **5.** (d) **6.** (a) **7.** (a) **8.** (a) **9.** (c) **10.** (d)

Worked-Out Problem

1. An investor could invest a dollar in Canada and end up with \$1.12. Alternatively, she could buy 2 marks and end up with DM2.2. For the DM2.2 to equal \$1.12, the exchange rate at the end of the year must equal 51 cents.

Chapter 7

Graph It 7

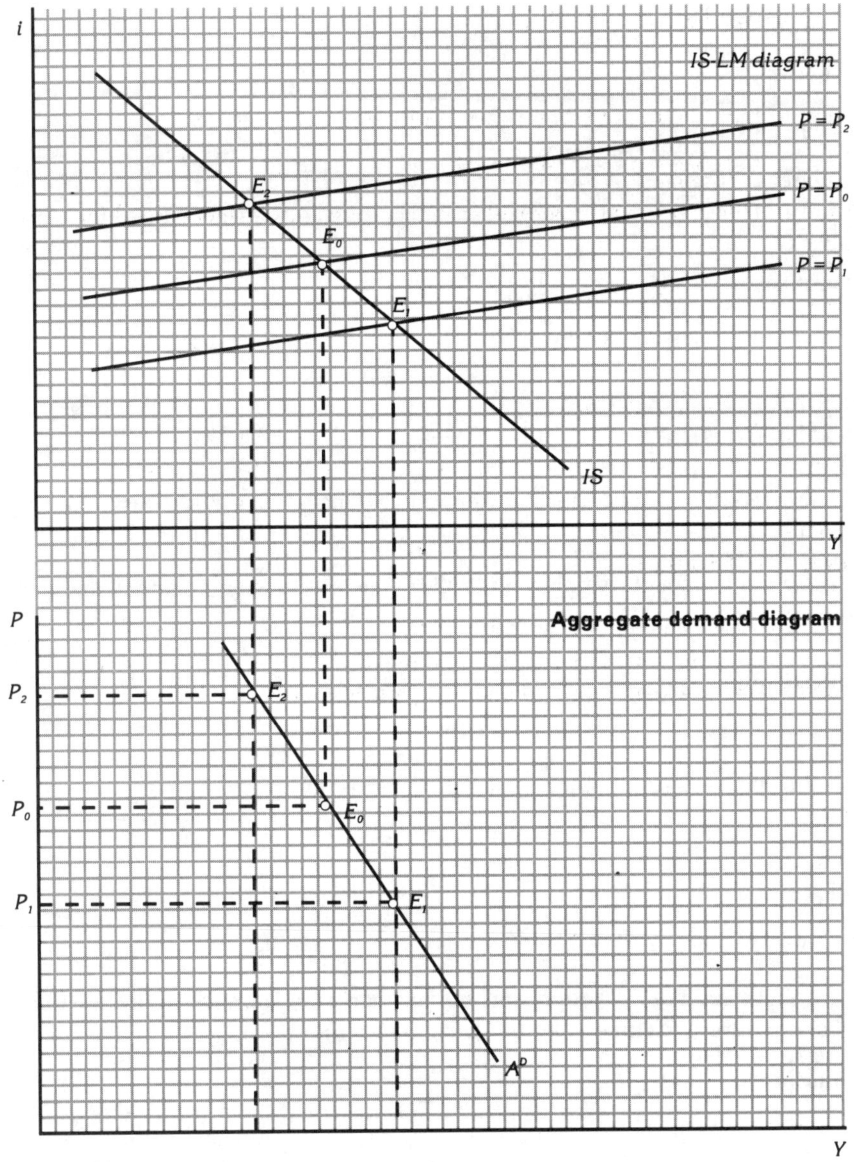

Chart 7-1

Fill-In Questions

1. autonomous spending
2. the money supply
3. *IS-LM*
4. crowding out
5. neutrality
6. aggregate supply
7. aggregate demand
8. horizontal
9. vertical
10. frictionless classical model

True-False Questions

1. False. Higher prices mean lower real balances. The *LM* curve moves left, increasing interest rates.
2. False. A low monetary policy multiplier means a steep aggregate demand curve.
3. True.
4. False. Same as question 2.
5. True.
6. False. The aggregate demand curve.
7. True.
8. True.
9. True.
10. False. Prices rise in proportion to the increased money supply, so that real balances are unchanged and the *LM* curve is unmoved.
11. False.

Multiple-Choice Questions

1. (c) **2.** (c) **3.** (b) **4.** (a) **5.** (a) **6.** (d) **7.** (b) **8.** (d) **9.** (b) **10.** (b) **11.** (b).

Worked-Out Problems

1. $Y = 2(1500) + 4(50\,000/P_{-1}) = 5000$
$P = P_{-1}[0.2 + 0.8(5000/4000)] = 120$

Next year:

$Y = 3000 + 4(50\,000/120) = 4667$
$P = 120[0.2 + 8(4667/4000)] = 136$

Year after:

$Y = 3000 + 4(50\,000/136) = 4471$
$P = 136[0.2 + 0.8(4471/4000)] = 148.8$

2. In the long run, $P = P_{-1}$, and so $Y = Y_P = 4000$

$4000 = 3000 + 4(50\,000/P)$
$(1/P) = 1000/200\,000$ $\quad P = 200$

Y is at its original level. Consumption must also be at its original level. Since $Y = C + I + G$, if G is up 500, investment must be down 500. Therefore, the interest rate must be up 0.25.

3. $4000 = 2000 + 4(100\,000/P)$
$(1/P) = 2000/400\,000$ $\quad P = 200$

Investment and the interest rate are unchanged!

Chapter 8

Graph It 8

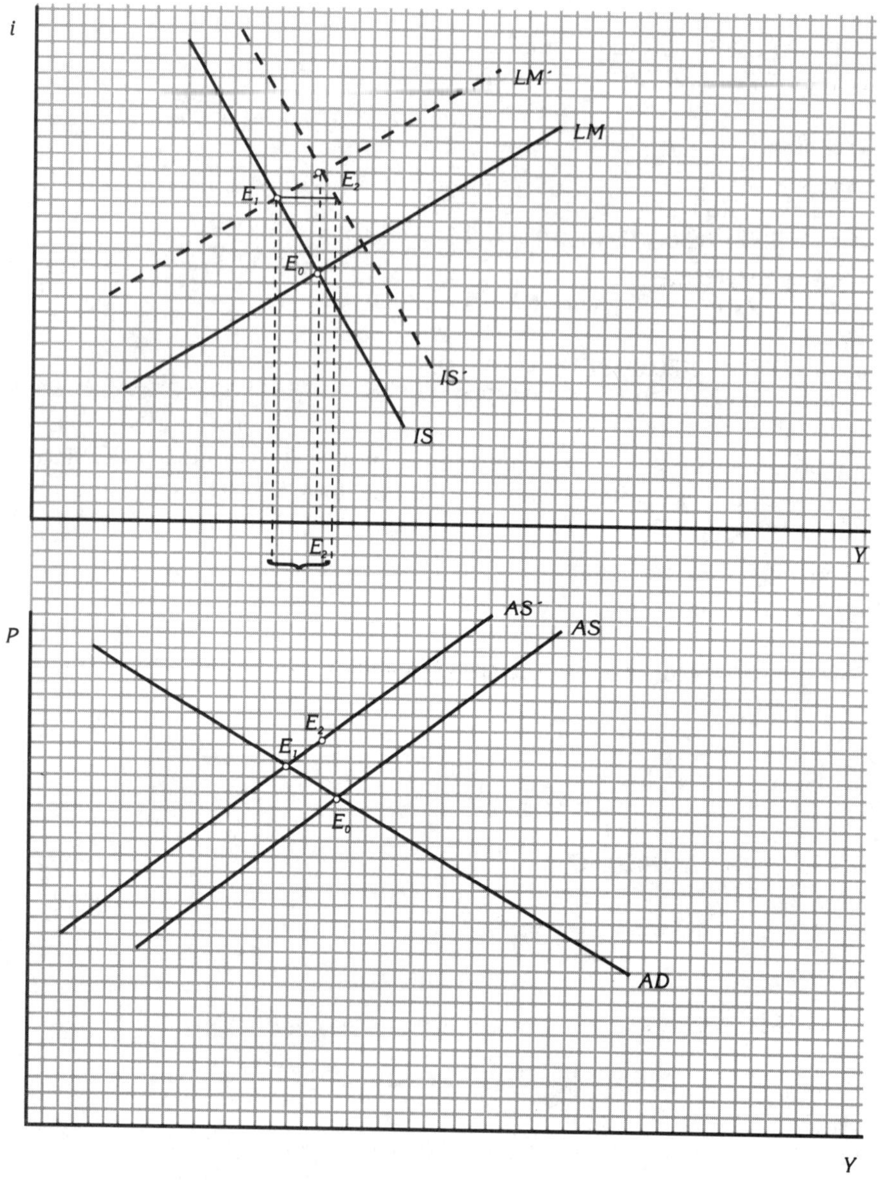

Chart 8-1

Fill-In Questions

1. long-term labour market relations
2. inflation
3. Phillips curve
4. systematically
5. labour productivity
6. markup
7. supply shocks

True-False Questions

1. True.
2. False. Adding a unit of labour increases output, though each additional unit adds less than the previous unit.
3. True.
4. True.
5. True.
6. True.
7. False. You cannot undo a shock that permanently lowers potential GDP.
8. True.
9. False.

Multiple-Choice Questions

1. (a) **2.** (c) **3.** (c) **4.** (a) **5.** (a) **6.** (c)

Worked-Out Problems

1. The aggregate supply curve in this case is

   $$P = P_{-1}[1 - 2(0.4)(1 - (1.1Y_p)/Y_p)] = P_{-1}[1.08]$$

   Since the initial price level is 100, the price level after 1 year is 108. In the second year, P_{-1} is therefore 108, so the second year's price level is 116.6.

2. The aggregate supply curve is given above. No inflation means $P = P_{-1}$. Therefore, the term in square brackets must equal 1, and so we must have $Y = Y_p$.

Chapter 9

Fill-In Questions

1. terms of trade

2. classical

3. Bretton-Woods system

4. purchasing power parity

5. J-curve

True-False Questions

1. False.

2. True.

3. False.

4. True.

5. False.

6. True.

Multiple-Choice Questions

1. (c) **2.** (b) **3.** (b) **4.** (d) **5.** (b) **6.** (a)

Chapter 10

Graph It 10

The completed graph appears below. You should have found the short-run *MPC* to be about 0.7 and the long-run *MPC* to be about 0.9. We made up the data by applying the following equation to each group of three points:

$$C = 0.4(Y_1 + Y_2 + Y_3)/3 + 0.5Y$$

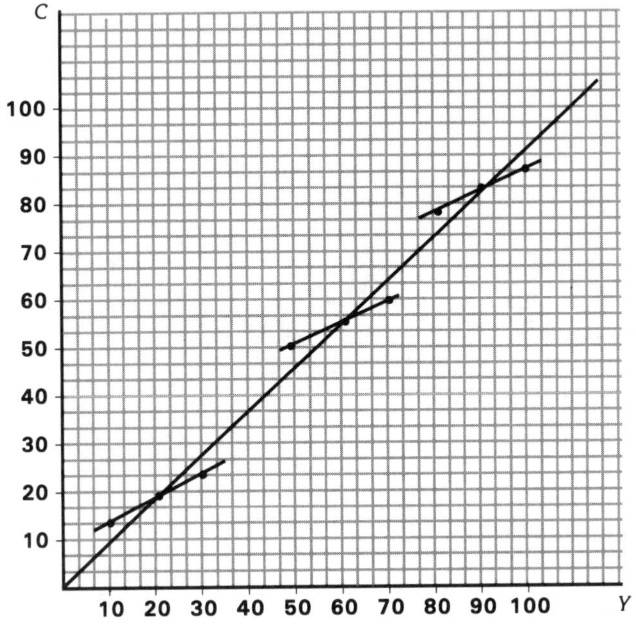

Chart 10-1

Fill-In Questions

1. life-cycle
2. permanent
3. dissavings
4. 0.90

5. 0.90
6. short-run
7. long-run
8. working, retirement
9. distributed

True-False Questions

1. False. It's just the other way around.
2. True.
3. True.
4. True.
5. True.
6. True.
7. True.
8. False. You have to save in order to have a bequest to leave, and so you reduce current consumption.
9. True.
10. True.

Multiple-Choice Questions

1. (b) **2.** (a) **3.** (c) **4.** (b) **5.** (c) **6.** (a) **7.** (c) **8.** (c) **9.** (c) **10.** (a)

Worked-Out Problems

1. Total resources are the sum of disposable income over the next 40 years. These resources must be spread out evenly over a 50-year period. A $100 tax cut that is permanent increases disposable lifetime income by a total of 40 times $100, or $4000. Spread over 50 years, this cut increases consumption by $80 each year.

   A cut that lasts only 1 year increases lifetime disposable income by $100, and so consumption increases by $2. A cut that is not in effect this year but is in effect for the next 39 years yields a total increase of $3900. Consumption increases $78 each year including the current one.

2. $\Delta C = 0.8(0.75\Delta YD + 0.25\Delta YD_{-1})$

(a) $\Delta C = 0.8[0.75(100) + 0.25(0)] = 60$
$\Delta C = 0.8[0.75(100) + 0.25(100)] = 80$

(b) $\Delta C = 0.8[0.75(100) + 0.25(0)] = 60$
$\Delta C = 0.8[0.75(0) + 0.25(100)] = 20$

Chapter 11

Graph It 11

Table 11-1

Year	GDP	I_t	$Y_t - Y_{t-1}$	$I_t - I_{t-1}$
1978	402.7	67.6		
1979	418.3	79.6	15.6	12.0
1980	424.5	77.7	6.2	−1.9
1981	440.1	87.0	15.6	9.3
1982	426.0	64.1	−14.1	−22.9
1983	439.5	72.7	13.5	8.6
1984	467.2	81.5	27.7	8.8
1985	489.4	85.6	22.2	4.1
1986	505.7	91.6	16.3	6.0
1987	526.7	102.9	21.0	11.3
1988	551.4	112.9	24.7	10.0
1989	565.0	119.2	13.6	6.3
1990	567.5	108.9	2.5	−10.3
1991	558.9	106.7	−8.6	−2.2

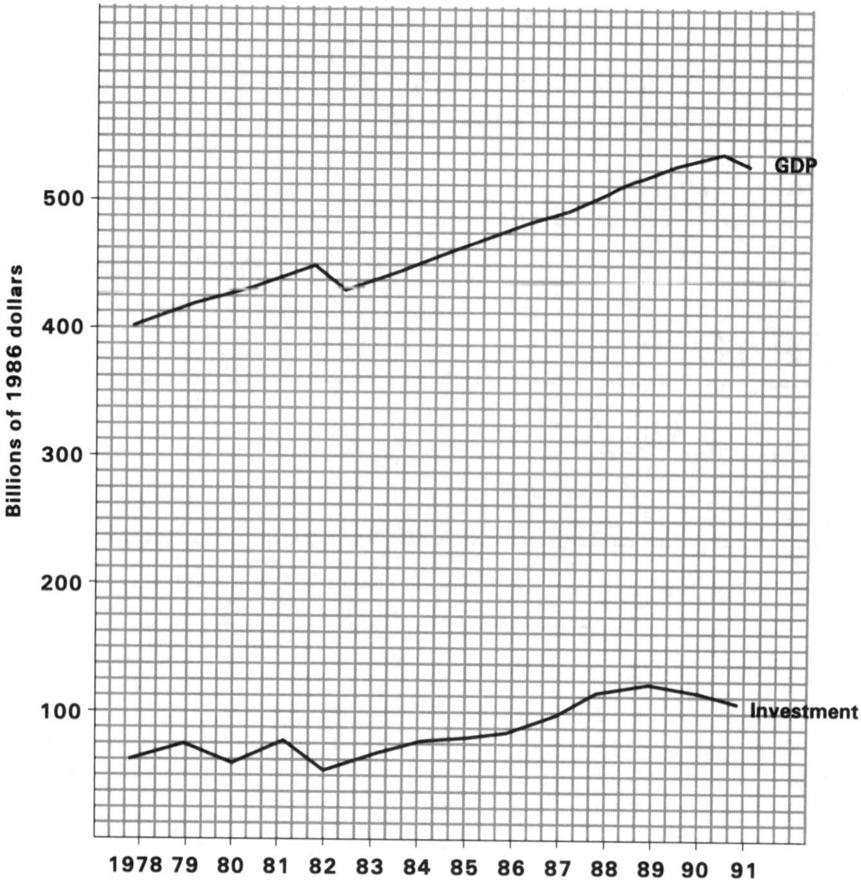

Chart 11-1

Fill-In Questions

1. business fixed, residential construction, inventory
2. flow, stock
3. marginal product of capital
4. rental or user cost of capital
5. expected future
6. investment tax credit
7. depreciation

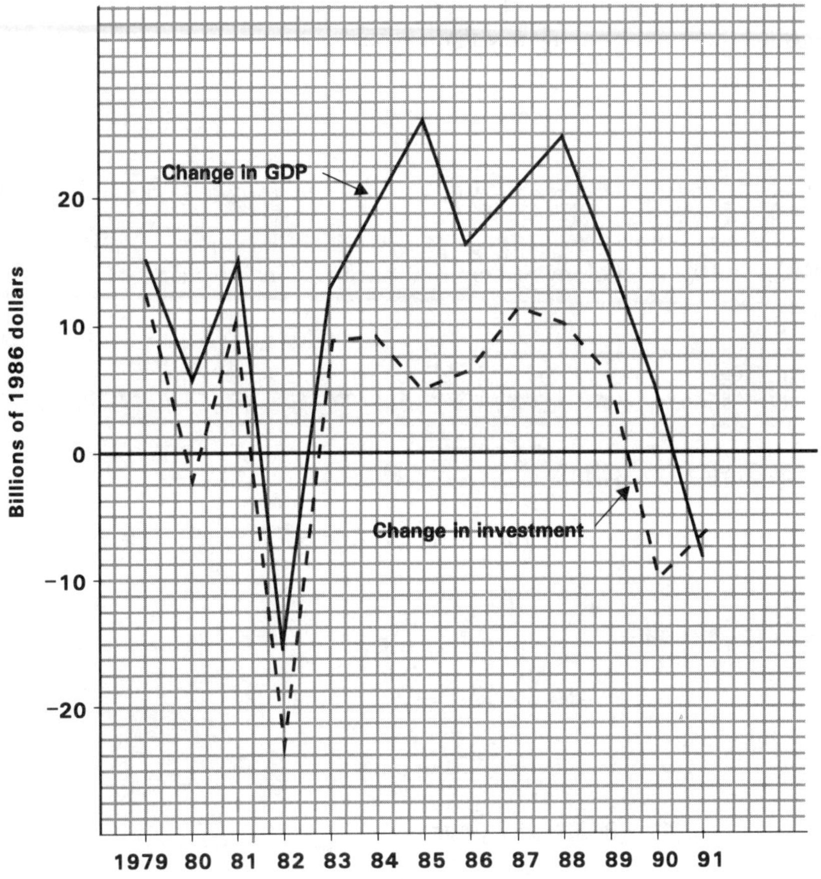

Chart 11-2

8. unintended
9. inventory cycle

True-False Questions

1. False. High interest rates make capital more expensive and thus lower investment.
2. True.
3. False. If the government pays for part of your equipment, you want to buy more.

4. False. If mortgage rates are high, your monthly house payment is high. People buy less housing, lowering residential construction.
5. True.
6. True.
7. False. If you expect sales to rise, you need more goods on hand, increasing inventory.
8. False. It's the level of investment that's proportional to changes in income.
9. True.
10. True.

Multiple-Choice Questions

1. (d) **2.** (b) **3.** (b) **4.** (c) **5.** (d) **6.** (c) **7.** (a) **8.** (c) **9.** (b) **10.** (a) **11.** (b)

Worked-Out Problems

1. $rc = i - \pi + d = 0.12 - 0.06 + 0.10 = 0.16$

   (a) $K^* = 0.25(16\,000)/0.16 = 25\,000$

   (b) $K^* = 0.25(32\,000)/0.16 = 50\,000$

   (c) $I_{net} = (K^* - K_{-1}) = 50\,000 - 25\,000 = 25\,000$
   $I_{gross} = I_{net} + dK_{-1} = 25\,000 + 0.1(25\,000) = 27\,500$

2. $I_{net} = K - K_{-1} = 0.5(K^* - K_{-1})$
   year 1: $I_{net} = 0.5(3600 - 2000) = 800$; $I_{gross} = 800 + 0.1(2000) = 1000$
   year 2: $I_{net} = 0.5(3600 - 2800) = 400$; $I_{gross} = 400 + 0.1(2800) = 680$
   year 3: $I_{net} = 0.5(3600 - 3200) = 200$; $I_{gross} = 200 + 0.1(3200) = 520$

   Notice that each year's net investment is added to the capital stock to determine the following year's capital stock.

3. A "fair" loan is one in which the amount of the loan equals the present discounted value of the payments.

   $$1000 = \frac{220}{1.1} + \frac{Q_2}{1.1^2}$$

   $Q_2 = 1.1^2(1000 - 200) = \$968$

Chapter 12

Graph It 12

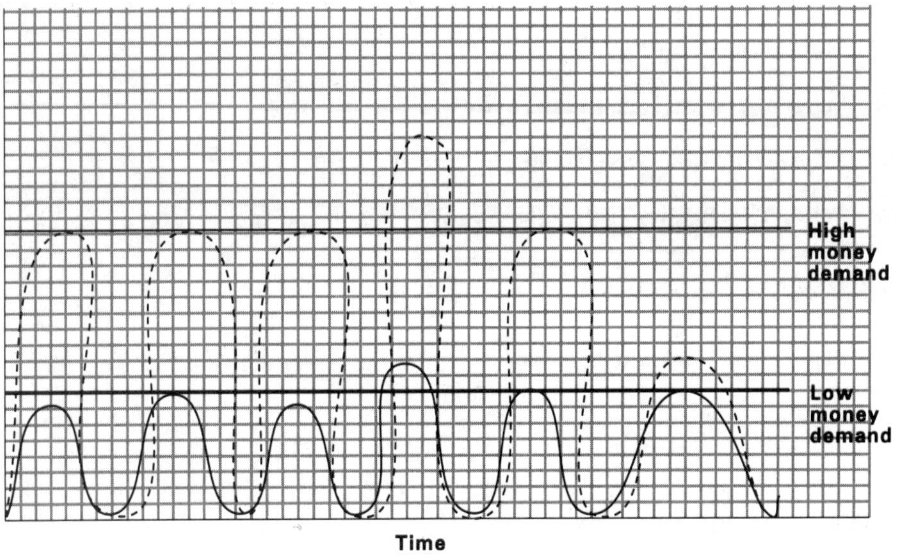

Chart 12-1

Fill-In Questions

1. real balances
2. currency and demand deposits
3. M1 plus savings accounts and notice deposits
4. transactions
5. velocity
6. velocity
7. precautionary
8. speculative
9. speculative
10. price level

True-False Questions

1. True.
2. True.
3. True.
4. True.
5. False. M1 is a strict subset of M2.
6. False. To do otherwise would show money illusion.
7. False. The Baumol-Tobin theory says money demand is proportional to the square root of GDP.
8. True.
9. False. This is just a switch between different components of M2.
10. True.

Multiple-Choice Questions

1. (c) **2.** (b) **3.** (c) **4.** (a) **5.** (b) **6.** (a) **7.** (b) **8.** (b) **9.** (c) **10.** (b) **11.** (b) **12.** (c)

Worked-Out Problems

1. Since the price level doubled, the $220 billion is only worth $110 billion in real, constant dollar terms. The change from $100 billion to $110 billion is a 10 percent increase. Since the Baumol-Tobin theory says that the income elasticity is 1/2, real money demand will rise by 5 percent.

2. This problem has to be worked backward. We know the amount we want the interest rate to change. We assume that interest changes by the amount given and see what change in the money stock this implies. We know, then, that if we change the money stock, the desired change in the interest rate will result.

   The interest rate is supposed to go from 4 percent to 3 percent. This is a drop of 25 percent. (The change is 1 percent; 1 percent over 4 percent is one-fourth, or 25 percent. A very common error is to think the change is 1 percent. The change is one percentage point of annual interest, not 1 percent.)

   Since we are told that the interest elasticity is –0.2, one-fifth of one-fourth is 5 percent. Thus, a 5 percent *increase* in the money stock will produce the desired interest rate change.

Chapter 13

Graph It 13

First Balance Sheets

Professor B		Bank	
Assets	**Liabilities**	**Assets**	**Liabilities**
Deposit $200	None	Reserves $200 (Required 20) (Excess 180)	$200 Deposit
	$200 Net worth		
$200	$200	$180	$180

Second Balance Sheets

Professor B		Bank	
Assets	**Liabilities**	**Assets**	**Liabilities**
Deposit $380	$180 Loan	Reserves $200 (Required 38) (Excess 162)	$380 Deposit
	$200 Net worth	Loan 180	
$380	$380	$380	$380

Third Balance Sheets

Professor B		Bank	
Assets	**Liabilities**	**Assets**	**Liabilities**
Deposit $542	$342 Loan	Reserves $200 (Required 54.2) (Excess 145.8)	$542 Deposit
	$200 Net worth	Loan 342	
$542	$542	$542	$542

Final Balance Sheets

Professor B		Bank	
Assets	**Liabilities**	**Assets**	**Liabilities**
Deposit $2000	$1800 Loan	Reserves $200 (Required 200) (Excess 0)	$2000 Deposit
	$ 200 Net worth	Loan 1800	
$2000	$2000	$2000	$2000

Fill-In Questions

1. high-powered money, the monetary base
2. required, excess
3. bank rate
4. open market sale
5. money multiplier
6. announcement effects
7. secondary reserve requirements
8. currency-deposit ratio
9. government bonds

True-False Questions

1. True.
2. False. A higher currency-deposit ratio means a lower money multiplier and so a lower money supply.
3. False. A higher reserve requirement means a lower money multiplier and so a lower money supply.
4. False. This also lowers *re* and thus the money multiplier.
5. False. Income has nothing to do with the money supply.
6. True.

7. False.

8. True.

9. True.

10. True.

Multiple-Choice Questions

1. (d) **2.** (d) **3.** (c) **4.** (c) **5.** (d) **6.** (a) **7.** (a) **8.** (c) **9.** (b) **10.** (b)

Worked-Out Problems

1. $CU = 0.4D$
$\text{M1} = CU + D = 0.4D + D = 1.4D$
$H = CU + 0.1D = 0.4D + 0.1 = 0.5D$

(a) $\text{M1}/H = (1.4D)/(0.5D)$
$\text{M1} = 2.8H = 2.8(100) = 280$ billion

(b) $H = 0.5D$; $\Delta D = 2\Delta H = 2(50) = 100$ billion

2. $\text{M2} = CU + D + SD = 0.4D + D + 2.5D = 3.9D$
$H = CU = 0.1D + 0.04SD = 0.4D + 0.1D + 0 .04(2.5)D = 0.6D$

(a) $\text{M2} = (3.9/0.6)H = 6.5H = 6.5(100) = 650$ billion

(b) $\text{M1} = [(0.4 + 1)/0.6]H = (1.4/0.6)(100) = 233$ billion

3. $H = CU + 0.1D = (0.5Y - 495i) + 0.1(Y - 50i) = 0.6Y - 500i$
$i = (0.6\text{Y} - H)/500 = 0.6(2.000) - (1.150)/500 = 50/500 = 10$ percent

Chapter 14

Graph It 14

Bank Balance Sheet 1

Assets		Liabilities	
Reserves	$ 200	$2000	Deposit
Treasury bills	400		
Loans	1600	200	Paid in capital
	$2200	$2200	

Bank Income Statement

Income		Expenses	
Interest on reserves	$ 0	$110	Deposit interest
Interest on T-bills	38	40	Stockholders' dividends
Interest on loans	224	120	Retained earnings
	$260	$260	

Bank Balance Sheet 2

Assets		Liabilities	
Reserves	$ 200	$2000	Deposit
Treasury bills	520		
Loans	1600	320	Paid in capital
	$2320	$2320	

Fill-In Questions

1. inside lag
2. outside lag
3. lags, expectations, uncertainty
4. action lag
5. recognition lag
6. decision lag
7. automatic stabilizer
8. activists
9. decision
10. outside

True-False Questions

1. False.
2. True.
3. False.
4. True.
5. False.

Multiple-Choice Questions

1. (b) **2.** (d) **3.** (a) **4.** (a)

Chapter 15

Graph It 15

Table 15-1

(1)	Estimate of potential GDP, 1982	380	390	400
(2)	Actual GDP, 1982	345	345	345
(3)	Gap [(1) – (2)]	35	45	55
(4)	Cyclical deficit [1/3 × (3)]	11.7	15.0	18.3
(5)	Actual deficit, 1982	20.3	20.3	20.3
(6)	Structural deficit [(5) – (4)]	8.6	5.3	2.0

Fill-In Questions

1. deficit
2. national debt
3. monetizing the debt
4. debt financing
5. money financing
6. primary deficit

True-False Questions

1. False.
2. False.
3. True.
4. True.
5. True.
6. False.

Multiple-Choice Questions

1. (c) **2.** (d) **3.** (d) **4.** (d)

Chapter 16

Graph It 16

Table 16-1

Asset	Beginning Value	End Dollar Value	End Real Value	Dollar Difference	Real Difference
Money	100	100	98.04	7.0	6.86
Bonds	100	107	104.90	5.2	5.10
Corn	100	112.2	110.00		

Table 16-2

Asset	Beginning Value	End Dollar Value	End Real Value	Dollar Difference	Real Difference
Money	100	100.0	89.29	17.0	15.17
Bonds	100	117.0	104.46	6.2	5.54
Corn	100	123.2	110.00		

Notice that the real interest rate is approximately 5 percent in each case (7 – 2 or 17 – 12), but that this is only an approximation.

Fill-In Questions

1. overshooting
2. rational expectations
3. expectations-augmented Phillips
4. Phillips
5. stagflation
6. credible
7. perfect foresight

True-False Questions

1. False. Rational expectations theory only says that predictable events don't move GDP away from potential.
2. True.
3. False. The real wage remains constant.
4. True.
5. True.
6. True.

Multiple-Choice Questions

1. (b) **2.** (b) **3.** (b) **4.** (c) **5.** (a) **6.** (a) **7.** (a)

Worked-Out Problems

1. $f = 500,\ m_{-1} = 0,\ \pi_{-1} = 0 \qquad \Delta\pi^e = 0$

$Y = 4000 + 2(500) = 5000$

$$\pi = 0 + 0.8\,\frac{5000 - 4000}{4000} = 0.2, \text{ or 20 percent per year}$$

Next period's expected inflation is this period's actual inflation, 0.2. Next year:

$f = 0$

$Y = 5000 + 0 + 2000(0 - 0.2) + 1000(0.2 - 0) = 4800$

$$\pi = 0.2 + 0.8\,\frac{4800 - 4000}{4000} = 0.36, \text{ or 36 percent per year}$$

Next year:

$Y = 4800 + 0 + 2000(0 - 0.36) + 1000(0.36 - 0.2) = 4240$

$$\pi = 0.36 + 0.8\,\frac{4240 - 4000}{4000} = 0.408, \text{ or 40.8 percent per year}$$

2. $f = 0_{-1}m_{-1} = 0.5,\ \pi_{-1} = 0 \qquad \Delta\pi^e = 0$

$Y = 4000 + 2000(0.5 - 0) = 5000$

The rest of the answers are identical to those for problem 1.

3. $Y = 4000 + 2000(0.5 - 0) = 5000$

$$\pi = 0 + 0.8\frac{5000-4000}{4000} = 20 \text{ percent per year}$$

Next year:

$$Y = 5000 + 2000(0.5 - 0.2) + 1000(0.2 - 0) = 5800$$

$$\pi = 0.2 + 0.8\frac{5800-4000}{4000} = 56 \text{ percent per year}$$

Next year:

$$Y = 5800 + 2000\,(0.5 - 0.56) + 1000(0.56 - 0.2) = 6040$$

$$\pi = 0.56 + 0.8\frac{6040-4000}{4000} = 96.8 \text{ percent per year}$$

Next year:

$$Y = 6040 + 2000(0.5 - 0.968) + 1000(0.968 - 0.56) = 5512$$

$$\pi = 0.968 + 0.8\frac{5512-4000}{4000} = 127 \text{ percent per year}$$

Chapter 17

Graph It 17

Table 17-2 ***"The New Days"***

	Unemployment Rate	Number in Labour Force	Number Employed
Male	2.80	1000	972
Female	5.50	800	756
Total	4.00	1800	1728

The "average" unemploymnent rate has risen, even though the typical individual, male or female, is less likely to be unemployed.

Fill-In Questions

1. unemployment, inflation
2. natural rate
3. perfectly anticipated
4. imperfectly anticipated, unanticipated
5. distributional
6. borrowers
7. lenders

True-False Questions

1. False. Aggregate policies have no effect on the natural rate.
2. False. Lost output is gone forever.
3. True.
4. True.
5. True.
6. True.
7. False. Those who are unemployed for a long time make up a large part of the overall average.
8. False. It makes sense for people to spend time looking around for jobs.
9. False. Job creation programs may lower the natural rate, and unemployment insurance programs definitely raise the natural rate.
10. False. Print enough money and you can get as much inflation as you'd like!

Multiple-Choice Questions

1. (c) **2.** (a) **3.** (d) **4.** (d) **5.** (d) **6.** (a) **7.** (b) **8.** (b) **9.** (d) **10.** (c)

Worked-Out Problems

1. Originally, $\bar{u}$ = 0.6(0.05) + 0.4(0.08) = 6.2 percent. Later, $\bar{u}$ = 0.5(0.05) + 0.5(0.08) = 6.5 percent. Of course, GDP will be much higher in the latter case, since so many more women are working!
2. The average duration of unemployment is (2 • 1 + 2 + 12)/4 = 4 months. In any given month, there will be two people undergoing a 1-month unemployment span, two people with a 2-month unemployment span, and twelve people with a 1-year stretch. Thus, 16 percent of the labour force will be unemployed.
3. At the end of the year you have \$107. The price level is now 1.1, and so the real value is 107/1.1 = \$97.27. In real terms, you have lost \$3.
4. In order to gain a 2 percent real return, you need 100(1 + *i*)/1.1 = 102, or 102(1.1)/100 = 1.122, or *i* is approximately 12 percent.
5. The price of your property will be rising 12 percent per year, so that after 2 years you will sell it for \$1.25 on the dollar, though it takes \$1.21 to be worth one constant dollar. Your nominal gain is \$0.25. The tax on this is approximately \$0.06, so that you are left with \$1.19, which is worth \$0.98 in real terms. Your 4 percent before-tax gain has turned into a 2 percent after-tax real loss.

Chapter 18

Graph It 18

Tables 18-1 and 18-2 follow. In nominal terms, the end-of-year debt in year 5 was only 530.81 without inflation as opposed to 850.26 with inflation. But as you can see, the real comparison shows little real difference only 530.81 versus 527.94.

Table 18-1

Year	1	2	3	4	5
Spending deficit	100.00	100.00	100.00	100.00	100.00
Beginning debt	100.00	202.00	306.04	412.16	530.40
Interest	2.00	4.04	6.12	8.24	10.41
Price level, end of year	1.00	1.00	1.00	1.00	1.00
Real debt, end of year	102.00	206.04	312.16	420.40	530.81

Table 18-2

Year	1	2	3	4	5
Spending deficit	100.00	110.00	121.00	133.00	146.41
Beginning debt	100.00	222.00	369.64	547.107	59.16
Interest	12.00	26.64	44.36	65.65	91.10
Price level, end of year	1.10	1.21	1.33	1.46	1.61
Real debt, end of year	101.82	205.49	311.04	418.52	527.94

Fill-In Questions

1. hyperinflation
2. inflation tax
3. seigniorage
4. inflation-corrected deficit
5. Fisher effect
6. liquidity effect
7. income effect
8. expectations effect

True-False Questions

1. True.
2. False. In the long run, GDP pretty much stays at potential GDP.
3. True.
4. True.
5. False. The nominal interest rate adjusts to expected inflation and the real rate is unaffected.
6. True.
7. True.
8. True.
9. False. However, they do tend to move together over long periods of time.

Multiple-Choice Questions

1. (c) **2.** (b) **3.** (d) **4.** (c) **5.** (c) **6.** (b) **7.** (a) **8.** (c) **9.** (b) **10.** (a)

Worked-Out Problems

1. We can use the formula $\pi = m - \eta g^*$, which shows that inflation is the rate of money supply growth less the rate of growth in money demand due to increased GDP. Inflation will be zero if the rate of money growth m equals the income elasticity of money demand, η, times the rate of growth of potential GDP, g^*. A good estimate of the income elasticity (from Chapter 12) is 0.7, with a range being between 0.5 and 1.0. A reasonable estimate for potential GDP growth is 3.0 percent, with a range of about 2.5 to 3.5 percent. So our best estimate of noninflationary money growth is 2.1 percent per year (0.7×3.0) with a range of 1.25 (0.5×2.5) to 3.5 (1.0×3.5) percent per year.

2. First, a minor point: 1000 percent annual inflation means the price level is multiplied by 11. (A 100 percent increase means something doubles, a 200 percent increase means something triples, etc.) We use the compound interest formula to solve this problem. Thus, $11 = (1 + r)\ 12$. Solving, we write $(1 + r) = 111/12 = 1.221$, or r equals 22 percent per month. We can solve the second question by writing $191 = (1 + r)365$ or $1 + r = 1911/365 = 1.014$. The daily inflation rate is 1.4 percent.

3. To be precise, the nominal value will have grown to $\$100 \times (1 + 0.50)10 = \$5766.50$. (Wow!) If we take today's price level as 1.0, the price level 10 years from now will have grown to $1.0 \times (1 + 0.48)10 = 50.42$. (Oh, dear!) The real value of the investment will be $\$5766.50/50.42 = \$114.37$. A quick and dirty way to find the same answer is to calculate the value of 10 years' compounding at the real interest rate, $0.50 - 0.48 = 0.02$. $\$100 \times (1 + 0.02)10 = \$121.90$. You'll note that using the real interest rate introduces a small error in the final answer, but certainly puts you in the right ballpark.

Chapter 19

Graph It 19

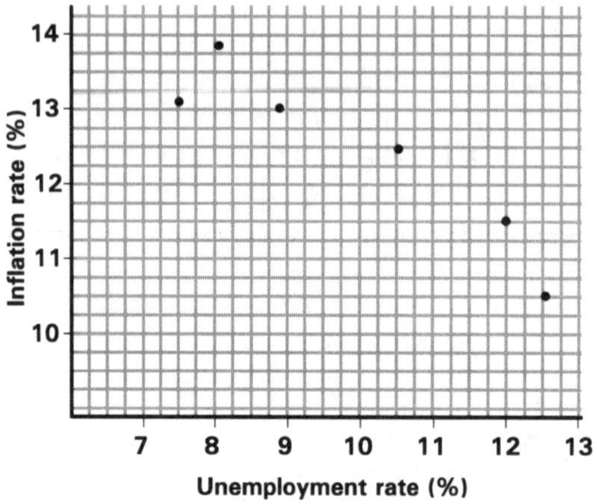

Chart 19-1

Fill-In Questions

1. monetarist
2. monetary growth rule
3. lomg and variable
4. short run/long run
5. monetary gradualism
6. rates of inflation

True-False Questions

1. False. They think it is relatively stable.
2. True.
3. True.
4. False. Nominal, not real, GDP.

5. True.

6. True.

Multiple-Choice Questions

1. (b) **2.** (b) **3.** (d) **4.** (b) **5.** (a).

Chapter 20

Graph It 20

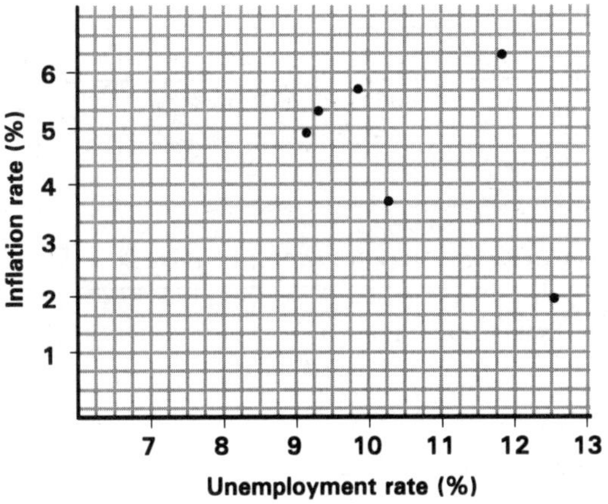

Chart 20-1

Fill-In Questions

1. rational expectations

2. real business cycle

3. efficiency wages

4. small menu costs

5. intertemporal substitution of leisure

True-False Questions

1. True.
2. False.
3. False.
4. False.
5. True.

Multiple-Choice Questions

1. (b) **2.** (d) **3.** (d) **4.** (a) **5.** (d).

Chapter 21

Graph It 21

Table 21-1 *Short- and Long-Run Increase in Aggregate Demand*

(1) 1979 investment (billions of 1981 dollars)	61
(2) 20% increase	12
(3) Increase in GDP [2 × (2)]	24
(4) Actual 1979 GDP	338

Table 21-2 *Short- and Long-Run Decrease in Aggregate Supply*

	1 Year	5 Years
(1) Increase in annual investment	12	12
(2) Cumulative increase in capital	12	60
(3) Total capital (roughly 3 × GDP)	1014	1014
(4) As percentage of capital	1.18%	5.90%
(5) Relative increase in production [1/4 × (4)]	0.30%	1.50%
(6) Increase in *AS* [GDP times (5)]	1	5
(7) As fraction of *AD* increase [100 × (6)/(3) above]	4.16%	20.80%

You can see from Table 21-2 that the aggregate supply effects of an increase in investment take many years to catch up with the aggregate demand effects.

Fill-In Questions

1. potential
2. per capita
3. productivity
4. production function
5. marginal product of capital
6. capital's share of output
7. constant returns to scale
8. steady state
9. technological change

True-False Questions

1. True.
2. False. Eventually, the additional capital stock gets depreciated away unless the saving rate rises.
3. False. It takes time for a higher saving rate to add to the capital stock.
4. True.
5. False. The growth rate depends only on technological change.
6. False. It takes time for the population to grow.
7. True.
8. False. More people, more output, though less output per person.
9. True.
10. True.

Multiple-Choice Questions

1. (b) **2.** (c) **3.** (b) **4.** (b) **5.** (a) **6.** (b) **7.** (c) **8.** (c) **9.** (b) **10.** (c)

Worked-Out Problems

1. GDP per capita is $y = Y/N$. Capital per worker is $k = K/N$.

$Y = AK^{a}N^{1-a}$
$Y/N = AK^{a}N^{1-a}/N = AK^{a}N^{1-a-1} = AK^{a}N^{-a} = A(K/N)^{a}$
$y = Ak^{a}$

2. One can prove directly that the marginal product of labour is $(1 - a)Y/N$. Total payments to labour are the marginal product of labour times the total amount of labour, $\{[(1-a)Y/N] \cdot N\}$. To find out what share of total GDP this represents, we divide by total GDP; finally,

$\{[(1-a)Y/N] \cdot N\}/Y = 1 - a = 1 - 0.25 = 0.75$

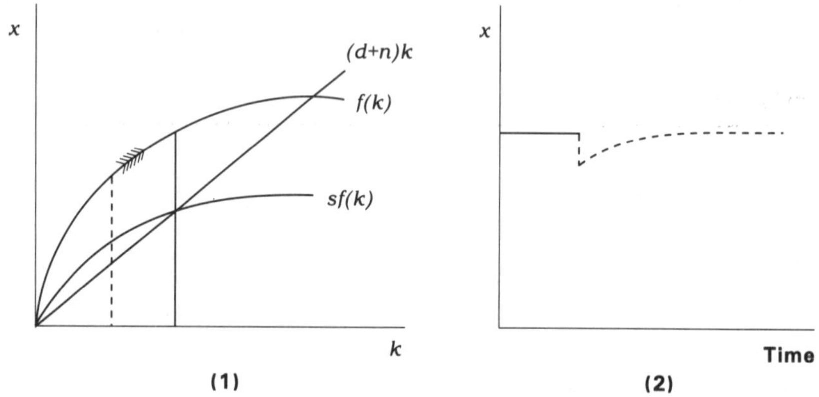

Figure d(1), (2)

3. Apply the formula

$$\frac{\Delta Y}{Y} = \theta \frac{\Delta K}{K} + (1 - \theta) \frac{\Delta N}{N}$$

where θ is capital's share, 0.25. In this case, 0.25(0.2) + 0.75(0.1) yields a 12.5 percent growth in GDP. Since population has grown 10 percent, per capita GDP grows 2.5 percent.

4. The path of per capita GDP is illustrated in Figures d(1) and d(2). $k = K/N$ falls to half its original value. Per capita GDP drops down the dashed line and then gradually returns to the steady state.

5. The path of per capita GDP is illustrated in Figure e(1) and e(2). The new saving curve is shown by the dashed curve. Per capita GDP gradually rises from the old steady state to the new steady state.

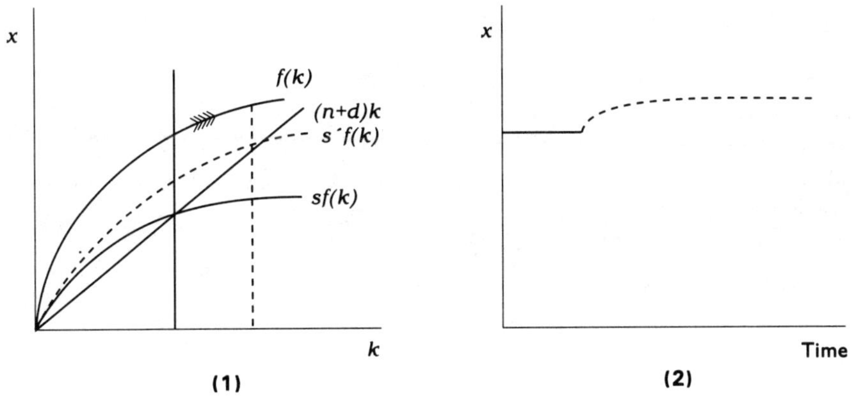

Figure e(1), (2)

ANSWERS *To Text Problems (even-numbered)*

Chapter 2

2. **(a)** $NX = \text{GDP} - (C + I + G)$
$= 240 - (150 + 40 + 48)$
$= 2$

(b) Indirect taxes = GDP – Net domestic income – Depreciation
$= 240 - 190 - (40 - 15)$
$= 25$

(c) Corporate profits = Net domestic income – (Wages and salaries + Interest income + Net income of unincorporated business)
$= 190 - (146 + 13 + 16)$
$= 15$

(d) Personal income = Net domestic income – Corporate profits + (Dividends + Interest on government debt + Transfer payments)
$= 190 - 15 + (5 + 7 + 25)$
$= 212$

(e) Personal taxes = Budget surplus – Indirect taxes + (Expenditure on goods and services + Transfer payments + Interest on government debt)
$= -15 - 25 + (48 + 25 + 7)$
$= 40$

Disposable income = 212 – 40
= 172

(f) Personal saving = Disposable income – Consumption
= 172 – 150
= 22

4. (a) In the former case it would count as investment, in the latter as consumption.

(b) GDP would increase. Household care is not counted in GDP unless there is a market transaction.

(c) It would increase net exports.

6. (a) The consumer price index (CPI) measures the cost of buying a fixed bundle of goods, representative of the purchases of consumers.

(b) $\frac{(5 \times 30) + (3 \times 20) + (4 \times 6)}{120} \times 100 = 195$

(c)

$$CPI_t = \frac{\Sigma P_t^i \; q_0^i}{\Sigma P_0^i \; q_0^i} \times 100$$

$$CPI_0 = \frac{\Sigma P_0^i \; q_0^i}{\Sigma P_0^i \; q_0^i} \times 100$$

$$CPI_t - CPI_0 = \frac{\Sigma q_0^i \; [P_t^i - P_0^i]}{\Sigma P_0^i \; q_0^i} \times 100$$

$$= \frac{\Sigma q_0^i \; P_0^i \; [(P_t^i / P_0^i) - 1]}{\Sigma P_0^i \; q_0^i} \times 100$$

8. (a) $YD = C + S \qquad S = \$15$

(b) $(S - I) = (G + TR - TA) + NX \qquad I = \$6$

(c) $C + I + G + NX = GDP \qquad G = \$27$

Chapter 3

2. (a) higher; 1500

(b) $Y = 2000 = 200/0.1$

(c) more; multiplier is higher ($\alpha = 10$)

(d)

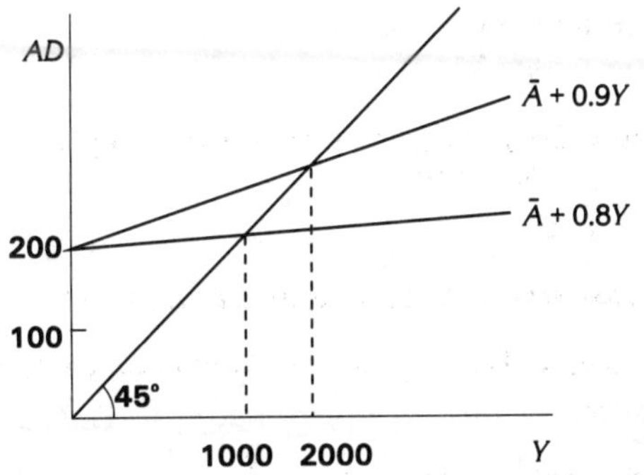

4. **(a)** $S = -\overline{C} + (1 - c)Y$

(b)

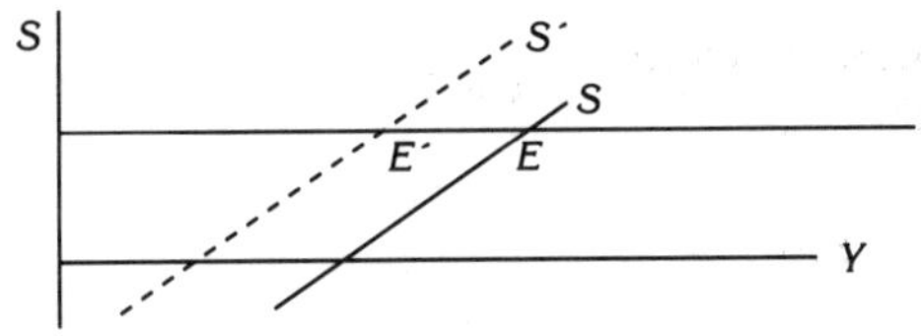

The saving function moves from S to S′.

(c) The economy moves from E to E′. The income level is lower, because an increased desire to save means that consumption, and so aggregate demand, is lower at every level of output.

6. $\overline{I} + \overline{G} + \overline{TR} + \overline{X} = \text{YD} - C + TA + Q$

$$= -\overline{C} + (1 - c)[Y - TA + \overline{TR}] + TA + Q$$

$$[(1 - c)(1 - t) + t + m]Y = \overline{A}$$

$$Y = \frac{1}{1 - c(1 - t) + m}\overline{A}$$

where $\overline{A} = \overline{C} + c\overline{TR} + \overline{I} + \overline{G} + \overline{X} - \overline{Q}$

8. **(a)** $Y_0 = \overline{C} + c(Y + \overline{TR} - bY - tY) + \overline{I} + \overline{G}$

$$Y_0 = \frac{\overline{C} + c\overline{TR} + \overline{I} + \overline{G}}{1 - c[1 - (b + t)]}$$

(b) $$\frac{1}{1 - c[1 - (b + t)]}$$

(c) Since tranfers rise when income falls, they reduce the effect of a change in total income on personal disposable income and spending.

(d) The countercyclical transfers operate just like the tax system. They act as an automatic stabilizer reducing the multiplier.

10. Use the numbers in problem 9.

Y_0^1 with $c = 0.8, t = 0.20, G = 200, = 1111.1$
Y_0^2 with $c = 0.8, t = 0.25, G = 250, = 1125$
$BS^1 = 0.2(1111.1) - \overline{TR} - 200$
$BS^2 = (0.25)(1125) - \overline{TR} - 250$

The budget surplus increases by approximately 9. The surplus rises because the increase in income results in more taxes for the government.

12. $\Delta Y = c\Delta YD + \Delta G$
$\Delta Y = c[\Delta Y - \Delta(TA - TR)] + \Delta G$
but
$\Delta G = \Delta(TA - TR)$
hence
$\Delta Y = c[\Delta Y - \Delta G] + \Delta G$
$\Delta Y = \Delta G \qquad \Delta Y/\Delta G = 1$

14.

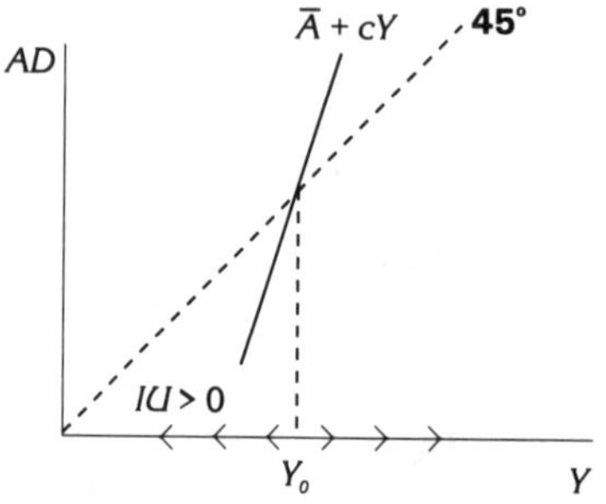

Here the marginal propensity to spend is greater than one and the equilibrium is unstable. Suppose we are at equilibrium and autonomous spending increases by \$1. On the next round it goes up by \$$c$. On the next round the increase is \$$c^2$, etc. If $c > 1$, each successive amount of spending is larger than that in the previous round, and the process will not converge. (See Section 3 of this chapter of the *Instructor's Manual* for discussion of the implications of nonconvergence.)

Alternatively, the adjustment process that focusses on inventories is unstable. To the right of Y_0, output is less than aggregate demand and firms therefore raise output to restore depleted inventories. However, this only causes aggregate demand to expand even more, and so on.

Chapter 4

2. **(a)** In Chapter 3 the multiplier with income taxes is defined as

$$\bar{\alpha} = \frac{1}{1 - c(1 - t)}$$

Thus, using the parameters of the consumption function specified in problem 1, we have

$$\bar{\alpha} = \frac{1}{1 - 0.8(1 - 0.75)} = 2.5$$

(b) In order to include the effects of the assets market on a change in government spending, solve the *IS* and *LM* equations from problem 1 simultaneously. In general terms:

The *IS* curve is $Y = \bar{\alpha}(\bar{A} - bi)$.
The *LM* curve is $i = 1/h\ (kY - \overline{M}/\overline{P})$.

By substituting the *IS* equation into the *LM* we get

$$Y = \bar{\alpha}\,[\,\bar{A} - \frac{b}{h}(kY - \frac{\overline{M}}{\overline{P}})]$$

or after collecting terms in *Y*,

$$Y_0 = \frac{h\bar{\alpha}}{h + kb\bar{\alpha}}\bar{A} + \frac{b\bar{\alpha}}{h + kb\bar{\alpha}}\frac{\overline{M}}{\overline{P}}$$

The terms that multiply the exogenous variables $\bar{A}$ and $\overline{M}/\overline{P}$ are the fiscal and monetary multipliers.

Therefore, by substituting the parameters *h*, *b*, and *k* from problem 1, and the value of $\bar{\alpha}$ calculated in **(a)**, the multiplier for government spending is

$$\frac{62.5(2.5)}{62.5 + 50(0.25)2.5} = 1.67$$

(c) From equation (11a) we have

$\Delta i = (k/h)\Delta Y = 0.004\Delta Y$

A fiscal expansion raises output by $1.67 per dollar increase in government spending, and therefore raises the interest rate by

$\Delta i = 0.004\ (1.67)\Delta G = 0.0067\Delta G$

Thus, a 149 dollar (= 1/0.0067) increase in government spending would raise the equilibrium interest rate by one percentage point.

(d) The difference in the multipliers calculated in **(a)** and **(b)** above arises from the impact of the fiscal expansion on income and interest rates and hence investment spending. The multiplier in **(b)** is lower because it incorporates the dampening effects of higher interest rates on investment.

4. The slope of the *LM* curve by 11(a) is equal to

$$\Delta i/\Delta Y = k/h$$

and thus depends on both the income and the interest response of money demand. Suppose there is an increase in income. Along the *LM* curve the equilibrium interest rate must rise more (a) the larger the increase in money demand, and hence the excess demand for money, induced by higher income, and (b) the smaller the interest response of money demand. With a small interest response of money demand it takes a large change in interest rates to eliminate a given excess demand for money.

6. Suppose our consumption function takes the form

$$C = \overline{C} + cY - gi \qquad g > 0$$

so that an increase in the interest rate reduces consumption and raises savings. This implies, in combination with the investment function, an aggregate demand equation:

$$A = \overline{A} + cY - (b + g)i$$

and hence an equation for the *IS* schedule of

$$Y = \overline{\alpha}[\overline{A} - (b + g)i]$$

Given b, there is now a higher interest response to aggregate demand. A given fall in the interest rate generates more of an excess demand for goods and thus requires a higher expansion in equilibrium output along the *IS* schedule. Thus the *IS* schedule becomes flatter.

8. The equation of the *IS* schedule is

$$Y = \frac{1}{1 - c(1 - t)}(\overline{A} - bi)$$

(a) For a given interest rate an increase in the tax rate, t, reduces the after-tax propensity to spend, $c(1 - t)$, and therefore reduces aggregate demand and thus the equilibrium level of income consistent with goods market equilibrium. The *IS* schedule will shift to the left and it will become steeper.

(b) For a given *LM* schedule that is upward-sloping, the equilibrium level of income must fall.

(c) The equilibrium interest rate will decline.

10. (a) This can be shown using equation 15a in the text. The smaller the coefficient, h, the larger the change in income for a given change in the money stock.

(b) Equation 16 in the text shows that the smaller h is, the larger the change in the interest rate.

12. (1) An increase in G raises aggregate demand and output: the larger is $\overline{\alpha}$, the more aggregate demand will increase; consumers are more responsive to a change in income level (the *IS* schedule is flatter, and the shift is greater).

(2) The increase in income raises money demand and hence interest rates: if k is small, the increase in in demand for money following the increase in income does not have a large impact on interest rates; likewise, if h is large, money demand is quite sensitive to the interest rate, and the change in i following the shift in money demand is small (the *LM* curve is flatter).

(3) The increase in interest rates reduces investment spending and dampens the output expansion: the smaller b is, the less sensitive investment is to the interest rate; the dampening effect of higher interest rates is smaller (again, a flatter *IS*). *Summary:* The change in equilibrium income following an increase in government spending will be greater when k and b are smaller and when h and $\overline{\alpha}$ are larger.

14. With the multiplier of 2, equilibrium income will increase by \$2 billion. For interest rates to remain constant, the real money supply must increase by k times the change in income.

$0.5 \times \$2 \text{ billion} = \$1 \text{ billion}$

Chapter 5

2. (a) $$Y = \frac{\overline{A} - hi_0 + \overline{X} - \overline{Q}}{1 - c + m}$$

$$Y = \frac{400 - 30(0.5)}{1 - 0.8 + 0.2}$$

(b) $NX = \overline{X} - \overline{Q} - mY$
$= 250 - 192.5 = 57.5$

(c) $\Delta Y/\Delta A = 1/(s + m) = 1/0.4 = 2.5$

(d) $\Delta Y = \Delta X[1/(s + m)] = 2.5$
$\Delta NX = \Delta X[s/(s + m)] = 0.5\Delta X = -0.5$

(e) $\Delta NX = -m\Delta Y = [m/(s + m)]b\Delta i = 15\Delta i$

When interest rates increase, investment falls; hence, income falls. Since imports are dependent on the level of income, they too fall, while exports are unchanged. Thus the trade balance improves.

(f) A country can use a combination of tariffs, export subsidies, devaluations, and quotas, along with some expansionary fiscal or monetary policy.

4. **(a)** This leads to both a decline in income and an external deficit — a dilemma. Use a tariff and increase government spending.

(b) This leads to an increased deficit and output above full employment. No dilemma — just cut spending.

(c) Same answer as **(b)**.

(d) This creates a trade surplus and increases income above full employment. This is a dilemma. We need a cut in spending and an expenditure switching policy.

(e) There will be no change in income, but there will be a balance of trade surplus. Lower tariffs and cut income taxes at the same time to increase imports while keeping Y constant.

6. $$\left(0.85\frac{1.146}{1.200}+0.05\frac{2.028}{2.429}+0.10\frac{0.693}{0.532}\right)100=98.4$$

Chapter 6

2. For all answers, use the following diagram:

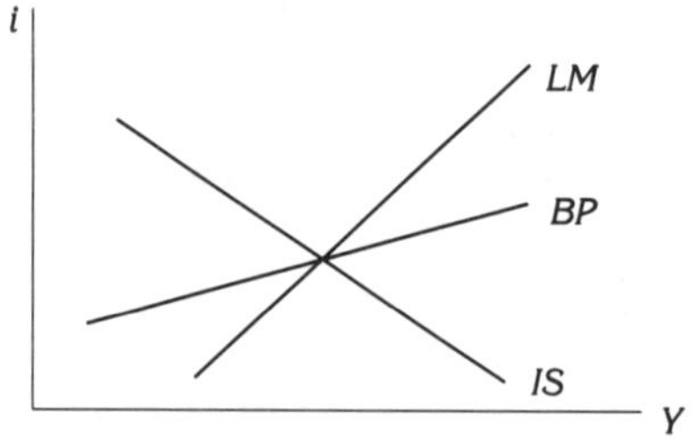

(a) This will temporarily shift the IS curve to the right and the BP curve down. Since it is temporary, no action need be taken, but a temporary export tax might be used.

(b) Now the shifts of the curves described in **(a)** are permanent. Income is above full-employment level, and we have a balance of payments surplus. Spending must be cut more than the increase in exports, and the money supply should be expanded.

(c) Here just the *IS* curve moves to the left. Policy moves it back to its original position by increasing government spending.

(d) Here we have an autonomous increase in capital outflows. This means that along the old *BP* schedule we have a deficit. Thus, the *BP* schedule schedule shifts up. Expansive fiscal policy and tight money will raise interest rates and maintain the level of income, and thus put us on the new *BP* schedule with higher interest rates and unchanged output.

4. With perfect capital mobility (given prices), a monetary expansion lowers interest rates and induces capital outflows and currency depreciation. The depreciation raises net exports, thus increasing demand and raising income. Monetary policy raises output not because it ultimately lowers interest rates and raises investment, but because it induces a depreciation and thus raises exports.

6. Starting at the point *E*, an increase in exports shifts the *IS* curve to *IS′*, but it has no effect on the BP curve since it is horizontal at the foreign interest rate. At *E′*, the domestic interest rate exceeds the foreign rate, and we have an immediate capital inflow. With a fixed exchange rate, the money supply increases and the economy moves to *E″*. At this point the overall balance of payments remains at zero, but the trade account has improved as shown in problem 1 of Chapter 5. With a flexible exchange rate, the capital inflow causes an appreciation that shifts the *IS* curve back to its original position. In this case the appreciation offsets the increase in exports so that the trade balance is unchanged.

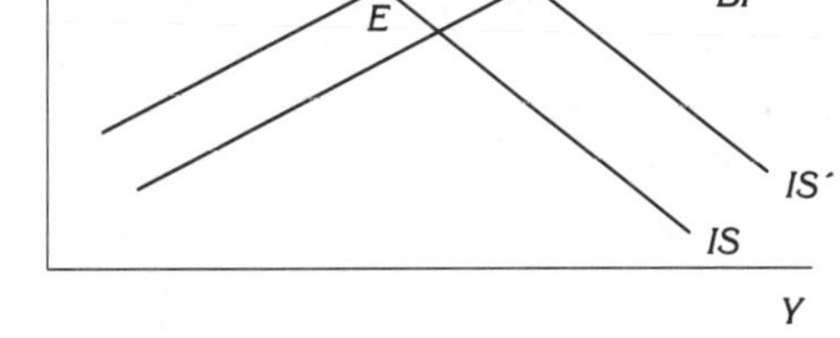

8. **(a)** The equation derived in the problem can be written in the form

$$(Y - \overline{C} - cY - \overline{G}) - (\bar{I} - bi) = -a(i - i^*)$$

The equation thus states that, in goods market and balance of payments equilibrium, saving minus investment equals the rate of capital outflow. The schedule is shown in the accompanying diagram as *AA* and is downward-sloping. A rise in income creates an excess supply of goods or raises saving above investment, thus giving rise to a current account surplus. To restore equilibrium, interest rates must decline, thereby raising investment and inducing a capital outflow to match the higher current account surplus. The schedule is drawn for given government expenditure and foreign interest rate.

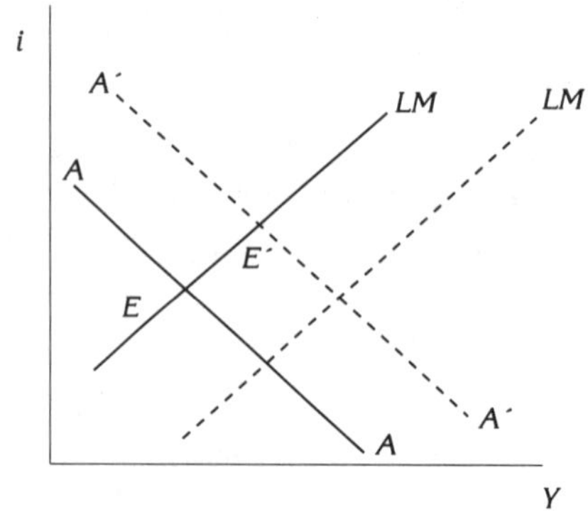

(b) The *LM* schedule is positively sloped as usual. At the intersection we have goods and money market equilibrium as well as payments balance.

(c) A fiscal expansion affects the *AA* schedule. A fiscal expansion raises aggregate demand and thus shifts the *AA* schedule upward. To maintain goods and payments balance, interest rates must rise or income must expand. The new equilibrium is a point *E′* with a higher interest rate and an expansion in income.

(d) A monetary expansion corresponds to a rightward shift of the *LM* schedule, thus reducing interest rates and raising income. The capital account worsens, but there is an offsetting increase in net exports that adds to demand. We showed above that a monetary expansion raises income and reduces interest rates so that it must lead to a depreciation. A fiscal expansion, by contrast, leads to higher income and higher interest rates. Here the effect on the exchange rate is ambiguous. If capital mobility is very high there will be appreciation; if it is very low there will be depreciation.

Chapter 7

2. The classical supply curve is vertical because it is based on the assumption that the labour market is always in equilibrium with the labour force fully employed.

Since there is no more labour available to produce any extra output, output cannot expand if the price level increases. The model also assumes that wages adjust quickly to changes in demand. If the demand curve shifts to the left, at the existing price level the quantity of goods demanded falls. Firms lay off labour, but these workers, anxious to remain employed, accept a lower wage. Because wages are lower, firms can charge a lower price and output remains unchanged. (This is the reverse of the case given in the book.)

4. An increase in the productivity of labour will cause the vertical aggregate supply curve to shift to the right. Prices will fall. The size of the rightward shift, and hence the fall in prices, will depend on the slope of the labour supply curve.

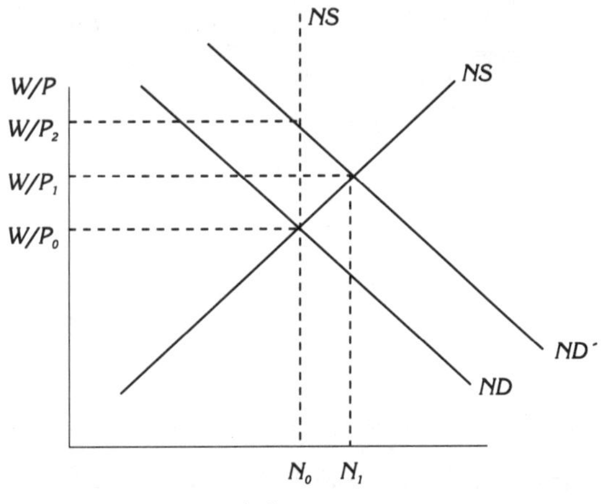

6. **(a)** The *LM* curve is flatter when the interest responsiveness of money demand is large. An increase in real balances (following a price decrease) causes a smaller increase in equilibrium output and spending, and a steeper aggregate demand curve.

8. $S + T = I + G$
$S + T - G = I$

Let G increase to G' (a fiscal expansion). Then

$S + T - G' = I' \quad G' > G$

I' must be less than I by the amount that G' is greater than G. There is full crowding out.

10. **(a)** A decrease in the personal income tax rate will shift the *IS* curve to the right; the aggregate demand curve also shifts to the right.

(b) As equilibrium Y increases, the demand for real balances increases. Since M/P is fixed, the interest rate must rise to restore equilibrium in the money market.

(c) Investment will fall in response to the higher interest rate.

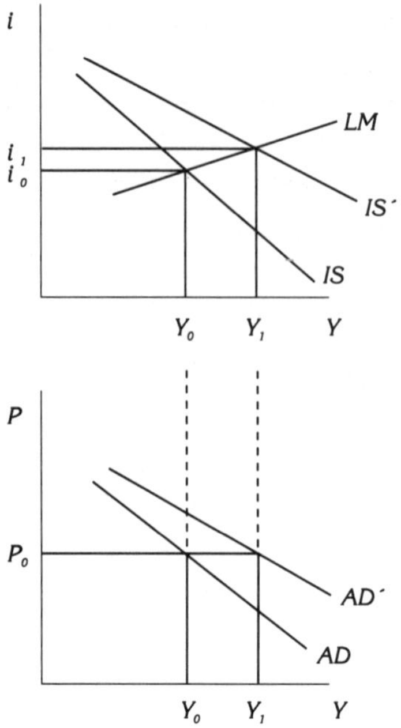

12. A decline in the demand for money implies an increase in velocity. If $MV = PY$, at a given income a decline in the demand for a given stock stock of money will cause prices to increase. (This, of course, isn't the strict quantity theory.)

14. (a) The strict quantity theory maintains that prices move in proportion to the nominal money stock. Velocity must be constant and output must remain at full employment for the theory to hold.

(b) Monetarists (modern quantity theorists) do not insist on the strict quantity theory, but they see changes in the money stock as the most critical single determinant of price level changes. A changing money stock may have real short-run effects, but monetarists believe that, in the long run, money is neutral.

Chapter 8

2. In the short run, real balances fall, but not by as much as the change in the money stock; this is because prices also fall. In the medium run, the level of real balances rises as prices fall, but they are still below the original level. In the final, long-run equilibrium, real balances are at their original level.

4. In the short run, increased government spending shifts *AD* to *AD′*. Output, employment, and prices all increase. Real balances fall and the interest rate rises. The new equilibrium is at E′.

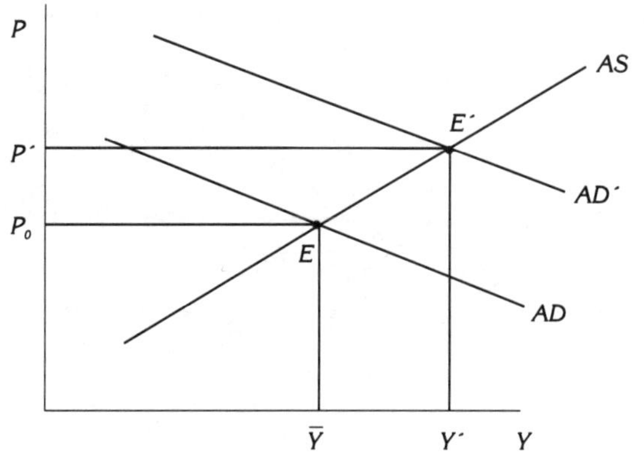

In the medium term, output is greater than normal and wages rise. Prices rise in response to the cost pressures of overemployment. The aggregate supply curve shifts up, passing through the full-employment level at *P′*. Output falls (from *E′*), and real balances continue to fall and the interest rate to increase.

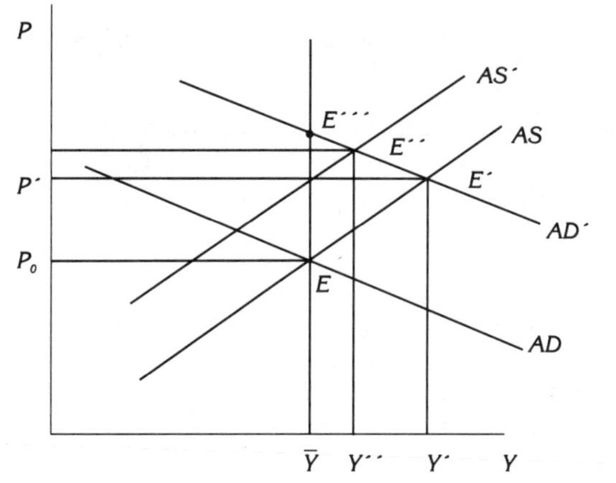

As long as output exceeds the full-employment level, wages and prices continue to rise and *AS* continues to shift to the left until the full-employment equilibrium is reestablished. Real balances are lower than their original level and the interest rate is higher.

6. An increase in income taxes causes a fall in consumption; the *AD* curve shifts to the left.

(a) In the short run, output and prices fall. Real balances increase; hence the interest rate falls.

(b) In the long run, output returns to the full-employment level. Wages and prices fall. Real balances increase further; thus the interest rate also declines.

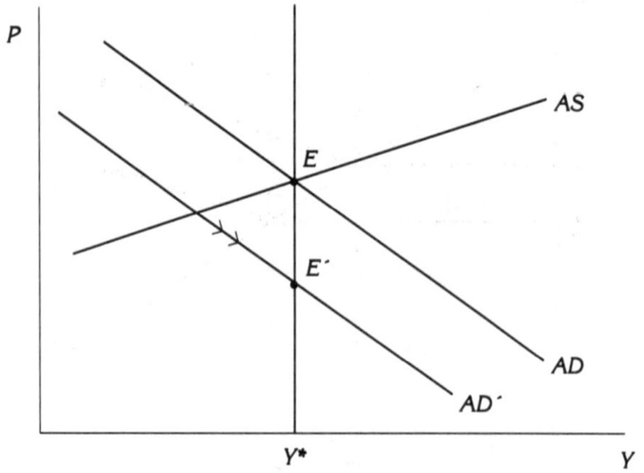

8. A decline in the real price of materials will shift the aggregate supply curve to the right, from *AS* to *AS'*.

(a) In the short run, output increases and prices fall as the economy moves to E'.

(b) In the long run, there is upward pressure on wages and hence on prices. *AS* shifts back toward its original position. The long-run equilibrium is reestablished at *E*. Real wages are higher than at the outset.

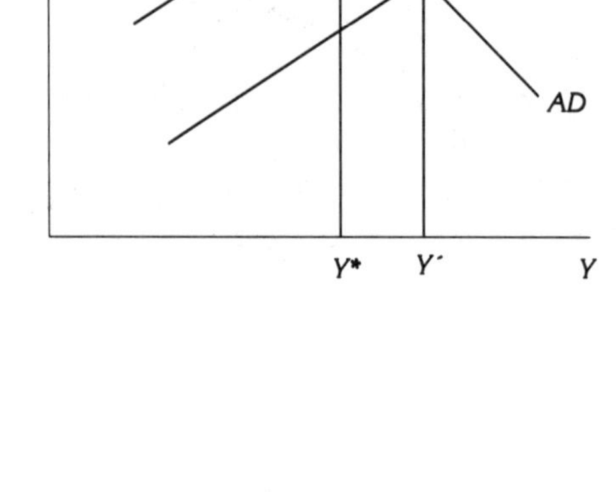

10. **(a)** The long-run effect of a materials price increase that is accompanied by a fall in the level of potential output given aggregate demand is shown in the figure. This differs from the case in the text (without the increase in *AD*) because in the long run prices increase and output is also reduced.

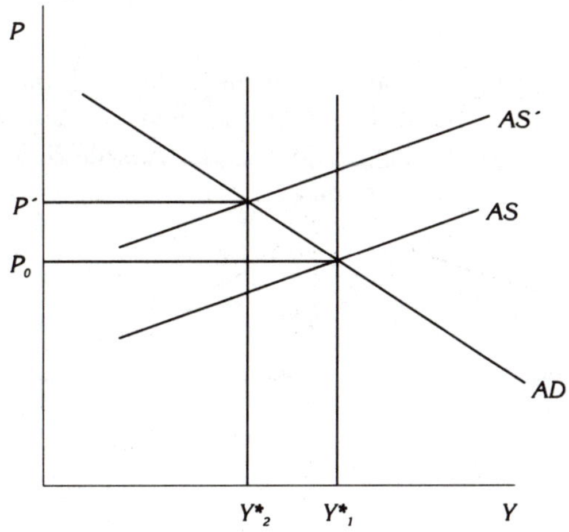

(b) As shown in the figure, the original materials price increase shifts the *AS* curve to *AS′*. Output has declined to below the new potential output level. Over time, wages will decline because of unemployment, but the economy will expand only to point *E′* because firms no longer find it profitable to supply the same level of output as before at full employment of labour, given the increase in costs.

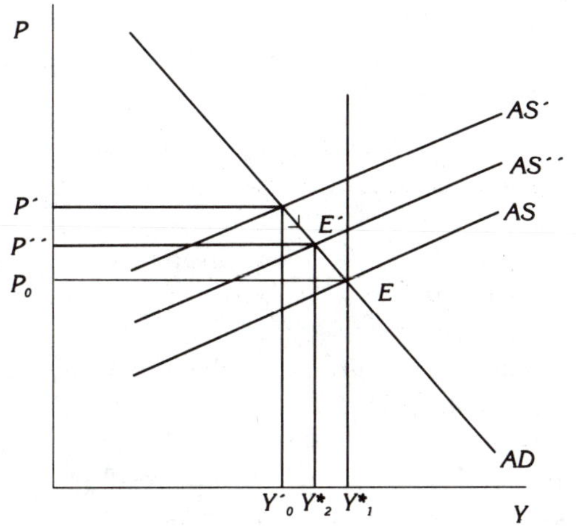

12. **(a)** The *AS* curve shifts up by the same amount as the *AD* curve, since the effect on the price level will be anticipated. An equation for the expected price level can be obtained by setting *AD* equal to full-employment output (see footnote 5 in the text).

(b) In this case only the *AD* curve shifts in the short run, so that output and the price level both rise.

(c) The diagrams will be the same as those shown in the text for the case of a money supply increase. The difference between the answers to (**a**) and (**b**) arises from different assumptions about whether or not the implications of a demand shift are incorporated into price level expectations.

Chapter 9

2. The equation of the *AS* curve given in Equation 9 of Chapter 8 is:

$$P = P_{-1}\,[1 + \lambda(Y - Y^{*})]$$

The other relationship required is the *IS* schedule shown in the figure. It is described by Equation 6 in the text:

$$Y = \bar{\bar{\alpha}}(\bar{A} - bi^{*} + q\frac{eP*}{P})$$

4. A tariff (with the proceeds redistributed so as not to have a simultaneous fiscal contraction) raises the relative price of imports and thus operates like a depreciation. Income tends to rise, leading to higher interest rates and thus to capital inflows and currency appreciation. With perfect capital mobility, the appreciation will proceed to the point where the change in net exports is zero and there is no effect on income or interest rates.

6. Purchasing power parity implies that on average, over long periods (five years?), exchange rate trends mirror differentials in national inflation rates. There are divergences from PPP to the extent that real disturbances intervene (changes in comparative advantage, oil discoveries, differentials in productivity growth) or that monetary events lead to a transitory, though quite possibly protracted, overdepreciation or real appreciation. A country that experiences a dramatic outburst of inflation (with uncertainty about how far the inflation will go) typically experiences an overdepreciation of its currency. When firm anti-inflation policies are instituted and nominal and real interest rates are raised sharply, so much capital flows in that an overappreciation results. These are important (and technically subtle) side problems in stabilization.

8. There would be an immediate depreciation and the short-run equilibrium would be at the point E' as in Figure 6-15. Along the adjustment path, the *LM* curve shifts back as the *AS* curve shifts up and the price level rises. At the new long-run equilibrium, the price level is higher but the initial levels of income and the interest rate are restored.

Chapter 10

2. (a) Since consumption is constant over the lifetime and assets are accumulated during working life and decumulated during retirement, the consumption-asset ratio falls (with increasing assets) during working life and rises (as assets decrease) during retirement. This can be shown formally by starting from the value of cumulative saving in year T of working life, which is equal to $T[(NL - WL)/NL]YL$. Hence the ratio of consumption, $(WL/NL)YL$, to assets is given by $WL/[T(NL - WL)]$. As T goes from 1 to NL, this ratio moves from $WL/(NL - WL)$ to $1/(NL - WL)$.

   (b) At retirement, $T = WL$ and thus the ratio is equal to $1/(NL - WL)$. During retirement we have a stock of assets equal to the number of years left, $NL - T$, times consumption $(WL/NL)YL$, or $(NL - T)(WL/NL)YL$. The ratio of consumption to assets thus is $1/(NL - T)$. At retirement we have $T = WL$, and as retirement proceeds T approaches NL. In the last year, $T = NL$ and the consumption-asset ratio approaches unity.

   Example: Suppose $NL = 8$ and $WL = 6$. Call X_T the ratio of consumption during the year to assets at the beginning of the year. Then we have

					WL		NL
T = 1	2	3	4	5	6	7	8
X_T	3	1.5	1	0.75	0.6	0.5	1

4. The propensity to consume out of income is WL/NL; the consumption ratio depends on the number of years' income available to finance lifetime consumption. Accumulated wealth is consumed over the life cycle. Therefore the propensity to consume is equal to one over the number of years left in life. The fewer the number of years left, the larger the fraction of wealth that can be consumed in the remaining years.

6. The permanent income hypothesis implies that consumption is proportional to permanent income, $C = kYP$. How does a Christmas bonus affect permanent income?

(a) A bonus every year is a permanent bonus; accordingly it will be treated like any other systematic part of income and will be consumed according to permanent income.

(b) A random or one-time-only bonus is spent over the lifetime. Only a small fraction of it will be consumed; most will be saved.

8. Gamblers have a high variability of income compared with those in stable professions such as civil servants. Their consumption is geared to their average or permanent income, and transitory bouts of winning or losing will not greatly affect their consumption behaviour.

10. To maintain income constant in the face of an increase in wealth we have to maintain constant consumption. The effect of higher wealth on consumers must be offset by increased income taxes. From Equation 14 we thus have

$$\Delta C = 0 = a\Delta(WR) - b\theta YD\Delta t \text{ or } YD\Delta t/\Delta(WR) = a/b\theta$$

for year 1. In the long run the tax change would be

$$\Delta C = 0 = a\Delta(WR) - b\theta YD\Delta t - b(1-\theta)YD\Delta t$$
$$\text{or } YD\Delta t/\Delta(WR) = a/b.$$

Suppose $a = 0.05$, $b = 0.5$, $\theta = 0.6$, and $Y = 2000$ billion. Then a 10 billion change in wealth requires a change in the average tax rate of $\Delta t = (a/b\theta)10/2000 = 0.0008$. In the long run the tax change is $\Delta t = (a/b)(10/2000) = 0.0005$.

12. **(a)** Saving may either increase or decrease following an increase in the interest rate. A higher interest rate may attract more saving through the higher return; the cost of not saving rises. But a higher return also means that a given amount can be available at some time in the future with less saving now.

(b) The amount of investment in an economy depends on the savings of the economy. A low saving rate leads to reduced investment and diminished future production.

Chapter 11

2. **(a)** The fact that permanent income and output determine consumption and investment means that the links between current income and consumption and investment are more complicated than they are in the *IS-LM* model of Chapter 4. If expectations are formed as in Chapter 10, as a weighted average of current and lagged income, then both consumption and investment spending will be less sensitive to current income than in the previous *IS-LM* analysis. It also means that the positions of the *IS* and *LM* curves shift over time, even in response to a one-time change in, say, tax rates or the money supply.

At a deeper level, the dependence of consumption and investment on permanent income means that considerable thought has to be given to how changes in policies affect expectations of permanent income. For instance, a temporary tax cut will have very different effects on consumption demand in the current period than will a permanent tax cut, and so on.

(b) Once the emphasis shifts to permanent variables, policy makers have to worry much more about the effects of their policies on expectations. In an particular case, as already noted, the effects of a policy change will depend on how the private sector interprets its permanence. Over the long run, the success of policy will in part depend on how much the policy authorities are believed, because the private sector eventually begins to understand recurrent patterns of public sector behaviour. For instance, if the monetary authority over long periods has followed inflationary policies, then a mere declaration that policy has now changed would be unlikely to be believed, without the support of experience.

4. An increase in the demand for a firm's product would raise the firm's expected level of future sales to some degree. The firm would then desire to have a larger capital stock and start to invest to reach this new capital stock. The speed of its reponse would depend both on how permanent it believed the change to be and on the costs to the firm of adjusting its capital stock quickly.

6. Animal spirits enter the analysis through the expected income variable. Presumably when entrepreneurs are optimistic, they believe they will be able to sell a lot and undertake a lot of investment; when their spirits are low, so are their sales expectations and they invest relatively little.

8. In the neoclassical theory of investment, the size of the desired stock depends on the firm's expected output and the rental cost of capital. For firms using the present value method of evaluating projects, increases in the cost of capital generally reduce the present value of a given cash stream and allow fewer projects to pass the positive *PDV* test: the rate of investment is inversely related to the cost of capital. When a firm anticipates an increase in output, the cash flows associated with a project will be larger and the *PDV* will rise: investment demand is positively associated with expected output. The decision-making of firms is consistent with neoclassical theory.

10.

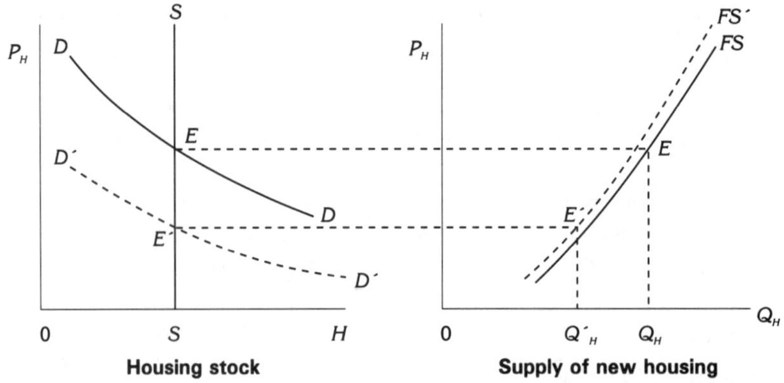

An increase in interest rates will reduce demand for the stock of housing, shifting the *DD* curve in the figure down to *D′D′*. At the same time, the increase in interest rates raises the financing costs of builders, and shifts the flow supply curve, *FS*, up slightly to *FS′*. The economy moves from point E in both figures to *E′*. The price of housing falls, and the rate of production of housing — the rate of housing investment — likewise falls, from Q_H to Q'_H.

12. **(a)** The desired capital stock is given by

$$K^* = \frac{aY}{i_C}$$

Filling in the specified numbers, we have

$$K^* = \frac{0.3 \times 250}{0.15} = \$500 \text{ million}$$

(b) If Y rises to \$300 million, K^* rises to \$600 million.

(c) With $\lambda = 0.4$, we have investment given by

$$I = \lambda(K^* - K) = 0.4(600 - 500) = \$40 \text{ million}$$

By the beginning of the second year, the capital stock is \$540 million. Thus second-year investment is

$$I = 0.04(600 - 540) = \$24 \text{ million}$$

(d) The answers give net investment. Gross investment continues to take place to restore depreciating capital even when the capital stock is at its steady-state value.

Chapter 12

2. **(a)** This decreases the need for holding large amounts of currency for *precautionary* purposes and also cuts the inconvenience cost of going between your savings and your chequing account, thereby reducing *transactions* demand. This would decrease the demand for M1 and not have much effect on the total demand for M2, since the reduced demand for M1 would be offset by the increased demand for savings deposits, a component of M2.

(b) This might make it less costly to make transactions between demand and savings deposits, and thus have the same effects as outlined in the answer to part **(a)** of this question.

(c) An increase in inflationary expectations would lead to an increase in nominal interest rates, thus reducing the demand for M1 — as in the answers to parts **(a)** and **(b)**.

(d) Credit cards cut into the transactions demand for money. Therefore, the demand for M1 would be reduced. People might shift into savings accounts away from M1, since they would want a convenient way of paying their credit card charges monthly.

(e) It all depends. If the collapse of the government meant a radical change in government, all money would lose value under the new government and prices would rise (i.e., there would be a drop in the value of money) when the fear of governmental collapse developed.

(f) If the interest rate on nonchequing savings deposits increased while other rates were held constant, then funds held in other assets would be transferred to these deposits. Therefore, the demand for M2 would increase and the demand for other assets would fall.

4. Travellers' cheques are an alternative to cash and are cheques that must be paid for at the rate of approximately 1 cent per dollar. The cheques, however, are insured and generally negotiable. The cost of the cheques must be weighed against the probability of having cash stolen or not having a personal cheque honoured. The higher the latter two probabilities, the greater the relative benefits of travellers' cheques.

6. For a given price level, a certain nominal money stock will be desired, given income and interest rates. At a higher price level, but with the same interest rates and income, the same level of real balances will be desired, so the nominal money stock would increase in the same proportion as the price level. However, a *continuing* increase in the price level, or inflation, will be reflected in an increase in nominal interest rates. This of course increases the cost of holding money, and therefore real balances will be reduced. Alternatively, in countries where the financial markets are not well developed, increasing inflation makes it expensive to hold money relative to real assets, such as land and houses, and individuals reduce their demand for real balances in order to hold more real assets.

8. The total interest earned is that on the amount *not* transferred at the beginning of the month. This is $(1 - t_0)Y_n$. It is held as bonds, earning i, for fraction t_0 of the month. Thus total interest earnings is

$$IE = i(1 - t_0)Y_n t_0$$

The interest earned as a function of t_0 is shown in the following table:

Value for t_0	Interest Earned
0	0
1	0
1/2	$\frac{Y_n}{4} i$
1/4	$\frac{3Y_n}{16} i$
3/4	$\frac{3Y_n}{16} i$

It looks as though interest earnings are maximized for $t_0 = 1/2$. This can be confirmed using calculus. Maximizing IE with respect to t_0 gives

$$0 = iY_n [-t_0 + (1 - t_0)]$$

or

$$t_0 = 1/2$$

Chapter 13

2. Δ Loans = (1 – 0.1) 0.95 = 0.855

$$\Delta M = \frac{1 + cu}{cu + re} = \frac{1.0526}{0.1526} = 6.9$$

4. Credit cards and ATMs should reduce the desired currency-deposit ratio, thereby increasing the money multiplier.

6. **(a)** **(1)** $M1 = CU + DD$

(2) $B = CU + R$

$R = R_n + R_d$ (where R_n and R_d are reserves held against notice and demand deposits respectively)

$R = r_n ND + r_d DD$

Now let $DD/ND = d$.

(3) $R = r_n DD/d + r_d DD$

Divide (2) into (1) and use (3).

$$\frac{M1}{B} = \frac{CU + DD}{CU + r_n \frac{DD}{d} + r_d DD}$$

$$M1 = \frac{1 + cu}{cu + r_n/d + r_d} B$$

Note: $CU = cu \times DD$

(b) $M2 = CU + DD + ND = CU + DD + DD/d$

$$\frac{1 + cu + 1/d}{cu + r_n/d + r_d}$$

(c) An increase in the demand deposit-notice deposit ratio will increase M1 and lower M2. The first effect can be seen by inspection, but for the second effect you can try a numerical example or differentiate the multiplier with respect to d.

Chapter 14

2. **(a)** In period 1 decide to make $1 billion expenditure in the next period.

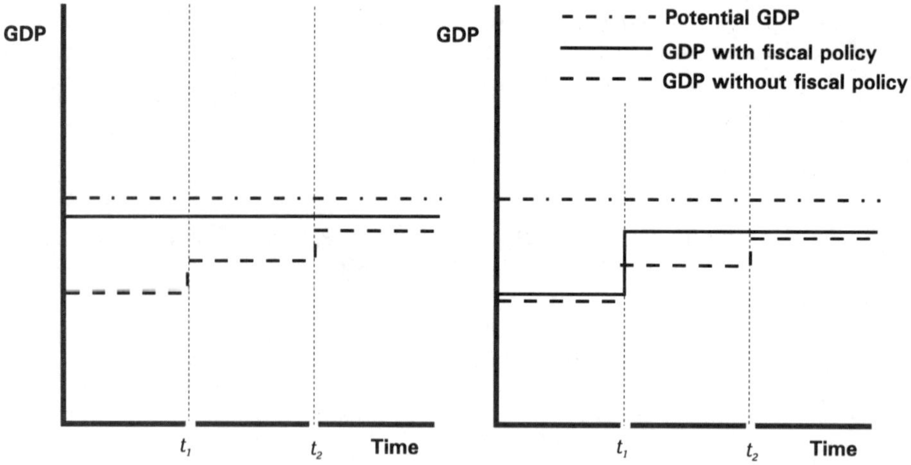

4. Caution is the key when there is multiplier uncertainty. Since the maximum multiplier is 2.5, in the first period government spending could increase without hazard by \$1.6 billion. In the next period the very cautious, forecasting an early return to potential GDP, would do nothing rather than run the risk of exceeding potential, although \$0.8 billion would be a reasonably safe expenditure.

6. First, be sure that you are distinguishing between arguments for and against policy rules and arguments for and against activism. It is possible to design activist rules. Since the economy, as well as our knowledge of it, is not set in stone, it is difficult to argue for hard and fast rules. Such rules incapacitate policy makers in times of major disturbances. One argument for a monetary rule or at least the announcement of future policy is that such knowledge reduces the uncertainty in the system. It is easier for individuals to forecast policy behaviour and to form their plans accordingly; they are not playing a guessing game with the government.

These statements apply to fiscal policy as well as to monetary policy; however, the long inside lag associated with fiscal policy makes it a better candidate for rules such as the automatic stabilizers.

Chapter 15

2. During the 1960s, the economy grew above potential — there was too much aggregate demand. A permanent tax increase should have been implemented by at least 1967. Of course, these policies would not have prevented inflation in the 1970s, but they would have meant that the economy entered the decade with a lower inflation rate than it actually did, and presumably, therefore, that the inflation rate in the 1970s would on average have been substantially lower. Those who emphasize expectations also believe that inflationary psychology would not have become deeply ingrained if the central banks had shown in the 1960s that they were serious about fighting inflation. This type of issue will be taken up in Chapter 20 when we discuss rational expectations.

4. Any combination of interest rates and income can, in principle, be achieved by use of monetary and fiscal policy. A high interest rate policy will mean low investment and high consumption for a given level of income. A low interest rate policy will reverse the roles of investment and consumption. Using the *IS-LM* model:

$M' > M^0$
$G^0 > G'$

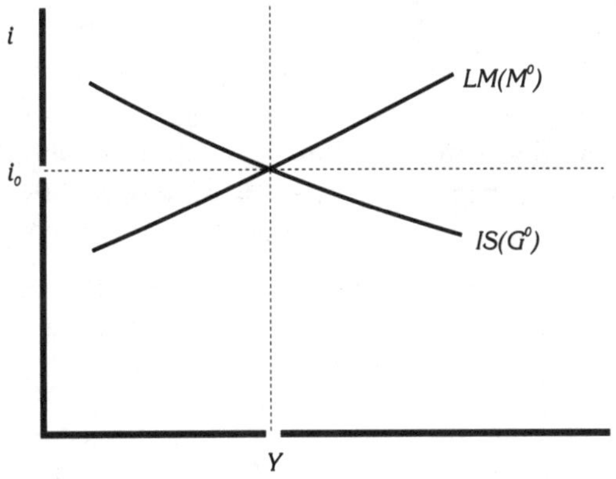

Low investment, high Interest "tight" Money, high spending

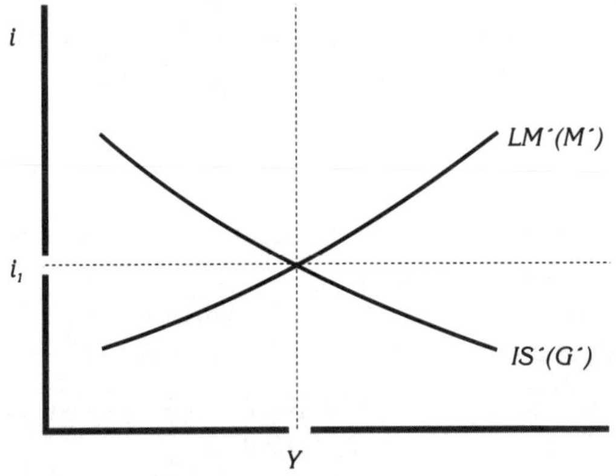

High investment, low Interest "loose" Money, tight spending

The 1981 mix had tight monetary policy and expansionary fiscal policy, corresponding more to the top diagram. In 1971, fiscal policy was relatively tight and the other diagram would have been more applicable.

6. By selling $300 million in treasury bills to the Bank of Canada, the government has effectively borrowed $300 million from the bank and $700 million from the public.

8. The people who own the government debt will receive interest payments and thereby will have future income — thus the debt is wealth to them. Of course, they sacrificed current income to buy the bond so that their wealth does not change. But everyone in society must pay taxes to pay the interest payments. So on average, for the entire economy there is a debt consisting of future taxes, corresponding to the wealth the debt represents to its owner. Once the debt is in existence, the interest payments must necessarily equal the tax payments so that the existence of a debt merely necessitates *transfers* from one group to another. As the text notes, if there is a burden of the debt it arises from the effects of the debt on the capital stock.

10. Since the debt-income ratio compares the size of the debt to the level of income, even if both are growing, the ratio will fall when income grows faster than debt. This was certainly the case during the period from 1950 to the early 1970s.

Chapter 16

2. **(a)** The long-run aggregate supply curve describes the tradeoff, if there is one, between inflation and unemployment when the expected inflation rate is equal to the actual rate.

   (b) In the long run, there is no tradeoff between unemployment (or output) and inflation according to the expectations-augmented aggregate supply curve. The expected growth of prices equals the actual growth rate:

   $$\pi_e = \pi$$

   The aggregate supply curve is vertical and intersects the horizontal axis at Y^*. In the long run, the actual unemployment rate is equal to the natural rate regardless of the inflation rate, since expected and actual inflation rates are the same.

   (c) Because the economy is constantly undergoing various economic shocks, it never reaches the long-run equilibrium.

4. Use Figure 16-7 as a reference. The first period would be identical to the text analysis. In the second, however, the demand curve will shift strongly to the

left, since $f < 0$; in fact, it will move to the original demand curve. Meanwhile the short-run supply curve will move up in response to the increase in inflation. The new equilibrium will be at a *higher* inflation rate and a *lower* output than the original equilibrium. Because output has fallen, the demand curve will again shift to the left, but now short-run supply is moving out in response to the lower inflation rate. The eventual equilibrium is back at point E.

6. **(a)** Inflation would rise immediately to 8 percent, and output would remain unchanged at Y^*.

(b) Using the equation from footnote 11:

$$\pi_1 = \frac{4 + 0.4(0.5)(8)}{1 + (0.4)(0.5)} = 4.67$$

8. Either a fiscal expansion or an increased monetary growth will shift the short-run aggregate demand curve to the right (accommodation). This stimulates output during the same period that it is falling due to the supply shock. Remember that this is achieved at the cost of higher inflation during the period if it is a one-time shock. If it is permanent, accommodating policy can soften the blow, although it won't alter the final outcome.

Chapter 17

2. **(a)** There is some controversy on this issue. If unions tie up "good jobs" (i.e., stable jobs), they may increase the secondary sector and thereby increase the natural rate. The real question is whether eliminating unions would allow more workers to have good jobs. In any case, there would be large redistributions of income as the union-nonunion wage differentials disappeared.

(b) At least initially until women achieved more stable labour force patterns or until "good" jobs became open to them, the natural rate would tend to increase.

(c) Less stable aggregate demand would mean that fewer jobs could offer stable employment. It would thus probably be less valuable for individuals to acquire the skills to go along with a particular job. The size of the secondary labour force and the natural rate or unemployment would increase.

(d) This would make it cheaper for individuals to search longer for jobs and for firms to lay off workers when demand for their product falls and thereby increase the natural rate.

(e) A high minimum wage makes it uneconomical for employers to hire workers they would be willing to hire at a lower real wage, and therefore it increases the natural rate.

In addition, Feldstein has argued that the minimum wage discourages the type of apprenticeship system used in other countries, in which individuals buy on-the-job training by accepting very low initial wages (sometimes they have to pay to be apprentices). With a higher level of skills, he contends, the natural rate would be lower.

(f) This would necessitate larger shifts of workers from sector to sector and would increase the natural rate.

4. While we could eventually reduce the inflation rate to zero by restrictive monetary and fiscal policy, and get back to the natural rate of employment, there is no serious reason to think that this could happen without substantial unemployment and excess capacity in the short run. The benefits of a *permanently lower* inflation rate have to be weighed against the transition costs of high unemployment. Answers vary depending on (a) individuals' evaluation of the relative social costs of inflation and unemployment, and (b) their estimates of how long it would take to get the inflation rate down to zero.

Judging from the behaviour of policy makers in the major countries, most have judged the cost of inflation is less than that of the unemployment that would ensue if tough anti-inflationary policies were followed. However, Canada, the United States, and Britain have come close to a hard-line monetary policy in recent years.

6. Using the average unemployment rates for 1966–70 as shown in the table, for 1990 we have an unemployment rate of:

$$(0.453)(3.3) + (0.333)(3.4) + (0.214)(7.4) = 4.2\%$$

This calculation gives a lower estimate of the natural rate, since the actual unemployment rates were lower in 1966–70 compared with 1971–75.

Chapter 18

2. Nominal interest rate in the long-run will be equal to $r^* + m$. During the adjustment period the rate falls and then rises, reflecting both the change in real rates and the change in inflationary expectations. The Fisher liquidity effect would indicate that the initial fall would be dramatic.

4. (a) When inflation is present, a dollar today can buy more than a dollar in the future. A person making a loan will estimate the growth in prices and charge this estimate as a premium over the rate he would get if there were no inflation. He intends the amount that is repaid to have the same

purchasing power as the amount lent. Why is the borrower willing to pay this inflation premium? If she is using the proceeds in a business she realizes that she will be able to sell her products at higher prices. If she is using the loan to make a consumer purchase, she knows that if she delayed the purchase by the period of the loan she would pay the inflation premium to the merchant rather than the lender.

(b) To determine the real interest rate, subtract the inflation rate from the nominal interest rate. The vertical distance between the two is the real interest rate. Figure 18-8 clearly shows the disparity in inflation and nominal interest rates in the early 1980s.

6. **(a)** The Bank of Canada may decide to fund the deficit with money rather than debt. If not, it may get worried if debt financing drives interest rates up and respond by a latter-day monetary expansion. If the Sargent-Wallace approach holds, we are bound to be worried sooner or later.

8. Total deficit = primary deficit + interest payment

$$4\% = \text{primary deficit} + \text{interest payment}$$
$$4\% = \text{primary deficit} + (30)(0.12)$$
$$4\% = \text{primary deficit} + 3.6$$
$$\text{primary deficit} = 0.04$$

In real terms:

$$\text{Total deficit} = (0.04) + 0.05\,(30)$$
$$= 1.9$$

10. People worry about deficits and debts because they accept the statements that every citizen, young or old, owes so many dollars. An enlightened person would worry about how the financing is arranged. Are we to be crowded out or priced out of sight? Or both? Or neither? In the long run, should we have the option, serious deficits may require higher taxes or budget-cutting measures to counteract the high interest payments due on years of deficit accumulation. Additionally, there is long-run concern about the level of capital accumulation and economic growth. This was discussed in Chapter 15.

Chapter 19

2.

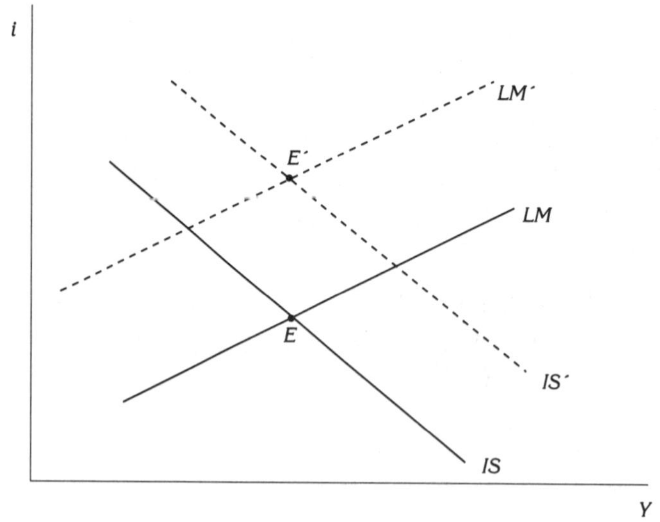

With tight money and easy fiscal policy, the economy moves to a point like *E′* in the diagram. In the late 1980s, monetary policy was tightened while the fiscal deficit remained high. Interest rates rose sharply.

4. Monetary policy was clearly more successful in bringing down the rate of inflation in the early 1990s, though at the cost of much higher unemployment rates. Money supply targets and gradualism were used in the 1970s, but were replaced by inflation targets in the early 1990s.

Chapter 20

2. The tenets of monetarism are:

   (i) The growth rate of the money supply is the sole determinant of long-run inflation.

   (ii) The growth rate of the money stock is the primary factor influencing nominal as well as real GDP (radical form) or (more moderately) it is an important short-run factor.

   (iii) The implementation of monetary policy has an undetermined and relatively long lag before it takes effect. At that time it may be inappropriate. Monetary policy should not be used for fine-tuning; rather, it should be a rule to keep the money stock growing at a constant rate.

(iv) The private sector of the economy is inherently stable. It should be left alone rather than subjected to attempts to use discretionary policies to manage it. The government should be small.

(a) The main disagreement between Keynesians and monetarists is over the relative impact of monetary and fiscal policy; otherwise they are much alike. Both feel that markets clear slowly.

(b) Both monetarists and those of the rational expectations-equilibrium school call for clear, undeviating government policy and a limited role for the government.

4. **(a)** In the Chapter 8 model, during a boom prices temporarily rise faster than wages, since the expected inflation rate is less than the actual rate. For that period we move upward along the short-run aggregate supply curve.

(b) The real business cycle approach explains that people spread a fixed amount of leisure across time by working more in booms, when they can earn more, and less during recessions.

6. If offered the opportunity to sell more at the current price, a monopolist will be willing to do so, since price is above marginal cost. Thus monopolistic competitors that find the menu costs of changing prices too high will sell more when the demand curve they face shifts as a result of the increase in the money stock.

8. Macroeconomics is a dynamic field evolving as new phenomena arise and require explanation. The basic framework derived by Keynes is still the foundation onto which economists add new extensions and revisions. These are the source of controversy. Time must pass and ideas must be tested in the real world before experience proves or disproves them.

The quote from Keynes alludes to the roles of economics and government in the world. Along with religion, these are the central forces in society. The philosophies that dominate them have an extraordinary influence on human life.

Chapter 21

2. Policies aimed at increasing the supplies of labour and capital are based on the premise that both respond positively to incentives — the former to work and the latter to save and invest. The after-tax wage is the major determinant of labour supply. A cut in the personal income tax increases this after-tax wage, and if substitution effects outweigh income effect, the labour supply will increase. One tax that has been pushed strongly is the flat-rate tax mentioned in the text.

Savings, too, can be encouraged by a personal income tax reduction, since savers look at their after-tax rate of return. The appeal of a consumption tax is obvious: money devoted to saving is exempt from taxation. Registered Retirement Savings Plans are an example of a policy designed to encourage savings. A smaller budget deficit would swallow up fewer private savings and allow them to fund private investment. Recall from Chapter 11 that businesses are concerned with their after-tax rates of return and that there are policies such as the investment tax credit that encourage additional investment. A final way of encouraging investment is to reduce the cost of regulations, but this must be traded off for a reduction in the social benefits of the regulation.

The outcome of each of these policies is uncertain and involves cost. Increased savings mean reduced consumption. A smaller deficit accompanied by tax cuts comes at the cost of deep cuts in government programs.

4. $\Delta Y/Y = (1 - \theta)\ \Delta N/N + \theta \Delta K/K \qquad \Delta A = 0$

$\Delta Y/Y = 0.6(-2) + 0.4(6) = 1.2\%$

6. **(a)** Output per head is constant, but output grows at the rate of population growth. This occurs because k is constant in the long run; thus $x = f(k)$ is also constant.

(b) An increase in the savings rate increases the *level* of output per capita, but the growth rate of output does not change.

8. With the production function

$Y = AF(K,N,Z)$

the growth rate of output is

$$\frac{\Delta Y}{Y} = \frac{\Delta A}{A} + \theta_1 \frac{\Delta K}{K} + \theta_2 \frac{\Delta N}{N} + \theta_3 \frac{\Delta Z}{Z}$$

where θ_1, θ_2, and θ_3 are the shares of output accruing to capital, labour, and natural resources respectively. The sum of the shares is unity:

$\theta_1 + \theta_2 + \theta_3 = 1$

(a) Suppose $\frac{\Delta K}{K} = \frac{\Delta N}{N} = g$. Also, we are told $\frac{\Delta Z}{Z} = 0$. Then

$$\frac{\Delta Y}{Y} = \frac{\Delta A}{A} + (\theta_1 + \theta_2)\, g$$

Since $(\theta_1 + \theta_2) < 1$, and assuming $\Delta A/A = 0$, output will grow more slowly than g. That means output grows more slowly than $\Delta N/N$, or that output per worker is falling.

(b) If $\Delta A/A$ were positive, then output could grow faster than g, and output per worker would be rising if technical progress were fast enough.

(c) In terms of limits to growth, it is argued that the fixity of natural resources means that output is bound to grow less rapidly than the labour input, and that we therefore cannot expect to continue to grow. The answer of the technology optimists is implied by **(b)**: if we can continue to make technical progress, then growth can continue even in the face of the drag implied by non-growing natural resources.

10. **(a)** x increases for every k.

(b) Savings = $s\tilde{f}(k^*) > sf(k)$ has increased.

Output per head is higher and the capital-labour ratio is higher.

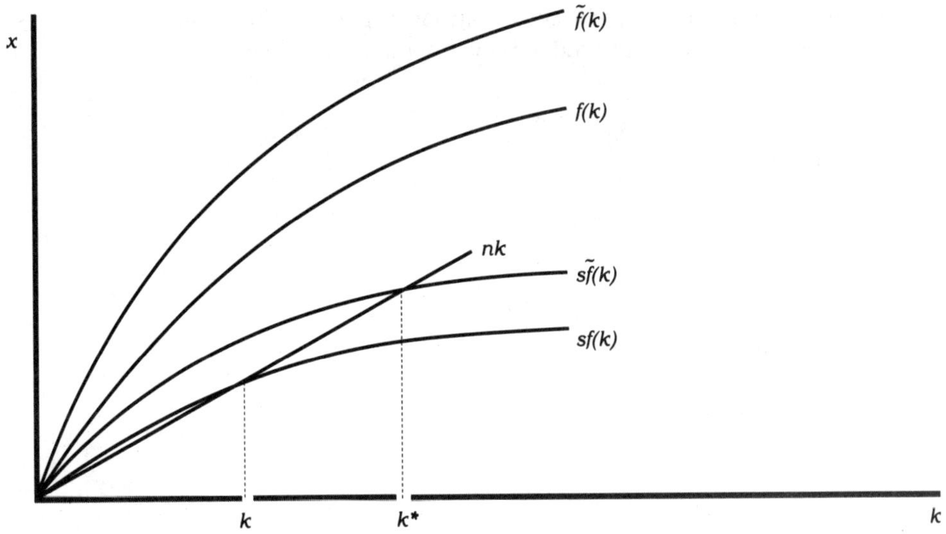

(c) After the increase in technical progress, savings and therefore investment increase. This allows the new k^* to be reached. The ratio of investment to capital is higher *in the transition* than in the steady state because more investment is taking place in the process of raising the per capita capital stock.

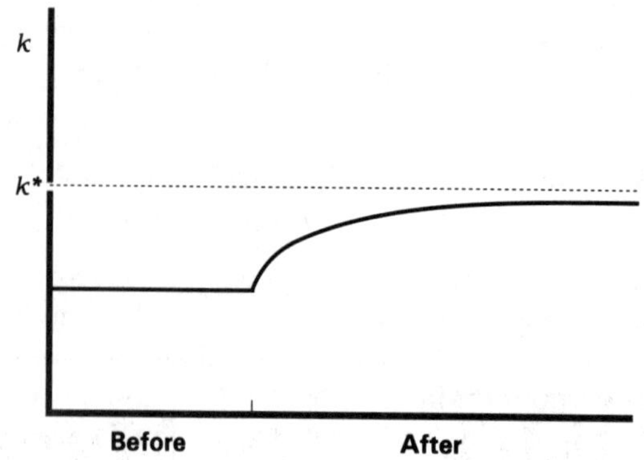

12. Lower per capita income is most often observed in countries with little industrialization. As countries begin to industrialize they are able to borrow technology from industrialized nations. At the beginning of industrialization, when income levels are still quite low, productivity will be very high. As the industrialization continued and incomes grow, these nations will eventually reach a point where they are "caught up," and productivity growth will level off.

NOTATION *In* Macroeconomics, *Fourth Canadian Edition*

Some General Rules

1. ′ (prime) denotes an alternative value of the same variable. For example, t' means an alternative value of the tax rate.
2. Upper bar (as in $\overline{A}$) means one of the following:
   (i) The variable is held constant.
   (ii) Autonomous portion of the variable.
3. Δ denotes the change in a variable.
4. A subscript means one of the following:
   (i) A subscript 0 (zero) usually means an equilibrium level.
   (ii) A subscript t means at date t; a subscript -1 means the variable is lagged one period.
   (iii) Alternative schedules (for example, AS_1 and AS_2).

5. A superscript * indicates:
   (i) An optimal, full-employment, or steady-state level.
   (ii) A foreign variable.
6. The letter *E* is reserved for equilibrium points.

Notation by Part

Part I

Basic National Accounts

Y	income or output
C	consumption
I	investment
S	saving
G	government expenditure on goods and services
Q	imports
X	exports
NX	net exports
YD	disposable income
TR	transfer payments to the private sector
TA	taxes

Determination of National Income

IU	unplanned additions to inventory
AD	aggregate demand
c	marginal propensity to consume
s	marginal propensity to save
A	autonomous portion of aggregate demand
α	multiplier

Public Sector

t	tax rate
$\overline{\alpha}$	multiplier with income tax
BS	budget surplus
BD	budget deficit

Monetary Sector

i	interest rate
M	money stock

Foreign Sector

m	marginal propensity to import
$\bar{\bar{\alpha}}$	multiplier with foreign trade
CF	net capital inflow
BP	balance of payments surplus
e	exchange rate (domestic currency price of foreign exchange)
P^*	foreign price level

Part 2

Aggregate Supply

P	price level
AS	aggregate supply
P^e	expected price level

Labour Market

ND	demand for labour
NS	supply of labour
N	employment
W	wage rate
W/P	real wage
u	unemployment rate
g_w	rate of increase of wages
LF	labour force

Part 3

Consumption

WR	real wealth
YL	labour income
NL	length of life in years

WL	working life in years
YP	permanent (disposable) income

Investment

K	capital stock
rc	rental cost of capital
d	rate of depreciation
r	real interest rate
π^e	expected inflation rate
q	Tobin's *q*

Money Supply and Demand

V	velocity of money
D	bank deposits
CU	currency
B	monetary base
R	cash reserves
L	bank loans
cu	currency-deposit ratio
re	reserve-deposit ratio

Part 4

Inflation and Output

π	inflation rate
m	growth rate of the money stock
f	change in fiscal policy
DAD	dynamic aggregate demand
SAS	short-run aggregate supply

Long-Term Growth

F	production function
A	technology term in production function
n	rate of population growth
s	saving rate
x	per capita output
k	capital-labour ratio

ECONOMIC DATA *Tables*

Table A *GDP, Prices, and Employment*

	GDP (billions of dollars)	GDP in Billions of Constant 1986 Dollars	GDP Deflator (1986 = 100)	Unemployment Rate (%)	Inflation Rate (% change in CPI)
1926	5.4	44.0	12.2	—	—
1927	5.8	48.1	12.1	—	–1.7
1928	6.3	52.6	12.0	—	0.3
1929	6.4	53.1	12.1	—	1.2
1930	6.0	51.3	11.7	—	–0.7
1931	5.0	45.5	10.9	11.6	–9.8
1932	4.1	41.3	9.9	17.6	–8.6
1933	3.7	38.3	9.7	19.3	–4.8
1934	4.2	42.3	9.9	14.5	1.5
1935	4.5	45.4	10.0	14.2	0.7
1936	4.9	47.5	10.3	12.8	1.9
1937	5.5	51.7	10.6	9.1	3.2
1938	5.5	52.3	10.5	11.4	1.0
1939	5.9	56.3	10.4	11.4	–0.8
1940	7.0	63.7	11.0	9.2	3.9
1941	8.5	72.2	11.8	4.4	5.9
1942	10.5	85.0	12.4	3.0	4.6
1943	11.3	88.2	12.8	1.7	1.8
1944	12.1	91.4	13.2	1.4	0.5
1945	12.1	89.2	13.5	1.6	0.5
1946	12.2	87.2	14.0	3.4	3.4
1947	13.9	91.6	15.2	2.2	9.3
1948	16.0	93.1	17.2	2.3	14.5
1949	17.3	97.2	17.9	2.8	3.1
1950	19.1	104.9	18.3	3.6	2.8
1951	22.3	109.6	20.4	2.4	10.6

	GDP (billions of dollars)	GDP in Billions of Constant 1986 Dollars	GDP Deflator (1986 = 100)	Unemployment Rate (%)	Inflation Rate (% change in CPI)
1952	25.2	118.7	21.2	2.9	2.5
1953	26.4	124.5	21.2	3.0	−0.9
1954	26.5	123.2	21.5	4.6	0.6
1955	29.3	134.9	21.7	4.4	0.2
1956	32.9	146.6	22.5	3.4	1.4
1957	34.5	150.8	23.0	4.6	3.2
1958	35.7	153.5	23.3	7.0	2.7
1959	37.9	159.5	23.8	6.0	1.1
1960	39.4	164.2	24.0	7.0	1.2
1961	40.9	169.3	20.1	7.1	0.9
1962	44.4	181.3	24.3	5.9	1.2
1963	47.7	190.7	25.0	5.5	1.8
1964	52.2	203.4	25.7	4.7	1.8
1965	57.5	216.9	26.5	3.9	2.4
1966	64.4	231.6	27.8	3.4	3.7
1967	69.1	238.4	29.0	3.8	3.6
1968	75.4	251.2	30.0	4.4	4.0
1969	83.0	264.5	31.4	4.4	4.6
1970	89.1	271.5	32.9	5.7	3.3
1971	97.3	287.0	33.9	6.2	2.9
1972	108.6	303.5	35.8	6.2	4.8
1973	127.4	326.9	38.9	5.5	7.6
1974	152.1	341.2	44.6	5.3	10.9
1975	171.5	350.1	49.0	6.9	10.8
1976	197.9	371.3	53.2	7.1	7.5
1977	217.9	385.1	56.6	8.1	8.0
1978	241.6	402.7	59.9	8.3	8.9
1979	276.1	418.3	65.9	7.4	9.2
1980	309.9	424.5	73.0	7.5	10.2
1981	356.0	440.1	80.9	7.5	12.5
1982	374.4	426.0	87.9	11.0	10.8
1983	405.7	439.5	97.3	11.9	5.8
1984	444.7	467.2	95.2	11.3	4.3
1985	478.0	489.4	97.6	10.5	4.0
1986	505.7	505.7	100.0	9.6	4.2
1987	551.6	526.7	104.7	8.9	4.4
1988	605.1	551.4	109.7	7.8	4.8
1989	649.1	565.0	114.9	7.5	5.5
1990	671.6	567.5	118.3	8.1	4.4
1991	679.2	558.9	—	10.3	5.8

Source: Statistics Canada, 11-210; *Bank of Canada Review.*

Table B *Financial Data*

	Money Supply* (billions of dollars)		Interest Rates		
	M1	M2	Treasury Bills	Long-Term Govt. of Canada Bonds	Exchange Rate (U.S. cents)
1951			0.79	3.22	94.8
1952			1.07	3.56	102.2
1953			1.69	3.71	101.7
1954			1.46	3.18	102.8
1955			1.55	3.14	101.4
1956			2.90	3.63	101.6
1957			3.78	4.14	104.3
1958			2.29	4.11	103.0
1959			4.81	5.07	104.3
1960			3.32	5.19	103.1
1961			2.83	5.06	98.7
1962	6.1		4.00	5.10	93.6
1963	6.3		3.57	5.09	92.5
1964	6.7		3.74	5.18	92.5 (Fixed rate)
1965	7.1		3.97	5.20	
1966	7.7		5.00	5.68	
1967	8.3		4.59	5.90	
1968	8.9	23.4	6.25	6.73	
1969	9.2	25.3	7.15	7.56	92.5
1970	9.7	27.6	6.10	7.97	95.8
1971	11.5	30.8	3.60	6.95	99.0
1972	13.0	34.7	3.55	7.23	101.0
1973	14.5	41.0	5.39	7.55	100.0
1974	15.3	47.4	7.80	8.87	102.3
1975	18.9	55.2	7.37	9.00	98.3
1976	19.2	63.1	8.90	9.22	101.4
1977	21.5	70.8	7.35	8.69	94.0
1978	23.3	79.6	8.59	9.24	87.7
1979	24.1	94.0	11.55	10.17	85.4
1980	26.6	110.6	12.75	12.33	85.5
1981	26.9	123.9	17.77	15.03	83.4
1982	27.6	133.7	13.81	14.36	81.0
1983	29.9	138.4	9.32	11.77	81.1
1984	30.0	148.4	11.11	12.74	77.2
1985	32.8	164.1	9.44	11.11	73.3
1986	34.6	179.8	8.99	9.54	72.0
1987	37.5	190.5	8.19	9.95	75.4
1988	40.1	213.4	9.48	10.22	81.2
1989	41.2	243.1	12.05	9.92	84.5
1990	40.4	266.2	12.81	10.68	85.7
1991	42.1	281.5	8.76	9.72	87.3
1992	41.3	280.9	6.92	8.92	85.6

*Average of Wednesdays for December.

Source: Bank of Canada Review.

Table C *Balance of International Payments (millions of dollars)*

	Current Account					Capital Account		
	Merchandise Trade	Services	Investment Income	Transfers	Current Account Balance	Net Official Financing	Net Capital Movements*	Statistical Discrepancy
1963	494	–297	–848	–24	–521		489	32
1964	696	–341	–909	–7	–416		311	105
1965	143	–394	–992	6	–1 098		1 369	–271
1966	266	–413	–1 119	29	–1 109		1 344	–235
1967	563	25	–1 240	49	–491		1 000	–509
1968	1 474	–530	–1 220	158	–86		881	–795
1969	911	–771	–1 206	110	–956		1 136	–180
1970	2 951	–702	–1 349	134	1 033	–1 530	–717	–316
1971	2 468	–827	–1 507	236	370	–778	919	–1 289
1972	1 951	–993	–1 460	219	–283	–218	1 874	–1 565
1973	2 923	–1 179	–1 730	298	312	467	538	–850
1974	1 835	–1 394	–2 237	497	–1 299	–25	2 331	–1 032
1975	–345	–2 063	–2 537	314	–4 631	404	5 957	–1 326
1976	1 559	–2 586	–3 536	467	–4 096	–522	7 876	–3 779
1977	2 972	–3 041	–4 571	318	–4 322	1 421	6 546	–2 225
1978	4 312	–3 212	–5 949	–54	–4 903	5 818	8 049	–3 146
1979	4 424	–2 627	–7 154	494	–4 864	–73	7 372	–2 507
1980	8 778	–3 131	–7 826	1 048	–1 130	1 496	2 306	–1 176
1981	7 292	–3 414	–11 337	1 328	–6 131	–862	14 587	–8 457
1982	17 654	–3 601	–12 670	1 440	2 824	1 352	–713	–2 111
1983	17 457	–3 846	–11 601	1 056	3 066	–1 033	2 626	–5 692
1984	20 237	–4 066	–13 513	778	3 437	1 888	3 615	–7 051
1985	16 926	–4 564	–14 333	787	–1 186	3 844	6 991	–5 805
1986	10 388	–4 253	–16 886	1 482	–9 268	1 141	13 219	–3 951
1987	10 341	–5 343	–16 671	2 073	–9 601	–5 391	14 293	–4 692
1988	10 422	–5 606	–18 953	3 614	–13 883	–11 683	18 120	–4 237
1989	7 045	–6 982	–21 149	3 568	–20 723	–3 085	25 088	–4 365
1990	10 925	–8 876	–23 933	4 252	–22 036	–1 222	28 359	–6 323
1991	9 164	–9 865	–23 289	3 797	–26 471	–399	7 791	–1 516

*Includes net official financing.

Source: Bank of Canada Review.

cut here

STUDENT REPLY CARD

You can help us to develop better textbooks. Please answer the following questions about the *Study Guide* to accompany *Macroeconomics*, Fourth Canadian Edition, and return this form via Business Reply Mail. Your opinions matter—thank you in advance for sharing them with us!

Name of your college or university: ______________________________

Major program of study: ______________________________

Course title: ______________________________

Were you required to buy this *Study Guide*? ________ yes ________ no

Did you buy this book new or used? ________ new ________ used ($________)

Do you plan to keep or to sell this book? ________ keep ________ sell

What did you like most about this *Study Guide*?

cut here

fold here

What did you like least?

Were there topics covered in your text that are not included in this *Study Guide*? If so, please specify:

Did this *Study Guide* assist you in learning concepts and techniques used in the text?

How could we make this *Study Guide* more useful in future editions?

cut here

cut here

fold here

BUSINESS
REPLY MAIL

No Postage Stamp
Necessary If Mailed
in Canada

Postage will be paid by

McGraw-Hill

Canada Post Corporation • Société canadienne des postes

7115

Attn.: Sponsoring Editor, Economics
The College Division

McGraw-Hill Ryerson Limited
300 Water St.
Whitby, ON
L1N 9Z9

tape shut